Dancing Culture Religion

Studies in Body & Religion
Series Editors: Richard M. Carp, Saint Mary's College of California and Rebecca Sachs Norris, Merrimack College

Studies in Body and Religion publishes contemporary research and theory that addresses body as a fundamental category of analysis in the study of religion. Embodied humans conceive of, study, transmit, receive, and practice religion, with and through their bodies and bodily capacities. Volumes in this series will include diverse examples and perspectives on the roles and understandings of body in religion, as well as the influence and importance of religion for body. They will also move conversation on body and religion forward by problematizing "body," which, like "religion," is a contested concept. We do not know exactly what religion is, nor do we know exactly what body is, either; much less do we understand their mutual interpenetrations. This series aims to address this by bringing multiple understandings of body into an arena of conversation.

Titles in the Series

Dancing Culture Religion, by Sam Gill

Dancing Culture Religion

Sam Gill

LEXINGTON BOOKS
Lanham • Boulder • New York • Toronto • Plymouth, UK

Published by Lexington Books
A wholly owned subsidiary of The Rowman & Littlefield Publishing Group, Inc.
4501 Forbes Boulevard, Suite 200, Lanham, Maryland 20706
www.rowman.com

10 Thornbury Road, Plymouth PL6 7PP, United Kingdom

British Library Cataloguing in Publication Information Available

Library of Congress Cataloging-in-Publication Data

Gill, Sam D., 1943-
Dancing culture religion / Sam Gill.
p. cm.
Includes bibliographical references and index.
ISBN 978-0-7391-7472-2 (cloth : alk. paper) -- ISBN 978-0-7391-7473-9 (pbk. : alk. paper) -- ISBN
978-0-7391-7474-6 (electronic)
1. Dance--Anthropological aspects. 2. Dance--Social aspects. 3. Dance--Religious aspects. I. Title.
GV1588.6.G54 2012
306.4'846--dc23
2012019985

Printed in the United States of America

For Fatumata

Contents

v

Preface

I have been to Bali several times. Upon arrival I am invariably whisked off by my friends to a temple festival or they incorporate me in preparing for an upcoming festival. These festivals are amazingly elaborate events that last days on end often with months' long preparation. They seem to be occurring constantly in Bali. With thousands of temples and each temple having an annual (on a Balinese calendar of 210 days) temple festival, I wonder how such effort required for preparation and performance is even humanly possible. Indeed, one might propose that ritual preparation and ritual performance is the principal occupation of most Balinese. Dancing is ubiquitous to temple festivals and many other religious events in Bali. And the dancing is not simply a group of grooving social dancers bouncing around to music. It is precise trained dancing performed in elaborate costumes and accompanied by the performance of live music— gamelan or other types of music ensembles. There is a remarkably close relationship between Balinese religion and dance performance.

I have spent many a day perched on a pueblo rooftop overlooking the dance plazas at numerous villages at Hopi and also at Zuni and other villages among the eastern Pueblo peoples where dancing is the principal ritual activity that goes on all day long. The sheer beauty is stunning and enthralling.

The eerie falsetto animal-like vocalizations of Navajo *yeibichai* dancers are something, once heard, never forgotten. Buckskin masked dancers dancing in the firelight casting surreal shadows; quintessential Navajo.

Having woven my way through noisy street protests in Yogyakarta I found the Sultan's palace where in quiet and calm contrasting with the cacophony in the surrounding streets the dancers entered the dance pavilion waddling in deference to the Sultan, though he wasn't present. The female dancers' faces appeared as masks fixed in an expression suggesting calmness, yet intense presence. As they danced, I found it difficult to even grasp that these were young women dancing; they transported me into the Javanese mythology, into an ideal Javanese world.

Lunchtime in Mali was a time for drumming and dancing, but then any time is a time for music and dancing. This group of Malians was assisting me and several other Americans to learn Malian dancing and drumming and even though we had been dancing and drumming all morning, the midday rest period was invariably filled with the sounds, gestures, and images that are Mali. I can't remember a time when there wasn't dancing and drumming and music; that is how one enacts being Malian.

These are but several experiences among many I have enjoyed as I have visited communities across the world. Dancing and music are invariably central to religious and cultural action and identity. Indeed, when I have inquired about upcoming religious activities upon arrival at a new location I have often been referred to dance events.

Outside of European and American Christian communities it is difficult to find a religious tradition that does not incorporate dancing and for many communities dancing is considered essential.

The world over dancing is associated with cultural identity. Travel brochures often include prominent images of costumed dancers along with distinctive natural features including landscapes, plants, and animals as well as cityscapes and distinctive architectural features. The opening and closing ceremonies of the Olympics feature dancing on a spectacular scale with the dances performed selected because they are iconic to the host countries. Some traditions hold dancing as fundamental to cosmogony and cosmology suggesting a highly sophisticated understanding of dancing. Dance is commonly used metaphorically as identified with life, with interrelationships, and with abstract concepts.

Danced movement patterns, gestures, postures, costumes, ritual, sensory experiences are inseparable from religious and cultural identity, value, and meaning. Yet, there is little to no dance theory that adequately supports the comparative and interpretive study of dance traditions. Our inherited folk theories and understandings (views of dancing we simply inherit without much reflective awareness) of dancing often claim high value for dancing while coincidentally our cultural and social practices often limit dancing to the fringes, the frivolous, the "just" or the "mere," the unnecessary. We have yet to develop and articulate a deep and rich understanding of dancing, what dancing does and how it does it, how dancing enacts and reveals fundamental dimensions of being human, and how we actually comprehend the nature of the movement that is distinctively dancing.

The perspective of this book is that dancing is fundamentally important to the study of culture and religion. Like so many other things dancing is remarkably complex when we attempt to understand it in depth. Yet, quite clearly dancing is marginalized even among the arts in Western cultures and is ignored if not forbidden by European and American Christian traditions. Dancing has never been taught in public schools as an important or essential subject and it has long been eliminated from the curricula of most schools. Dancing is strongly aligned with female gender; boys are limited to a few specific dances and men who dance are rare. Dancing is illegal in places like the Jefferson Memorial where people have been arrested for dancing. Dancing is a sport yet not a recognized sport. Dancing is often the core of cultural spectacle, yet otherwise marginalized. In "the dance world" ballet is considered "the dance." Yet, this dance world pretty much ignores the countless cultural/religious dance traditions throughout the world and history. Dancing is considered expressive, a language, a universal language, yet few seem to have any idea what precisely it is saying. Dancing is considered spiritual, yet dancing is an act wholly of body movement. It is thought to be healing even the core of certain therapeutic approaches, yet how this result is gained, if indeed it is, is poorly understood.

The academic studies of dancing, both theory and ethnographic, are overwhelmingly focused on the high culture art and entertainment forms of Western dancing. Dance anthropology is a small field populated largely by scholars who were dancers of ballet or modern who have continued their interest in an academic environment. While there is an enormous body of dance ethnography it is almost all incidental to general ethnographies and methods of adequate documentation of dancing in a cultural context have never been fully developed. Dance notation is remarkably complex; taking months to gain proficiency to notate dancing or even to read dance notation. Video recordings of dancing now exist on YouTube for tens of thousands of dances, yet few of these dances are studied with adequate theory or with sufficient attention to cultural historical context. Despite the near synonymy of dancing and religion in cultures the world over (the major exceptions are European and American Christianities), the academic study of religion has all but ignored the inclusion of dancing as a subject, and as an aspect of religion theory.

Looking back over the interests I have enjoyed in my career, it is remarkable that dancing was something I was attracted to from early in my days of studying Native American cultures. One of my first publications was a little editorial piece on dancing I wrote for the popular journal *Parabola*. Hopi and Zuni as well as the Yaqui village Guadalupe were places I regularly visited to attend ritual dance events while I was teaching at Arizona State University. I often ventured to the eastern Pueblos and to other Native American communities in the American Southwest where dancing was invariably part of what I enjoyed. My academic study of dancing came as an outgrowth of my studies of Native American religions as well as the associated interests in ritual, masking, and performance.

I didn't get personally involved dancing until, during one of my mid-life crises, it dawned on me that I had become a totally sedentary academic well on my way to a permanently pear-shaped kyphotic body. Efforts to "get in shape" quickly connected me with dance activities and I became obsessed with movement, an obsession yet to subside. Since I found myself willing to sacrifice faculty meetings (not much of a sacrifice really) and I came close on occasions to missing teaching my classes if there was a conflict with my schedule of movement activities, it became essential to keeping my job that I incorporate dancing somehow in my academic work. I recall first teaching a religion and dance class as a summer course in the early 1990s. Students were assigned thousands of pages of ethnographic materials that connected dancing with religion; I'd read little of it, but wanted to read it with students. We were all overwhelmed yet excited by every possibility. This was long before YouTube so we mostly had to imagine what these dances were like and we sat in our chairs reading and talking, stumbling along the best we could. One class during a discussion of Greek dance, I think, a woman in the class mentioned that she happened to know the dance we were talking about. The chairs were quickly moved aside and I immediately understood that to study dancing without dancing is like studying music by reading musical scores never hearing the music. This revelation set off more than a decade of the progressive development of my teaching religion and dance classes that eventually grew to a yearlong course covering more than thirty dance traditions associated in some way with cultural and religious identity and action. The course featured a studio a week in which students experienced dancing most of the dances we discussed taught by people from the respective cultures and traditions. And over the years it became increasingly clear to me that, as academics, we simply do not have adequate theory for studying dancing, especially as a cultural and religious form. This desire to understand dancing from a theoretical and academic perspective, an effort that has finally produced results that I present in this book, has consistently complemented my passion for dancing and teaching dancing.

Somewhere along this road I had come to know so many dancers and musicians from cultures the world over that I decided to open a school called *Bantaba World Dance & Music* that operated for eight years until I ran out of money to support it. It was an important community cultural center and attracted teachers and dancers from all over the world. Eventually it was also the context in which I began to dance and to teach salsa in various forms. I've now taught salsa dancing for over ten years. I have a performance group. I teach at high schools and in my own classes at the University of Colorado and I have written extensively related to many aspects of salsa social dancing. My studies of dancing have taken me several times to Bali and Java, a couple times to West Africa (Ghana and Mali), several times to Latin America (Puerto Rico, Costa Rica, and the Dominican Republic) where I have observed dancing and music in cultural contexts as well as participated in dance/music training. My studies of Australian Aborigines, while not focused directly on dancing, eventually incorporated the inclusion of dance studies although from historical sources rather than participation or observation. And, of course, before all of this for many years I enjoyed extensive experience in many Native American communities where dancing was invariably happening.

This book evolved from a growing collection of essays written over a considerable period of time brought together, rewritten, revised, and reconceptualized to comprise something of a book. I have not only wanted, but have also found it appropriate, to incorporate not only my academic work and my dancing and dance teaching experience. Importantly, when I am dancing or teaching dancing I rarely if ever give the academic issues a thought, yet I fully believe that twenty-five years of dancing and other movement activities have not only enriched my knowledge, but far more importantly they have also reconstructed me as a human being. My specific self-moving activities have constructed body concepts and gestural patterns. The experienced relationships and structuralities of the dancing movement have completely shaped me as a person including my academic and intellectual work. Increasingly over this quarter century I have become convinced that the specific self-movement experiences we practice construct who we are and our understanding of the world. Our thinking and perception are interlocked with our self-movement life. Thus in my former highly sedentary low-level movement life, I believe that I was a different person in every way. I believe that what I have created in this book has been decidedly shaped by the practices of self-movement I have experienced now for decades. I also believe that such changes do not simply occur upon the brief encounter with self-moving practices, but rather these changes take a long time, years in fact, for them to effect in a deep and constitutive way who we are.

This book is organized into six chapters with my intent that each chapter builds and enhances those that have gone before. The first chapter is on self-movement and is somewhat different in intent and structure than the other chapters. While it engages a number of cultural examples of dancing, it is concerned more with moving in a larger context than dancing, that is, with the aspect of movement of animate organisms. This broader and deeply theoretical concern is, I believe, necessary both to establish the context for distinguishing dancing among all forms of human movement and to reveal some of the most profound and provocative attributes of dancing as a distinctive form of self-moving. This broad chapter also offers a context for me to comment on, make observations about, and engage the social and cultural importance of many aspects of dancing as it occurs in contemporary Western societies. The practical and political are interwoven with the theoretical. These sections deal with such things as dance and gendered behavior, the changing role of movement/dancing across the life cycle, and the popular roles dancing plays.

Each of the next four chapters is structured around the juxtaposition of a distinct dance tradition with a philosophical or theoretical perspective developed by academics with rare, if any, reference to dancing. This approach has emerged from my discovery that in the careful study of a particular culturally-identified dance tradition it is often possible to discern clear and insightful observations and understandings of dancing both as applicable to that specific tradition, but easily generalized also to dancing wherever it occurs. Further, because I am an academic and have

always loved that strange process of reading, thinking, creatively reflecting and extending ideas, and bringing together disparate materials
knowing that this is a method with high probability for some exciting
creative thinking and writing, I found myself often informed about my
constant thinking about dancing while reading and reflecting on theoreti-
cal/philosophical materials that in no way incorporated or were intended
to be relevant to dancing. I found that I could creatively engage these
materials, to comprehend them more fully and deeply because I was
constantly relating them to dancing. In this book I attempt to interrelate
dancing and these theoretical and philosophical materials with the specific intent of developing a rich understanding of dancing and to offer fuller
comprehension of the philosophical and theoretical materials from the
perspective of dancing. The topics I use to accomplish this interrelationship are gesturing, self-othering, playing, and seducing. In the final chapter I summarize and reflect on this study of dancing particularly as it
offers model and insight to the academic studies of religions and cultures.

I use the term danc*ing* throughout the book to designate the abstract
dynamic that characterizes all actual dances. My core interest is as much
in dancing as in gesturally posturally culturally religiously specific
dances. Dancing and dances are clearly distinguishable, yet they are inseparable. Unfortunately, in my point of view, dancing is rarely even
acknowledged. Yet any study of dances without a deep appreciation of
dancing is, I believe, sorely limited and particularly with respect to rendering dance an object that no longer dances; such studies take the dancing out of the dances. My challenge is to discover and to articulate ways
in which the dancing remains central to dances even as they are studied.

In teaching "Religion and Dance" for many years I am well aware that
connecting dancing and religion is for many an unexpected conjunction.
As students find it unexpected, religion scholars simply ignore dancing.[1]
As I have indicated, in my experience the presence of a near synonymy of
dance and religion outside European and American Christian communities indicates that dancing certainly deserves a prominent role in the
study of religion. Yet, dance must not be simply an added subject of
study for religion complementing, for example, the study of pilgrimage,
sacrifice, conversion, and rites of passage. My hope is that dancing might
contribute to and inspire some reshaping of what we understand religion
to be and how we go about the academic study of religion. My hope is
based on understanding both dancing and religion as distinctively human forms comprised of culturally, historically, and personally shaped
gestural, postural, self-movement practices. The hope is that by showing
how it is possible to keep the dancing in the dances as we study them we
might aspire to keep the religioning in religions as we study them.

It is also my hope to engage in a study that is, according to the current
style, assigned to a "body" category or a "materialist" theory, yet without

the unfortunate attributes that necessarily accompany these categorizations. I caution that there is an implication that focusing on the body assumes a separation of body and mind; that a materialist theory is apart from belief. This book begins with movement which holds that, from a neurobiological and a philosophical position, any separation into body and mind, brain and muscle, material and belief (text), visible and invisible, virtual and actual is either arbitrary or in service to comprehending movement itself, living movement, vitality.

For better or worse, most of my academic work is done alone or as preparation for teaching or simply because I feel compelled to write about what I am thinking. I am sure this style of working results in both foolish errors and lost potential, yet it is what it is. I follow where my interests lead me, always amazed that they seem to be heading somewhere. As I have come to appreciate movement itself I have come to appreciate that research/writing is movement and that finishing a work for publication is the moment you unplug yourself from this source of vitality. Fortunately interests seem always rising.

I am thankful for Jonathan Z. Smith's lecture "'Now You See it Now You Won't:' The Future of the Academic Study of Religion over the next Forty Years" which he delivered at the University of Colorado in April 2010. This lecture has energized my continuing pursuit of movement and gesture. I can see the vast potential of these approaches and I hope this book contributes in some ways to demonstrating their merits. Jonathan has been a teacher and an inspiration to me for over forty-five years; I am always deeply grateful to him.

I thank Richard Carp and Rebecca Sachs Norris, the editors of this series, for seeing promise in what began as a mixed collection of loosely organized essays. I hope that I have succeeded in some measure in shape-shifting the essays in the direction of something looking like a book that might serve their hopes and expectations for their series. I am honored to be a part of this series and wish them well as the series grows. Special thanks to Rebecca for her careful reading of the manuscript. Thanks to Melissa Wilkes and Alison Northridge at Rowman & Littlefield for their helpful support in getting the book through press.

John Minear was a student at the University of Colorado Boulder decades ago. I well remember the engaging chats we had back then, so I was delighted when John turned up on Facebook a year or so ago. Since then I have enjoyed a regular and often heartfelt correspondence with John. In my experience such interactions are rare. John patiently read manuscripts, listened to podcasts, and read sources related to my preparation of this book. His thoughtful comments, his constant encouragement, and his persistent interest have been deeply valuable to me throughout this process. John's eagerness to see the relevance of these topics to the broader context of life often initiated provocative and meaningful discussions of a more personal nature. Thanks, John. I also thank

Nancy Maxson, John's partner, for her thoughtful comments and encouragement.

Recently I have enjoyed the influence of a couple of students that have informed and inspired me. Gabrielle Biscaye assisted me in teaching the dance course as an online course and clearly the most fun I had getting that course ready to teach was when Gabi and I sat down and videotaped a number of lively conversations in order to give students that would never see either of us in person a sense of our being present. Thanks, Gabi, and best wishes. This last year I was assisted in teaching a couple of courses by John Thibdeau who is a graduate student in religious studies but is also in a certificate program in cognitive science. John appreciates that dancing offers an area of interest for cognitive scientists that is generally unfamiliar to them; some of his research is in making that connection. John has also quite graciously kept me informed about some of the important materials in cognitive science and related fields. I have been deeply impacted by some of these works and by John's subtle guidance. Thanks, John. I wish you well as you move toward what surely will be an amazing academic career.

I wish there was some way to acknowledge the many aerobics and fitness teachers and workout buddies that I have enjoyed and learned from over the years. I doubt any of them would ever run across this book, but I want to note that I consider these shared experiences invaluable and always fun. I am deeply grateful for all of the dance teachers I have learned from. I have also danced with and taught thousands of social dancers over the years. This has been a joy and I have learned from each one of them as they have shared something of themselves with me as we danced.

My daughter, Jenny, has been daughter, friend, business partner, dance partner, and fellow dance teacher since she joined me in our *Bantaba World Dance and Music* adventure that started in 1999. She is my constant most valued source of inspiration and personal support. To have such a rich relationship with an adult child is, for me, the greatest joy and it fills my life with the deepest satisfaction. Thanks, Jenny, love you.

And then there is Fatumata, my granddaughter, to whom I dedicate this book. She is Miss Smarty Pants (wow is she smart!), a crack-up comic, a thoughtful sweetie, a fun companion for our many outings to shows and performances, my teacher in so many ways, and an awesome dancer. Fatu moves through life with inspiring beauty and grace. She is the future. Love you, Fatu.

NOTES

1. A couple of recent academic books that connect dancing and religion are Kimerer L. LaMothe, *Nietzsche's Dancers: Isadora Duncan, Martha Graham, and the Revaluation of Christian Values* (New York: Palgrave Macmillan, 2006) and Kimerer L. LaMothe, *Between Dancing and Writing: The Practice of Religious Studies* (Bronx, NY: Fordham University Press, 2004).

ONE

Moving

DANCING IS MOVING, BUT NOT ALL MOVING IS DANCING

The title song and dance number of the 1952 classic American film musical *Singin' in the Rain* is memorable and much loved. The number was filmed in two days with Kelly suffering a fever and the filmmakers plagued by technical issues, yet the results are magical. My concern is to see dancing as movement, to place dancing in the larger context of human movement, and to try to understand what distinguishes certain movement as dancing, a form almost universally recognized.

This classic dance number offers some clues. It begins with Kelly telling Debbie Reynolds goodnight and then feeling so exuberantly in love, he dismisses his car and driver despite the rain and starts walking. Kelly's walking is energetic and rhythmic, but it is not dancing. He jumps up on the lamppost; his buoyant movement consistent with his mood. As he walks down the sidewalk there is a precise moment when he appears to "break into" dancing and the lyrics of the song mark precisely when it occurs. The lyrics shift from "I'm singing in the rain" and "I walk down the lane just singing in the rain" to "I'm dancing in the rain." And here the lyrics fall away, the music swells, and Kelly dances. Any sense of purpose such as going home disappears. His "dancing in the rain" is clearly reward enough in the dancing. Kelly seems to abandon himself to his dancing; there is nothing for him but his dancing. As the dancing progresses it shades into playing as Kelly pretends to walk the curb edge as a tightrope and then, like a little boy, stomps and splashes in puddles in the street. What is it in all this movement that we so easily and confidently identify as dancing? It must be, in part, the nonquotidian aspect of the movement. Yet what exactly marks it? It must be, in part, something of the over-plus or transcendence of the movement, what I call "other" or "othering." Yet, how does this othering occur and what precisely gives rise to it? It must have something to do with it being autotelic, done just for the sake of dancing. But what about dancing makes it so self-fulfilling? Perhaps it is because dancing is movement that is about movement itself as much as anything. Thus dancing has the peculiar quality of incipience and anticipation in that it is always about to be something yet that thing passes in its becoming; dancing never resting with anything that has become. Perhaps it is that there is no abiding object made by dancing. Thus in dancing there is a sense of virtuality, an unfolding in the manifesting moment, something that is coming into being, but is never actually there. How is this quality, seemingly so paradoxical, possible? Perhaps it is because there is a sense of danger that accompanies dancing in which we sense that without the constant effort to keep dance manifesting it will be lost. Or the danger associated with dancing may be, as portrayed in the 1948 classic film *The Red Shoes* based on a Hans Christian Anderson fairy tale, that the dancing has taken control of the dancer; the dancer is somehow at the mercy of dancing's enchantment. And in Kelly's dance we experience his having been under the control of his dancing when he falls out of dancing back into just walking. At this moment he becomes aware of what he has been doing, that he had become something other in his dancing, that he had lost himself in a way yet had coincidentally somehow also realized himself most fully. This small moment of realization is, we can see, when, under the suspicious eye of the cop, Kelly seems almost embarrassed. He seems to be thinking "oops, was I really doing that?" a small sense that perhaps "dancing should somehow be illegal"; that humans should not be capable of actually doing such a thing! And this is precisely the emotion of wonder and fear that drives my study of dancing.

There is a comparable scene in Sally Potter's 1997 film *The Tango Lesson*. As the star of her own film Sally is learning to dance tango. Her relationship with her Argentine teacher, Pablo, is quite rocky until they come to an understanding of the balance and equity of the power in their relationship. She is making a film about Pablo who is teaching her to dance tango. Thus the film *The Tango Lesson* is in a sense a film about the making of the film which it is. The scene I want to consider takes place as Sally and Pablo are walking down a Parisian street. They chat and then they break into dancing for a few steps and then they separate briefly and fall out of dancing. Then they reconnect in a tango frame and again break into dancing for an extended dance sequence moving down the walkway finally ending in a tango pose. With the dancing movement now ceased, they find themselves a bit surprised to be back in their quotidian reality; it seems they have only at this moment, after the dancing has stopped, become aware of the wonder of being absorbed in their dancing. As they look about them they discover that the world has changed; indeed it has, it is now snowing.

While these dance film scenes are exciting and engaging, I do not select them because they illustrate something unusual about dancing. Quite the contrary, they show something I think common to all dancing and that will serve as one premise that is the basis for this chapter. Dancing is certainly moving, it is a form of movement, but not all movement can be considered dancing. In this chapter I will focus on the larger more pervasive sense that human movement constitutes the grounding context for a more precise and provocative consideration of dancing. Everything that can be discovered about moving also pertains to dancing, yet it does not alone distinguish dancing among movings. I will frequently use dancing examples to discuss moving, thus suggesting possible distinctions of dancing.

PRIMACY OF MOVEMENT

Some years ago I taught a course on the importance to the study of religion of the developments related to brain and body achieved in various scientific and philosophical fields. Many times before this term I had taught courses on various topics around the theme religion and body intended to complement what I felt has been a marked disregard of the body by academic studies of religion. I had tentatively titled the course "Brain and Body," but then in the last weeks before the course began, reflecting on my interest in dance and in the moving body, I decided I should include something specifically on movement and began searching for relevant materials. I frankly saw it then as a small complement to the other topics; a complement that I felt personally obliged to add. That I did not act in terms of what I then knew, but somehow could not acknowledge, is now something of an embarrassment; indeed, I now see that from the perspective of movement the entire approach grounded on the assumed separation of mind and body, even if my efforts were to integrate them, is an unnecessary confusion; indeed, now I think this approach does more harm than good. Teaching that course I began to realize that, while we are generally still locked into the uncomfortable and unresolvable binary oppositional terminology of brain and body, to center studies of religion and culture, including dancing, on movement circumvents the need for this binary oppositional distinction in the first place. There is, as I came to appreciate it then and increasingly since, a primacy of movement. I will make a stronger and hopefully compelling case for revisioning religion and the study of religion in these terms.

A provocative general work on human movement is Maxine Sheets-Johnstone's 1999 book *The Primacy of Movement*. An interdisciplinary scholar who has written extensively on dance and philosophy, Sheets-Johnstone wrote,

> In the beginning, we are simply infused with movement—not merely
> with a propensity to move, but with the real thing. This primal ani-
> mateness, this original kinetic spontaneity that infuses our being and
> defines our aliveness is our point of departure for living in the world
> and making sense of it. . . . We literally discover ourselves in move-
> ment. We grow kinetically into our bodies. In particular, we grow into
> those distinctive ways of moving that come with our being the bodies
> we are. In our spontaneity of movement, we discover arms that extend,
> spines that bend, knees that flex, mouths that shut, and so on. We make
> sense of ourselves in the course of moving.[1]

There is a thrilling gravity and provocative insight in this brief passage.
According to Sheets-Johnstone, we are born into the world not with concepts and consciousness, but as moving bodies. We do not learn how to
move as we come to life even in the womb and after we are born; we
come with movement as identical to life itself. Life means moving from
beginning to end. Further, we come as a human body that has amazing,
but not infinite, potential for moving. Knees and other joints bend or flex
in just certain planes. Mouths open and close, but their movement has a
limited range and it is connected with specific events like eating and
speaking. Spines flex in remarkably complex ways, yet they are also mechanically and muscularly designed for specific and limited movements.
And Sheets-Johnstone reminds us of an elementary fact, infants move.
They do not move to accomplish anything in the sense of some "I can,"
but rather as an aspect of their being alive. In movement, however seemingly random in the beginning, we animate organisms discover and
create ourselves and our world; that is as we encounter through self-
movement and touch the world into which we are born. Sheets-Johnstone
may seem to be saying the self-evident; a reminder of what we already
know. Yet, the provocation is to comprehend how even at the most basic
neurobiological level movement leads to discovery and construction of
self and world. We must even ask, "What is movement, human self-
movement?" And we must pursue the implications of understanding
moving for our deeper understanding and appreciation of dancing.

Primacy of movement implies that such important concepts as self,
consciousness, awareness, knowledge of the world, perception, meaning,
and vitality are all grounded and realized in movement, or more specifically and accurately self-movement, and that we do not learn to move in
this primal sense; moving is living.

Sheets-Johnstone's work is in the lineage of phenomenologist Edmund Husserl and particularly important to her was his idea of "animate
organism."[2] One immediate importance of focusing on movement is that
we need not separate humans from other animate creatures who, according to Husserl, discover their own selves through their distinctive self-
moving. That they may not come to the same sort of perception and
awareness that humans experience is thus due to specific physical and

kinesthetic differences between the bodies of various animate species. Thus humans and other animate beings are alike with respect to the primacy of movement, yet different in the make-up and functioning of their moving bodies. The species and the character of their being and awareness are distinguished one from another by the morphology of their moving bodies. However inelegant is Husserl's term "animate organism," it declares the inseparability of all the organs necessarily integrated by their animateness, that is, as moving complexities of organs that, while analytically distinguishable, can never function in isolation from the complex organism.

Consider Sheets-Johnstone again.

> If we take seriously that the (experience) "I move" precedes the (conceptual realization) "I can do," and if we take with equal seriousness the fact that specific perceptual awarenesses of ourselves arising in everyday tactile-kinesthetic acts of doing something are the touchstone and bedrock of our discovery of "I cans" and in turn of corporeal concepts, then it is clear that movement is absolutely foundational not only to perceptual realizations of ourselves as doing or accomplishing certain things or making certain things happen . . . and to correlative cognitive realizations of ourselves as capable of just such acts or activities, but to perceptual-cognitive realizations of ourselves as alive, i.e., as living creatures, animate organisms, or animate forms. Aliveness is thus a concept as grounded in movement as the concept "I can."[3]

Sheets-Johnstone holds that movement is foundational to our perception of ourselves, to our perception of the world we live in, and to our ability to act in the world. Even more directly she contends that our sense of self, our self-awareness, our perceptions and perceptive knowledge, our ability to act in our world and our agency are all founded on self-movement and the experience we acquire through moving in and interacting (implying touching) with our bodies and the environment. She conjoins all of these attributes bound together in movement as "aliveness."

Lest we think that this primacy of movement is confined to the early infant pre-language period of human development, Sheets-Johnstone writes,

> In discovering ourselves in movement and in turn expanding our kinetic repertoire of "I can's," we embark on a lifelong journey of sense-making. Our capacity to make sense of ourselves, to grow kinetically into the bodies we are, is in other words the beginning of cognition. In making sense of the dynamic interplay of forces and configurations inherent in our on-going spontaneity of movement, we arrive at corporeal concepts. On the basis of these concepts, we forge fundamental understandings both of ourselves and of the world.[4]

In condensed form Sheets-Johnstone lays out the blueprint of the foundational role of movement in the constitution, development, and maintenance of our being human animate organisms. It is as she says "a lifelong journey of sense-making" with movement essential to "body concepts" that are operative at all levels of sense-making and even perception itself. I will follow this blueprint throughout the balance of this chapter to deepen our comprehension of the primacy of movement.

A more sophisticated exploration of movement than Sheets-John-stone's, but in continuity with it, is presented by French contemporary philosopher Renaud Barbaras who has written extensively on movement in the intellectual heritage of phenomenologists Henri Bergson, Edmund Husserl, and Maurice Merleau-Ponty. I will turn to Barbaras a number of times in this chapter and book, but in this section the issue is to establish the primacy of movement and the implications of this primacy for our study of dancing and our understanding of religion and the study of religion. I am eager to consider Barbaras in terms of the complex issue of how we might understand movement itself; that is, the dynamic proces-sual moving aspect of moving. But, first with regard to its primacy, Bar-baras wrote:

> movement is ontologically irreducible. With movement, we enter into another order of reality: in classical terms, movement cannot be a mode or an attribute; it is always substantial and necessarily engages the essence of the subject. It is thus not possible to conceive of the move-ment of animals as something that accrues to them because of their special situation, because of a need, because of something external to their essence. It is quite intrinsic to movement that it does not and cannot arise from something foreign to it; movement is not a mere contingent modality; it is not possible to enter into the sphere of move-ment if one is not already in it.[5]

Movement, or more accurately living movement or self-movement as I often term it, then is not something acquired by a living being nor is it a mode or attribute of a living being. An organism does not exist to then acquire movement or to have movement as one of its attributes. Rather movement is primary to and inseparable from the aliveness of animals. Not only is there a primacy of movement for animate organisms, there is an ontological irreducibility to movement itself. Movement cannot arise from non-movement; it is not contingent on anything outside of move-ment; it is not something that can be entered from outside of movement. Barbaras holds that for animals, including humans, moving or self-mov-ing is of their being, what constitutes them as animals, not something acquired or added on. Thus for animals there is a primacy of movement and an ontological primacy of movement itself.

Barbaras restates:

> a being can move itself only if it is able to move itself, in other words, to bring itself forward within the realm of mobility. A being can enter into movement empirically only on the condition of being characterized by

> a fundamental mobility: it has a movement only insofar as it is in some sense movement. . . . An essential feature of animals is that they move themselves, which means that they are the subject of their own movement.[6]

Self-movement is animal ontology, animal is animal only in terms of self-moving. Movement is for animals the primal phenomenological specificity, inseparable from life, animal aliveness. And in this statement Barbaras, like Sheets-Johnstone, connects self-movement as primary to perception and to the self, by holding that animals "move themselves." For Barbaras self-movement is profoundly constitutive of subjectivity, of the self. We can anticipate the complexity and richness associated with movement as Barbaras holds that a being can move itself, yet this self cannot be grasped phenomenologically apart from its self-movement. This notion of primacy is not a simple statement of definitive criteria; it impinges on and is inseparable from every aspect of perception and vitality.

As I discovered, to focus studies of dancing and religion and culture on movement is something totally different than a focus on body. I cannot overstate the importance of the difference. Recent studies of religion and culture are showing increasing interest in focusing on what is often referred to as "body" or "materiality."[7] While this new emphasis is offered as a development, the inclusion of what has been overlooked by an overly mind (text) focused approach, and it is, it nonetheless continues to affirm, indeed it presupposes, the classic Cartesian duality: body/mind, body/spirit, soma/psyche, body/text, matter/consciousness. Even cognitive science considers a fundamental capability required of any new paradigm is the resolution of "the mind body problem."[8] There is almost ubiquitous discussion of the mind/body separation as a "problem" often identified with Descartes. However, framing studies of religion and culture in an understanding of the primacy of movement, self-moving, there is no longer a need to solve this problem. We need not focus on the forgotten or overlooked body. We need not integrate mind and body. When we comprehend the primacy of movement the negative consequences of the so-called mind/body problem simply do not arise. I will develop and exemplify this approach throughout this book.

Later I will consider movement from a neurobiological perspective focused particularly on proprioception. In that context movement occurs neither as the result of the body whose muscles and bones enable it to move nor because the mind/brain serves as the master ordering the body to move. Rather, movement is constitutive of the proprioceptive organism. Movement is primary and, insofar as we care to analyze the neurobiological mechanics engaged in movement, we will need to incorporate the interdependence of every system and attribute of the entire animate organism. At the neurobiological nexus, proprioception, there is no necessary or clear separation or hierarchy of neurology and physiology. Self-movement is not something acquired or some feature displayed; it is ontological and also ontogenetic.

Here is how Barbaras describes this position:

> movement escapes the separation of interior and exterior, of lived experience and the living being. Movement is neither consciousness nor matter but another mode of being on the basis of which a fragment of matter present to itself, that is, a flesh, can probably constitute itself. This is why life can be equally grasped from the interior and from the exterior.[9]

Throughout life we depend on self-movement for our self-understanding and our understanding of the world because we are movement through and through, inside and outside. Later I will take up in more detail a neurobiological consideration of what Sheets-Johnstone means by "the dynamic interplay of forces and configurations." I will discuss how it is that our very perceptual faculties and processes are neurobiologically grounded in self-movement. And I will also consider in greater detail the notions of what she means by "corporeal concepts," particularly as this notion is developed by cognitive scientists George Lakoff and Mark Johnson as "image schemas" and "basic level categories."

Dancing is through-and-through movement, self-movement. As we comprehend the primacy of movement to animate life we cannot help but enrich our appreciation and comprehension of dancing. With dancing as a widely acknowledged religious form of movement, the insights gained have implications for our understanding of religion and the way we approach the study of religion.

THE DANCER'S SENSE

I regularly teach a course called "Religion and the Senses." In preparing for and teaching this course I have read a good deal not only on humans as perceptual beings, but also on the remarkable and amazing aspects of every one of our commonly designated five senses: taste, touch, smell, sight, and hearing. The study of the human senses is endlessly interesting to me and in ways that we all can almost always confirm through personal experience because we are sensory beings. Yet my efforts to discover a sense particular to dancers were long confounded. As I ticked through the various senses dancing did not seem to depend heavily on any particular sense. Taste seems negligible. Touch is certainly present in that dancers are always in contact with the earth or the floor and sometimes with one another, yet touch does not seem sufficient as the dancer's sense. Dancers sweat and can smell themselves and other dancers. Social dancers may enhance their presence with scents, yet clearly smell won't do as the dancer's sense. Dancers usually depend on sight to relate to the space and to other dancers, but seeing is certainly not necessary to dancing. I think fondly of the tango dance done by the blind and cantankerous Lt. Col. Frank Slade (Al Pacino) in *Scent of a Woman*. So we cannot depend on that one. That leaves only hearing. While dancing is most often done to the accompaniment of music, clearly one can dance in silence or without music or sound as some post-modern dancers intentionally do such as the Trish Brown Dance Company. And, of course, the deaf have no trouble dancing.

So what might serve as the dancer's sense, some combination of senses? That possible solution never satisfied me. Or perhaps, I mused, dancers don't really rely on senses in any distinctive way. But I hate that notion since dancing is such an obviously sense luscious action; how can we possibly ignore the senses in something so inherently sensual?

Then I discovered that some views on the sensorium do not consider the five senses we commonly list to adequately cover the full perceptual spectrum, the full perceptual capabilities of human beings. The sense most commonly invoked at this point is often referred to as the "kinesthetic sense" and sometimes as "proprioception."[10] Kinesthetic obviously refers to movement and that we somehow sense and are aware of our own movement, of the position of our bodies, and the various parts of our bodies. This perception of movement complements the common five senses. Proprioception is perception of self. Proprioception refers to neurobiological receptors located in the muscle fibers and the ligaments that sense load and tension on muscles and send that information to the spinal column and the brain to let the central nervous system know how things are going in the muscles and joints. Proprioceptors also communicate with the muscle fibers in directing movement. Proprioceptors functions to prevent injury, to maintain balance, to allow for awareness (usually unconscious) of the location of body parts relative to the rest of the body and to the surrounding space. Proprioception works in conjunction with and as a part of our sensorimotor system which both directs movement as well as monitors the consequences of movement resulting in movement adjustments as well as knowledge of interactions with self and world through movement. Very cool.

As I learned about proprioception I began to be excited that this sense might qualify as the dancer's sense, yet when paired with an appreciation of the "primacy of movement" this seemingly overlooked and relatively ignored sixth sense suddenly offers remarkable promise. Without even needing a detailed neurological description of the functioning of the sensorimotor system and how through signals sent from the brain to body parts (efferent) to initiate self-movement or the various afferent (towards the brain) neurological signals that come from the receptors in the muscles and joints back to the spinal column and the brain, we can realize that this neurobiological system is fundamental to everything we found associated with the primacy of movement for animate organisms. The link of the primacy of movement and proprioception is highly promising for our study of dancing.[11]

Extending Sheets-Johnstone a bit here, we are born into the world with sensorimotor programs already in place to move and to sense the physiological reactions we encounter, through touching, during movement. This process seems no different from being born with a heart that beats, lungs that breathe, or functioning arms and legs, indeed, movement is the functioning aliveness of all these. Our heart beats and functions to provide life because of its inseparability from preset neurological programming and physiological/muscular functions. So too we have neurobiological programs that operate, inseparable from life itself, as aliveness, to create movement, build awareness and knowledge, and in the response to the experience of movement gained when encountering the environment through touch. This process requires the looped interdependence of both brain-based direction of movement and muscle-based readings of the interaction with body and environment. Seen this way the sensorimotor system—comprised necessarily of neurology and physiology, of brain and muscles—is the "animate organism" described by Husserl and discussed by Sheets-Johnstone.

I will return later to proprioception because it is clear it must play a central role in our understanding of movement and human perception. It will be my task to apply this knowledge, these perspectives, also to dancing. At the moment, we must simply understand that, as living beings, we are foremost animate organisms. We come into the world moving and this movement is how we come to understand self and begin the lifelong process of building concepts and knowledge and skills by which we live in the world. The kinesthetic sensorimotor proprioceptive nexus requires no integration. The notion of body and brain, experience and conceptual knowledge, perception and the perceptible are actually backfilled territorializations from which movement has been removed. By focusing on self-movement enabled neurobiologically by proprioception there is no separation that needs to be overcome because all is integral to the animate organism. Dancing, as self-moving, both benefits from this aspect of all human movement and plays its own part in being heuristic as well as agentive, that is, dancing is a means of investigating the world as well as a way of impacting the world by performing valued actions. Dancing creates the foundation for meaning and value. Dancing is a form of movement that helps us articulate the distinctiveness humans enjoy among all other animate organisms.

Should we be even slightly convinced that what I am proposing is an important way to understand and appreciate dancing, we must immediately see the limitations on and the misdirection of many of the modern Western perspectives that dismiss dancing as being of little value whatsoever to education or production, that isolate dancing from religion because it is thought to be limited to a sensuous, sinful, mortal body, and that marginalizes dancing even among the arts.

A peek at the kinesthetic sense that is connected with human self-movement and allows us to identify a possible dancer's sense opens the door to a greatly expanded understanding and appreciation of dancing. I will continue to focus on aspects of self-movement trusting for now that they also apply to dancing, realizing that I must return to a more precise consideration of what dancing itself is that takes place when one breaks into dancing, when we start "dancing in the rain" rather than just "singing in the rain" as we walk rhythmically down the lane.

MOVEMENT AND PERCEPTION

I want to tell a story, a description of a scientific procedure really and the stunning results. It is not a story easily forgotten. It is even disturbing in some measure, but endlessly fascinating. So here goes. As we all know, newborn kittens take a few days to gain the perceptive ability to see. This scientific procedure separated newborn kittens and confined them to the dark for extended periods. When they were allowed to be in the light they did so under the following conditions. The kittens were divided into two groups. One group of kittens were allowed to freely move about their environment as any kittens do. We have all enjoyed watching newborn kittens as they crawl around and bump into things and explore with their cute little paws and noses and roll about seemingly randomly. The kittens in the other group, let's not forget them, were placed in little carts attached to paired mates from the first group. I have not seen a photo of this, so I can't quite imagine how these carts worked or what they looked like nor how the other kittens were actually so "free" to move about their environment having to drag a mate in a cart with them. Getting past these technical concerns and doing our best to ignore the sad feelings we have for this whole lot of kitties being subjects in experiments, especially when we learn the outcome, here is what was discovered. The self-moving kitties developed normally and were able to "see" after several days; however, the kitties that were moving, but not self-moving, were functionally blind and did not ever gain sight even as they grew into cats.

Yikes! If we are to believe these results, and the experiment is reported by respectable scientists,[12] there are striking implications that build directly on the point about movement I have been developing. The kittens in the carts supposedly moved through approximately the same spaces and in the same patterns as did their paired mates. However, the only kitties that gained functional sight were those that proprioceived their space, that is, that actually encountered their environment by an actively engaged sensorimotor system including touch and proprioception that both directs muscular actions as well as receives and responds to the consequent and related environmental interactions. Only the kitties that came into actual physical contact with their environment, only the kitties that experienced the environment through touching (groping) it, developed sight. Presumably the cart kitties' eyes were biologically identical to those of the cart-pulling kitties, yet they did not develop the neurobiological base programmings that enable sight. This story offers a rather literal and neurological understanding of Sheets-Johnstone's and Barbaras's notion of the "primacy of movement" and the "discovery of self and world" through self-movement. [13]

Similar results have been documented for the congenitally blind who have, through later life surgical procedures, gained the biological capacity for sight. Many of these people who, in a romantic view, should experience the miracle of sight by instantly being able to see everything, report that they see little more than annoying blotches. Most prefer to continue to act and live as though sightless, presumably because they are.

Thus, we begin to understand that sight, vision, the visual world, is not comprised of some objective images cast upon a screen in our brains that give us "pictures" of the world itself already divided into distinct visible order. Rather sight is based in proprioceptive sensorimotor experience and is actually dependent upon it. We also learn that there is a "critical period" during which the development of sight must take place or the capacity is lost.

Another important animal-based study involved ferrets. Apparently ferrets are born at a time when their neurological development is immature. Mriganka Sur at MIT surgically rewired the ferrets so that cells in the eyes were reconnected to the area in the brain that is normally dedicated to hearing. If the brain is the center and director of perception then the ferrets would actually hear with their eyes . . . huh? That would be expected because the eye cells are wired to the hearing area in the brain. However, as the ferrets developed they simply were able to see with their auditory brains. [14] The explanation then is that sight is a function not solely of the brain in the skull that determines and directs everything, but that sight for the ferrets occurs because the ferrets' interactions with the world shaped the brain itself. Neurobiologists show that perception arises from movement and interaction with the world and thus movement is primal. Perception develops as active self-moving bodies physically encounter their environments.

Such revelations are part of a major revision accelerating over the last century about how we perceive the world. [15] Still, in both quotidian and academic perspectives, we continue to hold to an understanding of perception in terms of the model of the simple camera obscura. Cognitive scientists refer to the parallel understanding of cognition as "representational" or "computational." We analogize our perceptive selves as being like the camera obscura, that is, we are like a box with a pin hole punched into it. Light reflecting off the object outside of our bodies (the box) passes through the hole (our eyes) and creates an image on some surface within the box (our minds, our memories, our brains). The image in the box, in our minds, is a replica or representation of the objectively given world outside the box, the observer.

In the simplicity of this analogy it seems actually rather silly to hold this view, but we need only remember how strongly attached we are to the truth of the "eyewitness" and to objectivity in education, law, and many other areas in society. I am endlessly badgered by my students when I ask them to write creative and engaging academic essays. Most hold to some identity of the academic with the objective with no room for creativity or subjectivity. The great majority of educational testing from the earliest levels through graduate school is based on the unquestionability of the objective measure even though philosophy and science, as is an implication of the examples I have just given, have shown for a century and more that such a position is untenable. I find it interesting that the examination of Supreme Court nominees always centers on the degree to which the nominee is deemed to be objective. Yet, every nominee is easily labeled as having certain leanings, and sitting justices each have a very consistent record of how they interpret the law. In light of some obsession of objectivity in this context, it is difficult I think for us to even understand what might be understood to be the meaning of the words "judge" and "judgment."

The kittens and ferrets demand the end of camera obscura and the end of objectivity. They demand the end of our assumptions that we are separate from our environment. They demand the end of the belief that the world is simply given, nicely divided into distinct objects available to be perceived. If any of the kittens can be said to have had an objective (i.e., not based on their own personal subjective experience) experience of the world it would be the cart-bound kittens, yet, as we learned they could not see at all. Most of us have defaulted to ride in the carts or worse to eliminate moving completely.

While the connection of movement and perception dates from Aristotle, Maurice Merleau-Ponty, an existential phenomenologist who died in 1961, building on Edmund Husserl and others, developed an entire ontology based on interaction between the percipient and the perceptible, that is, the one who perceives and the world that is perceived. I will take up his work in greater detail later, but for now it is important to note that since at least mid-twentieth century there have been many such as Merleau-Ponty who have demonstrated in increasingly undeniable terms that self-movement is essential to the development of even our most basic perceptual capacities and in the broadest sense shape the character of what we perceive and who we become.[16]

In the intellectual lineage of Henri Bergson and Merleau-Ponty the strongest connection between movement and perception has been articulated by Barbaras, the foremost authority on Merleau-Ponty. There is an obvious link between self-movement and perception in that self-moving beings (animal/human as discussed based on Barbaras above) are the same beings that perceive or, as Barbaras puts it:

> perception is essentially linked to movement. Beings capable of moving are the very ones that are capable of feeling; feeling and moving are the two aspects of the same mode of living, because movement assumes the desire for a goal, which itself requires the capacity for perceiving it.[17]

Yet, Barbaras acknowledges that more must be done to establish the constitutive relation between perception and movement beyond this fact of coincidence.

Barbaras looks to Goldstein's early twentieth century classic work on the holistic aspect of the life of organisms (important also to Merleau-Ponty) for the articulation what he called the "tonic phenomena," that is, the correspondence of sensory impressions with tension of musculature. Barbaras explains,

> This does not mean that sensation triggers a tonic phenomenon, nor that the muscular tension gives rise to a sensation, but rather that the sensation possesses a certain significance for the organism, a significance that is expressed also at the motor level. Movement on the one hand and the grasp of a determined quality on the other hand are two modalities by which the organism enters into a relation with the kind of event that makes sense for it.[18]

Goldstein's research, focusing particularly on optical and tactile impressions, demonstrated that these two modalities, movement and grasping qualities, are co-present and interdependent. Perhaps we can appreciate this connection most immediately in terms of our quotidian experience of touch. We can clearly understand that to perceive something by touch requires the movement of touching. I suppose the exemplar or prototype of touch most of us hold is to move one's fingertip back and forth across a surface in the act of touching to perceive qualities of texture. We have the same ordinary connections of seeing and moving as expressed in phrases like "Look over this." We are generally aware that because the eye has but a small area of the visual field in sharp focus and that peripheral vision is more of a perception of movement than any other quality, we understand that seeing is moving the eye about the object or visual field. But then there is the less commonly known phenomenon of the constant mostly unconscious micro-movements of the eyeballs in their sockets (saccades) without which vision blanks out.[19]

As this link of perception and movement is explored Barbaras comes to the position that

> the perceived necessarily possesses a dynamic significance; as the relation of an organic totality to an event[20] in its midst, perception involves

essentially an internal link with movement . . . if perception is a certain relation between the living subject and its surroundings, movement forms part of its essence.[21]

And Barbaras offers us other ways of understanding the inseparability of movement with perception. He holds that there is "a fundamental incompleteness at the heart of the living being."[22] This incompleteness arises because "life is from the start in touch with things other than itself."[23] In this separation whose connection Barbaras describes by a complex reconsideration of the term "desire," is the ground of an essential mobility of life. Desire for Barbaras is not a striving for the satisfaction of some need, but rather for manifestation or as he also puts it, "Life is not the satisfaction of needs but the experience of dispossession."[24] Perception is then the movement toward the other, the world, motivated by desire, that is, by a manifestation toward an incompleteness that can never be overcome. Barbaras continues,

> By going toward the world, the living being goes toward itself; insofar as the world is essentially inaccessible, the living being is, on the other hand, still always separated from itself. Thus, the relation of the world to the beings who appear in the world correlates exactly with the relation of the movement of existence to the acts in which this movement is accomplished.[25]

Perception and what Barbaras calls "living movement" are then two terms referring to the same amazingly rich and complex way of understanding ourselves.

One other way of comprehending the necessary inseparability of perception and movement begins to suggest to us something of what movement, particularly self-movement or living movement, is itself. I'll expand on this below, but to this point hopefully I have shown that movement, living movement or self-movement, is constitutive of and inseparable from our being animate creatures and our being perceiving creatures aware of our environment. Interestingly, on the one hand, isn't this just patently obvious? Yet, on the other hand, the primacy and constitutiveness of movement to being human is remarkably profound with implications that could easily take a lifetime to explore.

Again, this attention to movement is relevant to our efforts to understand and appreciate dancing. To see dancing as self-movement with qualities and patterns of moving and interacting with the environment that are invariably prescribed by culture and religion cannot be divorced from even our most basic experiences of perceiving the world in which we live. At this point in my presentation I expect that we can begin to appreciate that if, as a child, I study ballet I will literally perceive a different world than if I grow up in the streets defending my space by break dancing. I'll extend this example more fully.

THE KEY TO ACUITY

With the baby boomers entering retirement and their accompanying concerns about maintaining their mental health, a new multibillion-dollar industry has emerged related to brain acuity. The concerns seem to focus almost exclusively on memory, especially short-term memory. There is an unfortunate belief that is supported by high-powered medical establishments like Johns Hopkins that memory sharpness inevitably declines beginning at age 40. It's a long unavoidable slide, they say, to fuzzy-brained adults who arrive at this condition by their 60s. The rather unquestioned acceptance of this inevitability is supported by the widespread practice of telling self-ageist jokes, a practice that I admit I thoroughly detest. You know those little quips that refer to the supposed humor of lost capacities and lost memory. Phrases like "senior moment" are silly at best. I propose we reclaim this term "senior moment" and give it the value it deserves. Living for 60 or 70 or 80 years accumulates a goodly amount of experience and knowledge. Furthermore, over these decades we have hopefully adjusted expectations and gained a measure of perspective and patience. We should understand what is important and what is not. In many cultures around the world and certainly even in Western cultures a century or so ago, elders were those who were looked up to for their wisdom and their insight and their experience. So, I argue, those in their 60s and upward years should have regular occasions when they can say with great pride "now that was a senior moment" referring to an occasion when they used their experience and wisdom to handle a situation or to offer sage advice to another or to mediate a conflict with grace and peacefulness. Now that is what we should all look forward to, not some slide into irrelevance and forgetfulness and embarrassment.

Associated with this current eagerness to serve the forgetting is a plethora of books whose subject is the brain, how to understand it, how to care for it, how to nurture it, and so on. I have read quite a few of these and I am astounded that we still identify what I call "the brain in the skull" as the most important organ in the body and the only organ relevant to memory. The brain is seen as the controller and dictator of all a person is and does. The online branch of this brain industry offers, usually for a hefty price, exercises, games, and puzzles that claim to increase mental sharpness and memory. Independent research that has surveyed a great many of these mental exercises convincingly shows that while most lead to improved skill in the tasks that constitute the particular exercise—that is, with practice one can work certain types of puzzles better—the impact on overall memory acuity is not measurably significant. And, of course, all of this ignores that there might be any role of the body beyond the brain in the skull in this matter or even that perhaps there are roles for muscles and bones and proprioceptors in even shaping the brain.

In improving memory sharpness the only type of activity that has clearly demonstrable evidence of effect is physical exercise, moving one's body. The explanation for this finding is rarely even considered, but most commonly it is associated with the contribution of physical exercise to general health, to increased blood flow, and to a greater sense of vitality and motility. One clever scientist speaking in a National Public Radio interview recommended doing both, that is, the so-called brain challenging mental activities that rarely engage the body in movement as well as physical exercise.[26] When, at the end of the interview, he was asked what he personally did for his brain health and memory, he said that he did both at once, he walked on a treadmill while he read a newspaper.

Okay, I'm going to do my best not to be cynical or rudely critical, but I want to approach this matter of brain acuity and issues of memory in continuity with what we have discussed about moving so far. To briefly summarize the core propositions and observations: from birth (actually before) we learn, we gain a sense of self, we establish basic body concepts, we create fundamental neurobiological programming as an organism, through the sensorimotor-proprioceptive-touching-groping processes of moving ourselves in the world and encountering the world in physical ways. Furthermore, this process does not end at any particular age even though we have incorrectly believed that the brain is fully developed and thus set for life at around age seven. This process of human development continues in important ways throughout life, yet inseparable from self-movement. I will discuss later the notions of plasticity and how our lifestyle tends unnecessarily to support decreasing plasticity and the progressive decline of capacity and acuity.

An essential position we must gain from our discussion of the primacy of movement is that conceptual development, memory, acuity as an organism, and vitality are inseparable from sensorimotor-proprioceptive-touch activities. Thus, we may understand anew why physical exercise is so obviously important to brain acuity and memory. It is for all the reasons commonly given, but also because physical exercise involves self-movement and the essential proprioceptive-touch encounter with the environment. The experience of self-movement is the core of the process of learning and discovering and expanding and maintaining ourselves within the world.

While the scientific studies rarely differentiate types of exercise, usually limiting themselves only to the intensity and duration of exercise, it surely proceeds logically from our discussion that there are types of movement that are much more valuable than walking a treadmill while reading a newspaper. Remember the kittens! The point I want to make here is that while all forms of moving have documentable benefits, not all self-movement is the same particularly as a factor in mental capacity, recall, and acuity. Note that this "walking-while-reading" approach to "doing it all" is actually simple multitasking and that it is certainly not particularly challenging in either task because walking a treadmill is to call on extremely basic (well relatively speaking) sensorimotor programming unchallenged because of the total predictability of treadmill walking. The only mental challenge I could see in this activity occurs in the first minute or so on the first use of a treadmill when you have to figure out how to make it go and how to get walking on it so that you don't fall off. Beyond that, it requires no challenging attention. Isn't walking a treadmill functionally fairly equivalent to the kitties in the carts? Further, reading a newspaper or similar material has a proprioceptive dimension, but one isolated in the body to the eyes and thus the challenge is limited to mental comprehension of quotidian written language and reflections on the content. Furthermore, reading the news does not even engage the unexpected aspects that would accompany a human conversation about the news.

Taking inspiration from infants and kitties and ferrets, it is not difficult to propose that the most important type of action one may do to increase and maintain acuity (and this is acuity of the organism, incidentally, not just the brain) is challenging self-movement that engages an unknown or unpredictable environment, that is, physical movement that is challenging to the sensorimotor-proprioceptive-touch system. It is self-movement responsive to challenge from the environment requiring quick and varied movement responses, the more complex and challenging the movement, the better. This style of self-movement is an actively engaging challenging movement that demands one's attention to alter and adjust movement based on interaction with the environment. I have been interested in this idea for a long time and have surveyed a good many cultural activities to determine the presence of this more complete and effective form of activity and have found, interestingly, that many (yet fewer than might be expected) activities may have an initial phase when this occurs, but then quickly give way to simple repetition without much challenge.

Playing tennis (or similar competitive racquet sports) has a high measure of challenging self-movement because one must constantly adjust one's whole body movements in relentlessly unpredictable demands determined in response to the way the other player hits the ball. Riding a skateboard in a skate park or elsewhere is another example where balance, speed, and movement are constantly being impacted by the vastly changing terrain of the park or course, by the efforts of the rider to do particular tricks, and by the constant attention to other riders to avoid collisions. Basketball is another sport that demands constant engagement of the body based on environmental demands. And these principles can easily be applied to any activity.

Interestingly dancing is commonly identified as an activity that is engaging in this particular way. But not all dances are the same in this respect. I have developed a form of salsa that provides a fun way to accomplish this constantly challenging demanding self-movement. It is a form of *rueda de casino*, in which casino (or Cuban) style salsa is done in a circle with "called" moves (a caller shouts out the names of the moves in random sequences) that can be remarkably complex. The form I have developed engages every dancer in both the "lead" and "follow" roles and with the circle oriented to the inside as well as to the outside. Thus the movement is ambidextrous along two axes and has an environmental orientational challenge. The dance is done with partners so it requires touch encounters with multiple other dancers and changing of partners during dancing. And, of course, the dance is done to music. Thus, dancers must move in complex patterns while engaging partners to the music executing moves in both lead and follow roles immediately upon command and many of these moves involve changing partners or moving in complex interweaving patterns around the circle. I love this style of dancing and have taught it for years. However, I must admit that I have tried on many occasions to teach it to adults and found that adults tend, with few exceptions, to become frustrated and many simply cannot do it. Their frustration seems most fully associated with remembering movement on demand as well as the challenging ambidexterity and spatial orientation of the dance. Later I will take up the important topic of the cultural expectations and influences on our self-movement patterns during our life cycle. For many years I have taught *rueda de casino* to hundreds of high school kids and found that they love the dance and learn it with little difficulty, even though it seems that it is the penchant of teens to frequently vocalize their sense of how hard it is. I just laugh at them and keep them dancing. High school aged youth learn more rapidly than those college aged.

Another activity that I do regularly that I believe has similar characteristics is step aerobic exercise particularly when it is done in a "dancy" style and at the more advanced levels. Describing it offers further illustration. This is a movement form that is invariably found in fitness centers rather than dance studios. It involves moving on command in named patterns at medium speed on and off and around a piece of equipment (step) about 16″ by 42″. This step can be elevated to differing elected heights by the participant. A step class then involves called self-movement elements that build up into routines each comprised of perhaps half a dozen elements and then as many as five to seven of these routines are accumulated during an hour-long class. The named elements can be complex and the routines even more complex. The routines are always done both to the right and to the left (ambidextrous movement) and sometimes oriented both to the back of the step and the front of the step. The pace is constant throughout the class. In a class there are no ability levels, no breaks to teach elements, and no rest periods. A good step aerobics class provides an hour of constant challenging self-movement involving much of the body moving in complex and unpredictable ways. The instructor's call comes but a split second before the move is executed and the calls come fast and furious. Step aerobics is often referred to as a form of dance and that identification is worth reflection. A criterion commonly used to distinguish step classes is the level of danciness (if that is even a word). It seems to me what is being assessed here is the complexity, intricacy, variability, and unpredictability of the movement. A highly predictable step class tends to be more like walking a treadmill. With regard to acuity it is interesting that most dance forms, certainly not all, emphasize the lower body, the step patterns and sequences. The upper body is engaged for style or, in the case of step aerobics, to increase the level of exertion of the workout. Interestingly I have never heard but the vaguest mention of the contribution to whole body acuity that is gained from adding coordinated upper body movement or even to the advantages of the more dancy step classes.

So just to be sure that I am clear here: these challenging or demanding forms of self-movement require a person to respond to a stream of relatively random and frequent demands from the environment to immediately move many parts of the body at once in coordinated patterns with precision and intention and often in coordination with musical rhythm and to do so with an ambidextrous balance and in varying spatial orientations to the environment. Got it? Now compare this to walking a treadmill while reading a newspaper and you will appreciate that this step-aerobic self-demanding form of movement is in an entirely different universe. How could this form not produce much greater results related to acuity of the organism?

Like my efforts to teach *rueda de casino*, I've observed that step aerobics is a difficult activity for many people to enter. To come into the midst of this activity is daunting and can be discouraging. Many leave a step aerobics class in the first fifteen minutes. It takes considerable repetition before one can begin to feel that he or she knows enough of the moves in order to avoid finding oneself standing and watching others move or risking falling off the step. And a good class is so unpredictable that thankfully even the most experienced person will occasionally find a sequence challenging to follow on the first repetition. Step aerobics appeals primarily to women from college age through middle age. I will have more to say on this crazy gender situation.

The intense and rather exclusive focus on the brain currently so popular in the literature directed at intelligent generalist readers tends to ignore the essential importance of challenging self-movement. Further evidence is contained in this personal anecdote told by Pierce Howard, the author of *The Owner's Manual for the Brain* (2006). He writes,

> I've had many friends try to encourage me to take aerobic dance classes. For me, personally, that is a distasteful proposition—I don't

like the music most aerobics instructors use to motivate their partici-
pants, don't like the follow-the-leader format, don't like the emphasis
on dressing out for the event, don't like having to drive there. . . .
Instead I walk. I love to walk.[27]

I describe later why I think many of Howard's "don't likes" are based in
his gender and his age (he was early 60s at his writing), but the point here
is that neuroscientist Howard shows no awareness of the neurobiological
differences in the impact on organismic acuity between aerobic dancing
which is engaging the sensorimotor-interoceptive system in constant
creative stress and walking which, while an important form of physical
exercise, has little to no challenge to this system but relies on the most
common and simple sensorimotor patterns.

To summarize this discussion now: sharpness of animated organism
(what I used to refer to, yet now avoid, as brain/body acuity) is inseparable from challenging and demanding sensorimotor-proprioceptive-touch
self-movement. I will be unapologetically prescriptive. We should adopt
this form of self-movement as a lifestyle as early in life as possible and
not save it as a hedge against the mental decline associated with aging.
Dancing and dance-related movement forms often rank highly among
forms that offer the desired challenge, yet, of course, there are many
others.

MOVEMENT ITSELF

I have been talking about self-movement or living movement as though
we know what that is. Movement is a common term we use without any
need for explanation, yet not unlike so many things (dancing is certainly
an example), when we focus on what movement is itself, it is far more
complex than we might expect and yet the results of pursuing what
movement itself is are, I believe, remarkably rewarding. When we think
about it the actual moving part of movement is rather difficult to grasp.
The very word "grasp" suggests that movement is a thing that might be
held in one's hand or mind. Yet, the very idea of grasping[28] movement is
to deny the moving dynamic aspect of the movement we are trying to
understand. Typically we chart movement on a graph, or we think of a
trajectory, or we think of the point of initiation and termination of movement. These methods depend on traces of a movement event, a backfilling to account for action already passed, a way of describing or territorializing how movement unfolded over time and through space, but they
are not ways of actually understanding the moving aspect of a movement
event. Moving is associated with a transversal of time and space, yet it
cannot be said to be in some point in space and time because that would
take away its motion. Moving is incipience or coming into being. The

energy or tendency of moving is always denying place as it tends toward place. Desire for place is always unrealized. If considered manifest, that is, as occupying a space/time location, movement is no longer the movement itself but is only the trace or effect or remains of concluded movement.

Since dancing is moving, we can appreciate that we have a similar challenge in our study of dancing; a challenge we must see as an opportunity for insight. Indeed, we need begin to appreciate that it is a different thing to understand dancing (that incipient, almost becoming, always in the process, moving) than it is to understand a dance or dances, which are the basic patterns of movements and rhythms that comprise the distinctiveness of a dance among many dances. A dance is when it isn't dancing. I believe that it is first essential to be interested in understanding dancing because my use of the term dancing is to designate the vital active enactive aspect of all dances, and then, with the benefit of the insights and perspectives gained, to consider how it impacts our understanding of particular dances.

Let's look at this issue of movement itself a bit more carefully assisted by the 2002 book by Brian Massumi, *Parables for the Virtual*. He looks to the early twentieth century French philosopher Henri Bergson for revealing a way of comprehending movement itself in his discussion of Zeno's classic paradox. Zeno was a pre-Socratic Greek philosopher (5th century BC) who described the passage of an arrow from the shooter's bow to the target. He proposed that every space can be divided in half and that mathematically this division can continue infinitely. Given this property of space, an arrow would necessarily need to pass through any remaining space to get to the next. Yet since space can be infinitely divided the arrow would necessarily have to spend infinite time passing through subsequent endlessly divided segments of space and therefore, Zeno argues, could never reach the target; thus the paradox.

Bergson's analysis showed that Zeno's paradox arises from an analysis of a movement trajectory rather than the movement itself. Massumi describes Bergson's insight.

> If the arrow moved it is because it was never in any point. It was in passage across them all. The transition from bow to target is not decomposable into constituent points. A path is not composed of positions. It is nondecomposable: a dynamic unity. That continuity of movement is of an order of reality other than the measurable, divisible space it can be confirmed as having crossed. It doesn't stop until it stops: when it hits the target. Then, and only then, is the arrow in position. It is only after the arrow hits its mark that its real trajectory may be plotted. The points or positions really appear retrospectively, working backward from the movement's end. . . . A thing is, when it isn't doing. [29]

Movement, the moving itself, is necessarily prior to any grasping of or formulation of or analysis of the movement. This analysis of trajectory is a working back from moving itself having occurred in some post-movement construction of a trajectory. Perhaps this seems but a minor shift in perspective, one needed to help us keep from going crazy over Zeno's little mind-twister, yet Massumi goes on to outline the far-reaching consequences of this shift in perspective, and they are remarkably significant and important. The implications deserve extensive consideration, but let me just mention several of these consequences to help us grasp something of the importance of Massumi's and Bergson's revelation.

Movement is, in its becoming, absorbed in occupying its field of potential. Movement cannot be determinately indexed to anything outside itself. A proper study of movement emphasizes process before signification or coding. To do otherwise stops the movement, back-forms it into a grid. Thus, position is no longer the first concern with movement, but a problematic second. Position is retro-movement or movement residue. Positionality is an emergent quality of movement. Passage is primary in relation to position. Passage precedes construction. Grids happen. Movement is ontogenetic, that is, always a coming into being.

We can get a sense of the importance of Massumi's analysis by returning to the opening couple of sentences in his book:

> When I think of my body and ask what it does to earn that name, two things stand out. It moves. It feels. In fact, it does both at the same time. It moves as it feels, and it feels itself moving. Can we think a body without this: an intrinsic connection between movement and sensation whereby each immediately summons the other?[30]

Massumi discusses the implications of this shift through the balance of his book developing not only on Henri Bergson, but also on the work of such figures as Gilles Deleuze and Charles Sanders Peirce.

Something of the remarkable profundity of considering moving itself is addressed repeatedly in a number of Barbaras's works. Earlier in this chapter I began the presentation and consideration of Barbaras's understanding of movement, living movement, in terms of what he recognized as "a fundamental incompleteness at the heart of the living being." Thus, he writes

> to move is not to be what one is (or was); it is to be always beyond and therefore within one's self, to exist on the basis of noncoincidence. Within the "there is" there is negativity only as mobility, because the latter represents the only negation that is not based on a positive nothingness and therefore does not compromise the fullness of this "there is." This interior negativity in the world must be taken as attesting to the constitutive negativity of the subject insofar as it is subject for the horizon.[31]

Living movement then is that reaching always beyond attesting to an incompleteness, yet this is a negativity that is not a "positive nothingness" or a need that might be somehow fulfilled by the results of moving but rather accounts for moving itself, or living movement itself, or self-movement itself.

Barbaras develops this idea of movement in terms both of desire and distance which he carefully defines and discusses in his 1999 book *Desire and Distance: Introduction to a Phenomenology of Perception*. I introduced Barbaras's specific understanding of the term desire earlier in this chapter. To clarify his understanding of movement as well as my interest in appreciating movement itself as fully as we can, consider another Barbaras passage on desire.

> Desire is not an emotion subordinate to need, which allows need to be satisfied with maintaining the tension toward the future [*l'avenir*]. Desire defines the very essence of the living being. If the distinctive feature of desire is that the desired fuels it as much as it satisfies it, and if what is desired is always beyond that toward which it carried itself, so that nothing fills it in since it is not desire of anything positive, then desire exactly describes the mode of being of the living being as long as it manifests itself though a fundamental mobility.[32]

As I understand Barbaras, desire is not attached to the kind of positive need that might be filled as the result of some action. Rather Barbaras understands desire in the aspect that always demands a moving forward. Thus desire is associated with a need, an incompleteness, a nothingness, or negative need, that both creates the motivation for and opens the space for movement. Desire as movement *is* only so long as it isn't satisfied. Desire is then in some sense the fuel or the condition of movement set in a structurality that is endlessly, so long as there is life, self-perpetuating. Desire, this tension toward the future, is, as Barbaras puts it, "the very essence of the living being."

Shifting now to the language of distance, Barbaras reframes his discussion of living movement. The living being is from the beginning and always located in a world, an environment, that is separate, at a distance; yet this distance (I'll return to this idea later in term that Merleau-Ponty discussed as "pure depth") is then recognized as intrinsic to living movement. There must be a distance for movement to be motivated, yet this distance may never be closed or crossed for such would be the cessation of moving, and thus the loss of vitality. In a sense it is the endless threat of the collapse of this distance which is the constant motivation or *energia* of living movement. Barbaras addressed this aspect of movement further in these terms:

> conceptualizing living organisms on the basis of their constitutive mobility leads to recognizing that the intrinsic nature of living movement is such that it cannot be abolished, but on the contrary is ceaselessly

renewed, amounts ipso facto to recognizing that this movement never completely attains what it aims at, never comes to possess what it seeks to grasp; the object of this movement is irremediably situated at a distance. Because this Distance is manifestly irreducible, it is not spatial, which amounts to saying that this Distance is not to be confused with a simple empirically measurable length. . . . this Distance is ontological; it may give rise to a spatial approach, but it can never be abolished. In other words, there is an otherness [which I will discuss in a full chapter "Self-Othering"] about the world of living organisms that, far from being an obstacle or threat to life, is in reality its very condition of possibility.[33]

Distance in which movement occurs is space without dimension.

The following passage further deepens our understanding of Barbaras on movement. This remarkable account of the structural role of distance in comprehending moving itself anticipates topics that I will discuss at length in later chapters: self-othering, gap, seduction, playing, pure-depth. Clearly coming to terms with movement is invaluable to or study of dancing and also religion.

Movement serves the act of satisfaction and is the mediation between two states of completeness. Movement does not take root in life itself but in what puts life in danger. The living being is in movement, not insofar as it is living, but rather insofar as it is likely to cease living. Movement is the reply to an external threat, and as long as it is such, it is external to the essence of life. Consequently, if movement does not express life as much as the situation of precariousness in which life finds itself, we are led to wonder how movement is possible. How can a being that strives for self-preservation, which is repetition, be a mobile being? In truth, only a being that is originally capable of moving itself, that is essentially movement, is able to act to satisfy its needs; only a being that is originally in touch with exteriority is able to discover what is likely to suit it there. The empirical movement of the living being as displacement in space therefore refers to an essential mobility that is not explained by need but, on the contrary, makes its satisfaction possible.[34]

To keep dancing our central concern to the fore, lest we get lost in diversions, my point is that as it is important to comprehend moving itself rather than to be satisfied with an account of movement based on a back-filled trajectory of movement. Likewise, in order to develop an adequate understanding of dancing as fundamental to being human and as an important category for the comparative study of human cultures and religions, we must find ways of articulating dancing itself as necessarily prior to and constitutive of the study of dances, forms of dance, choreographers, and dance histories and traditions. It is in this endeavor that we will glimpse the inseparability of dancing from vitality, from energetics, from potentiality, and from a distinctively human engagement with "the essence of living being."

The body, or the animate organism as a physicality, that is, the thing moving and doing the moving, when seen in light of the transitional, processual, ungraspable aspect moving itself, demands to be broadly reconsidered. Massumi addresses this issue.

> To think of the body in movement thus means accepting the paradox that there is an incorporeal dimension *of the body*. Of it, but not it. Real, material, but incorporeal. Inseparable, coincident, but disjunct.[35]

The moving body is physical object but with an incorporeal dimension, that is, an otherness. It is at once a virtual and an actual body. Massumi goes on

> The body is as immediately virtual as it is actual. The virtual, the pressing crowd of incipiencies and tendencies, is a realm of potential. In potential is where futurity combines, unmediated, with pastness, where outsides are infolded and sadness is happy (happy because the press to action and expression is life). The virtual is lived paradox where what are normally opposites coexist, coalesce, and connect; where what cannot be experienced cannot but be felt—albeit reduced and contained. For out of the pressing crowd an individual action or expression will emerge and be registered consciously. One "wills" it to emerge, to be qualified, to take on sociolinguistic meaning, to enter linear action-reaction circuits, to become a content of one's life—by dint of inhibition.[36]

I think Massumi is discussing what Barbaras put in terms of the "precariousness" in which life finds itself, that external threat that seeks to collapse the virtual and actual in a seeming satisfaction that terminates movement that ends life. Movement is to live the paradox.

In my efforts to understand human movement and dancing and religion, I have become a huge fan of proprioception. Proprioceptors are the neuro-sensors that are wrapped around muscle fibers (muscle spindles) and are associated with ligaments in the joints embedded in the collagen of the connective tissue. They sense length and stress and communicate with the central nervous system to adjust sensorimotor programs to monitor and shape movement. Proprioceptors are commonly described as having only a feedback role secondary to the commands of the central nervous system, yet I much prefer to understand proprioceptors as the processual interstices where brain and muscle and bone are functionally inseparable in movement. Proprioception is the neurobiology of movement. Proprioception offers a parallel language rooted in neurobiology to investigate movement itself. It is little wonder that proprioception is the subject of deep contemplation by innovative thinkers such as Brian Massumi.[37] Proprioception, as Massumi explains it, folds tactility into the body, enveloping the skin's contact with the external world in a dimension of medium depth: between epidermis and viscera. The muscles and ligaments register as conditions of movement what the skin internalizes as qualities: the hardness of the floor underfoot as one looks into a mirror becomes a resistance enabling station and movement; the softness of a cat's fur becomes a lubricant for the motion of the hand. [38]

Massumi illuminates proprioception as an essential aspect of our "groping" [39] movements by which we discover self and other as we also create ourselves in the context of our exploration and discovery of the environment. Further, Massumi writes, "Proprioception translates the exertions and ease of the body's encounters with objects into a muscular memory of relationality. This is the cumulative memory of skill, habit, posture." [40] Massumi reveals the role of proprioception in gesture, a topic I will consider in much greater depth in the next chapter. Our encounter with the world creates movement patterned memories in our bodies which give us a sense of self and world, that is, proprioception "draws out the subject's reactions to the qualities of the objects it perceives through all five senses, bringing them into the motor realm of externalizable responses." [41]

There is a "double translation" offered by proprioception in movement that connects the self with the world, the body with the environment, translating both from the outside into the body and from the patterned movements of skill and gesture in the body outward to its agency and actions in the world. This double translation is always interactive and oscillatory. Appreciating this looping enaction gives us an understanding of movement itself. And further, as Massumi points out, proprioception is, in some sense, synaesthetic, in that it engages and integrates all of the common five senses.

Finally, proprioception is associated with affect, with feeling. In the simplest sense we often appreciate the sheer pleasure of moving. [42] This is something children clearly experience in that they seem to run everywhere they go. We need to recognize that the undeniable corporeality of feeling, of passion, of intensity, is inseparable from moving.

MOVEMENT AND MEANING

There is no meaning in movement itself. We cannot say what movement itself means in propositional terms. Yet in that movement is the manifesting of the desire to overcome the distance of virtual/actual, self/other, self/environment; it always trades in distinction and difference. Although movement is only when distinction and difference remain a negative need, that is, a need always almost fulfilled as it is seductively receding, never quite fulfilled, the distinction and difference are also necessarily valued and meaningful. The human propensity to backfill movement, to fulfill need, to satisfy desire, to close the gap, is as much a face of living movement as is its dynamical ceaselessness even as it is in a sense also its death. The primacy of movement and the ontogenetic character of movement itself (vitality) engages ontological primaries such as the self/other distinction and perception (a reversibility between perceiver and perceptible). Little surprise then that we find movement to be inseparable from meaning even though our efforts to comprehend the movement/meaning relationship is as rich and engaging as it is complex and elusive.

The next chapter "Gesturing" will explore aspects of movement and meaning in terms of gesture. Here I want to consider other dimensions.

The encouragement of movement among our children from infants throughout early childhood likely reflects our intuition that movement is essential to learning during this early and crucial period. In this period before language has been acquired or remains seemingly more pedestrian than the communication of concepts and ideas, movement seems the key to acquiring knowledge, learning language, and gaining and expressing meaning.

Mark Johnson discusses the relationship between meaning and the body in his 2007 book *The Meaning of the Body*. In his first chapter focusing on the role of movement he holds that *"from the very beginning of our life, and evermore until we die, movement keeps us in touch with our world in the most intimate and profound way. In our experience of movement, there is no radical separation of self from world."* [43] For Johnson this relationship between the human beings and the environment that is realized in movement is a relationship of meaning, meaning at all levels. It is in moving that, as we have already seen, we connect with the environment in ways that create and discover value and distinction, thus meaning. Johnson is not limiting this important role of movement to human development during those tender formative pre- or early-language years; he believes movement is essential to meaning "evermore until we die." It would seem that modern Western cultures have not adequately felt or understood this connection since they encourage progressively limiting and reducing movement with advancing age. Why then would we not expect an accompanying decline through life in vitality affects and the capacity to create fresh meaning? These presumptions need serious critical reconsideration.

Johnson charts quality aspects that associate movement and meaning using techniques similar to those Daniel Stern [44] uses to discuss vitality forms ultimately developed from Rudolf von Laban's system of movement analysis. This approach uses shaped lines to represent movement qualities such as explosive, graceful, halting, weak, or jerky. Sheets-Johnstone called these distinguishable patterns of movement that have both shape and quality as constituting "corporeal or body concepts." Johnson refers to them in the terms he and Lakoff developed, namely, "image schemas." He understands these image schemas to be foundational to, and constitutive of, all meaning, no matter how highly conceptual or seemingly abstract. While we may be comfortable with this sort of understanding of the acquisition of meaning for pre-language children, we may find that it challenges our understanding of how we acquire meaning in later life. We commonly think that meaning is contained in concepts that we are then taught through explanation and exemplification based in language. That is, we think of meaning as something delivered to us by means of language in terms of concepts. Johnson states his position quite clearly, *"The key to my entire argument is that meaning is not just what is consciously entertained in acts of feeling and thought; instead, meaning reaches deep down into our corporeal encounter with our environment."* [45] That is, all meaning is based in and founded on the experience of the human body moving in and interacting with its environment. Meaning is grounded in felt and experienced qualities and in principled relationships all established in movement.

Image schemas or body concepts are then foundational distinctions and relationships that are acquired through repetitive movement and, although they are invariably unconscious, serve as foundational to all constructions of meaning including logic itself. There are a number of essentials to constructing image schemas and how they come to construct meaning. They are inseparable from the moving body. They arise from repetitive movement that engrains patternings as sensorimotor programs or engrams. They are relative to species neurobiology. They are impacted by cultural/historical/individual experiences. In this respect they are among the means of fundamental transmission of culture. In being established in experience and remaining largely unconscious image schemas appear to us to be natural, real, true, obvious, without question or doubt.

Johnson invokes John Dewey's "principle of continuity" to argue that wherein image schemas function at the most basic level of meaning, they also inform in decisive ways meaning at every level including the most abstract conceptual levels.

The simple INSIDE-OUTSIDE image schema is an important example allowing us to appreciate the concept. Sheets-Johnstone holds that "in" is the first spatial concept humans develop. [46] Clearly from earliest human experiences, even prenatal, there is the experience of the distinction between inside and outside and qualitative associations are always present. Inside the womb is safe and nurturing. The movement from inside to outside is highly charged even in the preconscious experience of birth. Eating and excreting require movement from outside to inside to outside and these movements are highly charged emotionally from birth. The body and particularly movement patterns involving moving from outside to inside the body and the inverse are fundamental movement experiences in which we understand not only our bodies in relationship to the world, but the fundamental relationship with all the accompanying logic of INSIDE-OUTSIDE. In his classic book *The Hidden Dimension* (1982), Edward T. Hall documented wide cultural differences in the perceptions of and needs for personal space.

Then this inside-outside distinction supports the fundamental concept of container. The meaning and distinction of container is dependent on the INSIDE-OUTSIDE image schema. The CONTAINER metaphor in turn, that is, understanding abstract distinctions in terms of the entailments of CONTAINER, underlies everything from concepts of category to issues of definition and distinction. Yet, we can also appreciate that it is quite possible that variations in lived experience can lead to distinctly different experiential bases as well as relational principled understandings of this fundamental body concept or image schema. Consider how attentive we are to such things as setting "clear boundaries" and developing "inappropriate boundaries" or the "trespass of personal boundaries." We are concerned with touching others because this behavior establishes the experiences and principles of fundamental image schemas that then provide the basis for so much else of what we understand and experience. We often attribute personal difficulties or seeming aberrant behavior to such fundamental image schematic formations as INSIDE-OUTSIDE.

Image schemas are not usually constructed from a single experience or movement (although they may be powerfully shaped by a traumatic experience), but rather through high repetition of routinized movement, patterned movement. I'll take this repetitive or habitual aspect of movement up in much greater detail when I consider gesture, but it is clear that it is deeply relevant to dancing and to ritual. Dancing presents repetitive patterns of movement that are often strongly associated with quality and value, often culturally determined, and that establish specific sets of distinct image schemas or body concepts.

Maxine Sheets-Johnstone offered body concepts as foundational to human discovery of self and world. Mark Johnson, relying on his collaborative work with George Lakoff, developed this idea in the terms of image schemas. Image schemas are processes and relational, akin to verbs. Complementing these ideas is the notion of "basic level categories" developed by Lakoff and others relying on a history of the concept that stems from the middle of the twentieth century. This construct, focused on category formation and function, complements the "image schemas" by being more like nouns. It has been determined that in the development of categorical distinctions there is a mid-point in the hierarchy of related category terms that contains the most basic terms in the category set. For example, in the set that includes chair, there are a large number of sub-categorical terms that modify and refine this category such as bean bag chair, kitchen chair, lawn chair, and high chair. Further, chair is a category belonging to other categories such as the composite category furniture. It has been determined that basic level categories share a number of distinctive features. They are the first in the series acquired by children learning a language. They are the simplest of the terms in the series. And most important to our present concern is that basic level categories arise from and are based in movement patternings, that is, in the development of associated sensorimotor programs, or we might appropriately refer to them as gestures. Lakoff's understanding of basic level categories reveals that these foundational building blocks for the construction of meaning are grounded in movement; and that is a major revelation. For example the basic level category "chair" is bodily grounded in the gestural pattern of sitting. It is the gestural action of sitting that allows us to call by the same simple term objects as seemingly unrelated and physically different as a large bag of beans and an exquisitely fashioned and crafted wooden object. Notice that the higher level category "furniture" does not have a single gestural program associated with it, but many rather different movement patterns and would thus necessarily arise at a later stage. Also lower level categories such as "kitchen chair" or "bean bag chair" are connected with the general gestural program sitting yet have refinements or sub-programs that allow the subset distinction. Thus, there is strong evidence that basic level categories, foundational to the way we understand ourselves and our environment in terms of categorical distinctions, are based at once necessarily on both the distinctiveness of the human body (its distinctive neurobiology, its morphology) and also on movement/gestural/postural/touch interactional experiential processes.

Because basic level categories are grounded in human experience, the implications for category theory are deeply significant. The establishment of basic level categories serves to undermine classical category theory which is grounded on the notion that reality exists independent of human perception and is simply objectively available in the terms we grasp as categories and distinctions. The implications of basic level categories being constituted and discovered inseparable from distinctively human gestures then demands the construction of a new category theory in contrast to classical category theory. Lakoff and Johnson call this "prototype theory" and it is based on a category associated with specific human movement experience.

A major aspect of the development of category theory is the awareness that basic level categories are shaped to gradients of characteristics that correlate with experience. While all human bodies have closely similar neurobiology, clearly not all human experience is the same. There are obviously cultural, historical, and individual variations. These add a healthy messiness to category theory that is always unacceptable in classical theory. Lakoff[47] proposed that understandings and distinctions of categories are based operationally on best cases or prototypes rather than on logically defined distinctive features. A prototype is a loose idea of what a best representative of a category should generally look or be like and then other members of the category can be admitted or excluded based on some proposed likeness or difference to the prototype. Obviously this similarity/difference could be constructed in terms of limitless attributes of the prototype. The prototype arises based on the most common or natural gestural patterns, affordances (Gibson), enactions (Varela) one would have with a category delimiter and there are fairly clear grounds for how these prototypes are selected and function. Best examples usually function without awareness or consciousness to distinguish categorical boundaries. And, obviously, best examples (prototypes) are not the same from culture to culture; they are not necessarily universal. Yet, because of the foundational and constitutive role played by the distinctively human neurobiology there is compatibility despite cultural and historical determinations. This helps us appreciate the complexities of communication and the rich varieties of world views. It might be argued that if classical category theory held, there would be no need for comparative culture studies.

While movement itself does not have specifiable meaning, movement nonetheless is the stuff of which meaning is made. Johnson sums it up this way:

> We humans are live creatures. We are acting when we think, perhaps falling in and out of step with the environment, but never are our thoughts outside of it. Via the aesthetics of our bodily senses, the environment enters into the very shape of our thought, sculpting our most abstract reasoning out of our embodied interactions with the world.[48]

We now must appreciate that body concepts/image schemas and basic level categories are the mechanisms by which through movement/gesture/posture/touch we discover and construct ourselves and coincidentally our environment. Dancing as a repetitive culturally shaped human form of movement/gesture/posture/touch contributes to this most fundamental human meaning-making.

We often ask ourselves, "What is the meaning of that dance?" While we may sometimes even come up with some programmatic explanation or description, we are often confounded as to how to approach this question. In dancing the moving itself tends to discourage the backfilling needed to address specific meaning. Yet, as routinized patterned movement that in itself may not have specifiable meaning whatsoever, dancing can be understood in the terms of playing a role in establishing image schema and basic level categories as sensorimotor programs, the experiential and even logical reasoned basis for the very principles and foundations on which meaning can be acquired and expressed. Further, we may begin to understand that the analysis of meaning related to specific genres or types of dancing is not to offer some explanatory statement of its particular meaning (that is another matter), but rather in discerning the image schemas born in the specific dance movements.

While this proposition may seem rather abstract, perhaps an extended comparative example focusing on well-known dance forms might serve to clarify.

BREAKIN' AND BALLET

In the early 1980s a number of popular films contrasted "street" dancing, that is, hip hop and breakin', with "studio and art" dancing, that is, ballet, jazz, and modern. The trend of these highly formulaic films has continued to the present. An extensive review of these films would be fun and perhaps insightful (if rather repetitive), but here I'll just review several to help us understand how the differing movement styles and patterns construct and enforce image schemas that embody contrasting cultural meanings and values. Furthermore, since this film formula is broadly popular it is argued that the films support the images schemas represented.

Let's begin with the 1984 film *Breakin'* which was immediately followed by *Breakin' 2: Electric Boogaloo*. The break dance and hip hop in this film is west coast break dancing, often contrasted with east coast breakin' associated with the rise of rap, graffiti, and breakin' in the South Bronx in the late 1950s. In California breakin' in this period featured parachute pants, Adidas brand gear, and pastel colors. The film focuses on two black young male break dancers, Ozone and Turbo, who, practicing in their little garage apartments, are aspiring street dancers. A young white female studio-trained jazz dancer from the burbs connects with these guys and the dynamic tensions of the drama are set.

First, the chick has to gain some training in breakin' from these guys. When they first take her to a club battle including her as a dancer they are humiliated in a battle with another dance group. She wants them to enter her world by auditioning for parts in an upcoming jazz dance show. Her manager is concerned and offended by her hanging in the streets (well it is southern California so it is the beach walkway) and with untrained dancers. Yet, he is partially won over by attending the second club battle where they end up victorious. When the street boys come to audition for the jazz show they are rudely dismissed because of their street-dancer identities, yet they insist on showing their stuff and, of course, win starring roles in the show which, in the scenes that end the film, has been extensively reworked to incorporate the freshness of their street dance style. The audition scene is highly predictable (very much like the audition scene in *Flashdance*), yet demonstrates the contrast between the values of street dancers and those of staged art/entertainment dancers.

The values associated with these contrasting dances are clear and they correspond with movement and gesture. The obvious ones: studio-trained dancing—the ballet model no matter the dance—is art, high culture, trained, yet at risk of becoming stuffy and refined to the point of losing its energy and excitement and relevance. It focuses on formal rules, bodies trained to conform to specific movements, and has the potential to be predictable and boring. Street dancing however, as these films present it, is fresh, edgy, confrontational, energetic, improvisational, strong, unpredictable, and exciting.

Hip hop and breakin' are dances that are strongly in contact with the street both physically and culturally. These dances emerged in the South Bronx in 1950s where they were not only danced in streets and parking lots, they also literally take the dancer down on the street to spin and execute moves. This dance tradition has strong African and Latin American (itself strongly connected to Africa) influences, yet in the urban ghetto setting it takes on the postures and gestures of battle and combat. Dancing is done in a posse or crew (resembling, if not actually being, a gang), yet each dancer dances on his own. Only more recently and then in stage or formal competition settings have groups performed coordinated choreographed routines.

Hip hop and breakin' movement is forceful, masculine, confrontational, combative, aggressive, individual, improvisational, and virtuosic. It requires extensive physical strength and, somewhat unusual to dancing, particularly in the upper body (this may have some influence from capoeira, a Brazilian form of combative male dancing that arose over a century ago and has spread throughout the world). It involves extensive inversions in head spins and hand stands with the head closer to the street than the feet a good portion of the time. Training for hip hop and breakin' involves individual repetitive efforts in one's garage or on the street corner or while actually dancing in public. Dancers learn from one another perhaps stealing moves more frequently than learning them in a friendly exchange. Learning this sort of dancing is not done in studios; yet, of course, as with so many dances and musics (including rap) it eventually became commercialized and transmitted in this way.

The image schemas or body concepts are rather straightforward. Horizontal is the predominant plane of movement corresponding with values of confrontation and combat. The movement is muscularly powerful and masculine. It is down on the street. It is "in your face" and confrontational and full of "attitude." There is a circular image schema that includes the surrounding crew and opponents as well as the spinning on head and back. The circle and circular movement is dynamic and moving (spinning as a demonstration of strength and virtuosity and balance). Yet the circle is closed and is a container, which in social terms is exclusivist and associated with camaraderie. The circle encloses the dance where all are participant dancers. Improvisational movement and demonstrations of brute/physical strength are fundamental to winning and surviving. Individual improvisation for brief bursts of virtuosic dancing is typical.

Jazz/ballet trained dancing constructs quite different image schemas. Control, conformity to a long tradition of highly defined movement technique, verticality, feminine dancers and feminine values, orientation to a defined perspective (originally the king, now the audience in a theater with a proscenium stage), the conflict of good and evil yet it is not resolved through battle and competition but through magical kisses or cleverness, the color codes that correspond with the good/evil values and the associated elements of movement (where down and inversion are clearly associated with evil), and so on. These image schemas support values of hierarchy, aristocracy, conformity with and mastery of established rules and expectations, the power of ascendency both perhaps culturally and spiritually, and the perspectives of art as a showing to others. These dance movements are considered "high culture" and performed in glamorous venues on proscenium stages for well-dressed affluent audiences.

Many films fit this pattern, but I will consider one other from the same period, the 1983 film *Flashdance*. A girl living in a warehouse apartment who makes her living as a factory welder aspires to become a ballet dancer. Clearly she is untrained; her dancing confined to private dancing and sexy dance performances in a club. Eventually she obtains her longed-for audition. The audition scene that ends the film is, as I mentioned, similar to that of *Breakin'*. A tiny bit of background; earlier in the film there is a seemingly incidental scene where the principal character, played by Jennifer Beals, comes across a breakin' crew performing on the street. This is the Puerto Rican group "Rock Steady Crew." Apparently this street dance correlates with her sensibilities as an untrained dancer and she incorporates breakin' as well as hints of her exotic dancing in her eclectic audition piece. A backstory to this audition dance is pretty funny. Jennifer Beals is the actor playing the dancer, the dancing however is done by Tamara Rawlings and the surprise backspin in the piece is done by Crazy Legs Hirsh, a member of Rock Steady Crew. Predictably the stodgy audition panel members remain bored and unimpressed until the dance piece shifts to street/exotic inspired movement which leads, of course, to her success.

Based on these two representative film presentations it is clear that the gestures and postures that identify and distinguish these two dance genres establish image schemas that carry and ground differently valued understandings of society, relationships, authority, propriety, behavior, gender roles, and discipline. Being deeply embodied and not consciously selected these image schemas inform all of life's values and meanings for these respective dancers and associated cultures, even the rules of reason itself. These body concepts are inseparable from the basis by which these contrasting sub-cultures construct and recognize meaning and value.

It is perhaps too easy to overlook that in nearly every one of the films in this genre, while it appears that the street forms win and are superior to the trained high culture art forms, the image schemas most confirmed by these films are those associated with the formally trained dancers and the art/entertainment venues. My guess is that most viewers believe that these films confirm the superiority of the values of the street dancers, yet the recognition sought by all of the street dancers in these films, the measure of their success, is being admitted to the art/entertainment venues and forms. And, while none of these films offers any insights into this value system (they all end at the point of these dancers "success"), this inevitably requires these street dancers to learn choreography, to be trained, to dance together, to perform on a stage before an audience, to show up for rehearsal, to take criticism from non-dancing teachers, and to leave the street. The films show that the art/entertainment image schemas are capable of absorbing inspiration from and aspects of these street dances, yet transforming them into their own image schemas and the accompanying body concepts and values.

My friend, Kenny Jemenez, who taught me hip hop many years ago, always talked about taking hip hop to "a new level." The very verticality of this statement indicates an awareness that the horizontal values of street dance are, at some point, not adequate. Like a number of hip hop dancers, Rennie Harris has taken his hip hop to the stage as in his 2010 show *Puremovement*. The result is that the street dance is now done on stage oriented to the audience and choreographed. The battle or competition elements are gone except where they inform choreography. Individual performances, perhaps still improvised in limited ways, occur in the circle, yet now a circle of light projected on the stage. The music in this show is an upbeat electronic score rather than rap or hip hop perhaps so that it is more accessible to the culture of the theater audience. Capoeira and standard breakin' moves influence the choreography.

Since the 1960s hip hop and breakin' have moved to more formal battle scenes, especially competitions that may attract dancers from all over the world. These dances have also become standard in such competition environments such as the television show "So You Think You Can Dance?" where hip hop has developed to incorporate complex psychological dynamics in polished choreographed partner dances.

Girls have long been enrolled in ballet (and also modern and jazz) classes and programs to acquire the gestural/postural foundations bearing image schemas and body concepts appropriate to Western high and refined culture and exemplary femininity. Increasingly, boys are enrolled in hip hop and break dancing classes (an alternative or complement to martial arts I suppose) to learn through movement the traits appropriate for masculinity, but certainly not the masculinity of the streets. With an understanding that forms and styles of movement are constitutive of identity I want now to turn to a consideration of the implications of gendered movement practices.

I'D RATHER THROW LIKE A GIRL THAN DANCE LIKE A GUY

In 1990 Iris Marion Young published a provocative article titled "Throwing Like a Girl: A Phenomenology of Feminine Body Comportment, Motility, and Spatiality"[49] that, twenty years later, continues to attract discussion. At issue for Young is why girls tend to throw objects in a style differently from boys. The potential to go way wrong or into insensitive territory here is fairly high. The essentialist argument about gender and gendered attributes—that is, that girls are just made to throw in an "awkward inefficient" style, while boys are essentially strong efficient throwers is one I would think few would dare state these days, yet I think it rather clear that a fair portion of the general population continues to believe this. And, despite Young's expressed intent to dismiss the essentialist position, I think there is evidence that she actually held something of an essentialist view while justifying it by proposing that it is the result of the situation of girls being raised in a male-dominated patriarchal society. I'm rather astounded that Young framed her entire consideration by privileging the type/style of movement associated with males as the standard without analysis or criticism, even limiting the kinds of movement she considers to those in the movement category that might be labeled "throwing like a boy." It is these assumptions that I think reveal a hint of her hidden essentialism.

While Young went strongly in the direction of situational explanation, kinesiologists have resorted to exploring the difference in terms of body mechanics (bone length and muscle strength) which is fairly safe grounds given that since Title IX in 1972 girls have had by law opportunity in sports equal to boys, yet girls' activities are rarely merged with boys'. The Olympics continues to honor gender (if it can be determined) as a major categorical factor.

My developing perspective comes from somewhat different interests. I've been fascinated that in dancing and in demanding self-moving whole-bodied activities girls/women are, on average, far more adept than guys. I'm surprised and concerned that the bulk of the studies done on this "throwing like a girl" issue fail to evaluate movement style in the context of its relevance and importance to contemporary culture. Also yet to be done is to consider this issue in light of the recent alarming information about the massive and quite sudden shifts occurring in education, work, and social success that indicate the rapid decline of men in contrast to the rise of women. I believe there is a connection.

Some personal anecdotal observations. I have taught salsa dancing for years. Among the thousands of people I have taught, the girls/women far out-perform the guys in ability to move to rhythm, in the complexity of their awareness and control of the many parts of their moving bodies, in their ability to use various body parts simultaneously to do different things (like moving their feet one way while moving their arms another), in creating a sensitive responsive touch connection with their partners, and so on. I also teach a form of salsa called *rueda de casino* which I have described above. Again, on the whole women are far more adept at *rueda* than are guys. And the same holds, as I have noted, for step aerobics and Zumba forms of fitness exercise. I also observe gender correlations in the popularity of fitness classes that focus on building strength. These classes focus on lifting weights and there is no patterned foot movement, yet these classes are fast-paced, directed by an instructor, and coordinated with music. They are not popular among men and when men attend, they often move with little concern for the beat in the music.

Staying on a personal note for context, being confident that this is not simply personal to me or local to where I live, my granddaughter is a member of a dance company. The company is comprised of fifty girls from ages 5 to 17. No boys. I've attended many Denver area competitions for this company and among hundreds of girls participating in these events there are never more than a few boys. As a dance teacher I encounter hundreds of women who bemoan the fact that their male partners simply won't/can't dance.

Now, of course, there is no question that guys can dance well and guys can do step aerobics and Zumba well. Many dance and aerobics instructors are guys. I'm not trying to suggest any essentialist statement such as "guys can't dance," yet these observations regarding gendered preferences in movement forms/styles raise other significant issues and they cause me to ask why Young's essay and the entire issue was not framed using the female standard and focus on the issue "dancing like a guy?" I'm asking why guys tend toward some movement forms and girls others. While I can understand that male movement standards were once unquestionably accepted, I do ask now why they continue to be seemingly unquestionably accepted when it is so clear and obvious that there are many arenas where women on average have much greater movement abilities. This question also leads me directly to consider what movement forms are actually best for either gender relative to creating the postural/gestural movement patterns (image schemas) that establish skills valued by contemporary social and economic needs. And to ask what movement forms/skills best serve human development throughout life? In reading across the literature on these issues, I believe there remains a general bias against anyone that cannot perform some physical activity that involves the overhand hurling of a small object at enormous speed and force accurately at a target. Here is how Young described her criteria:

> I concentrate primarily on those sorts of bodily activities that relate to the comportment or orientation of the body as a whole, that entail gross movement, and that require the enlistment of strength and confrontation of the body's capacities and possibilities with the resistance and

> malleability of things. The kind of movement I am primarily concerned
> with is movement in which the body aims to accomplish a definite
> purpose or task. . . . Another aspect of bodily existence, among others,
> that I leave unconsidered is structured body movement that does not
> have a particular aim—for example, dancing.[50]

It is interesting that Young considers the hurling of a round object as
having "aim," whereas engaging a great many of one's various body
parts in artful movement does not. Young's selection of the movement
forms to consider and those to ignore is curious. Her selection criteria
lean decisively toward the types of movement that have long been identified as male. I'm surprised that, in the feminist environment in which
she wrote, she would so obviously accept male movement as the standard without even a careful critical discussion. The movement indicated
by the phrase "throwing like a girl" invariably recognizes that there is a
preferred style of throwing, that is, "like a boy," and any other throwing
styles are declared at the outset to be inefficient, untrained, awkward,
and identified by endless other pejorative terms perhaps appropriately
summed by Young herself as "women in sexist society are physically
handicapped."[51]

An interesting defense of the possibility that a girl might throw well,
in boy measures, is the softball pitcher Jennie Finch. Her ability to throw
a softball was engaged in a scientific test where her throwing was scien-
tifically compared with that of a male baseball pitcher. What fascinates
me about this example is that Jennie is measured and evaluated in terms
of her ability to hurl a small object with speed and accuracy. She, of
course, being a girl, hurls a softball and uses a girl style of underhand
throwing, but the main point is that she can generate object speeds and
force on a par with the best of the boys. What seems to amaze those
involved in this study and those that watch the video of it is how well
Jennie can "throw like a boy," even better than a boy, and there appears
to be no awareness that this whole study privileges a gender identified
cultural gestural pattern and that alternative values for throwing or moving might even be relevant. I cannot imagine any scientific studies performed to determine if boys can "dance like a girl." Gender identity tied
to gestural/postural self-movement is a fascinating issue. Clearly Jennie
Finch's identity as a female is not questioned by her ability to "throw like
a boy," yet it is quite likely that any male who "dances or moves like a
girl" is subject to questions of his gender identity and labeled a sissy or
gay.

The point I am lifting up for consideration here is that the unquestioned and unexamined standard that even gives rise to the phrase
"throwing like a girl" comes from the presumed superiority of not only
boy-style throwing, but perhaps boy-style everything else. This view
seems to suggest that for boys and girls to be equal is for girls to become

like boys, certainly not boys to become like girls, or boys and girls both
changing and expanding their styles of movement to include something
of the movement styles typified to the opposite gender. That the boy-
style remains the unquestioned standard one need only look at a bit of
the literature continuing to deal with the issues. Australian Greg Downey
recently (2009) attempted to approach the issue from the perspective of
neuroscience and to ask questions about girls' brains as part of the explanation. Let me quote just a single passage to demonstrate the unquestioned prejudice apparent in the language used. Downey writes

> If women can acquire the skill to throw overhand (witness Olympic
> softball fielders), then the question should be, instead of why do girls
> "throw like girls," why do some girls throw so poorly if they are ca-
> pable of throwing well? Most students of the biomechanics of throwing
> would argue that it is a technical problem: women don't throw proper-
> ly and the technique that they put together is hampered by a number of
> kinaesthetic problems, some of which obscure avenues of further skill
> development.[52]

The unquestioned use of evaluative terms pejorative to girls is shocking
as is Downey's apparent acceptance that it is the girls' problem.

Well, let me pose some alternative questions. We might simply ask,
"what does overhand hurling a small object at great speeds and with
enormous force accurately hitting a target prepare one for in our world?"
Hmm, let's see . . . I'm thinking . . . still thinking. Oh yes, to be a professional sports player in any of several sports. And . . . hmmm. Other than
that I can't seem to think of anything. Such skill was doubtless vitally
important in hunting societies where stones or spears were the main
weapons used to kill and bring home dinner to the little missus. When
was that last valuable? Perhaps we could revive it as an even more manly
way of hunting than archery or slingshots or rifles. We could lobby for
open stone hurling or spear throwing hunting seasons. Okay, I'm being
slightly silly, but only to make a serious point. It is seriously difficult to
think of any profession that is well served by the sensorimotor pattern of
throwing like a boy or by the body concepts (image schemas) that accompany these gestural/postural skills. Why should throwing like a boy be
the unquestioned standard for "proper" throwing?

Another perspective. The physical analysis of a baseball pitch reveals
it as taking upward of two seconds to complete involving complicated
biomechanics and sensorimotor neurological programming that takes extensive training to develop and practice to maintain. This sort of skilled
throwing, however long it might take to develop, eventually becomes a
complex sensorimotor program that is operated under some generalized
sense of mental control and focus. This kind of throwing activity, characterized by taking a long time to build up, to wind up in preparation for a
sudden release or thrust of violent proportions at some object at a dis-

tance, does seem in Western standards the quintessential male type of movement. I'd suggest this general characterization is appropriate for many predominantly male movement activities and even much that might be thought of as male style in quotidian movement. A slow build-up of energy with explosive outwardly directed powerful, even violent, thrust trajectory effect. It is a movement that is outward from the body. Even in the sensorimotor programming it requires primarily efferent (from brain to muscle) signals rather than depending on much proprio-ceptive feedback through the process of execution. It is movement that amasses the entire body to function as a single unit in effecting the action. It is a movement that is intended to impact the external world through force and power and manipulation. Aim, in the sense of focus and precise direction, is an integral distinction of the movement. The identity of dis-tinctive movement characteristics strongly correlates with, because they are identical, body concepts (image schemas) that are foundational to value and meaning-making.

Yet, consider this throwing movement compared with something like dancing or doing step aerobics, that is, self-movement on demand to ambient music. While it seems that a two-second act is a really short time to accomplish all that has to happen to throw an object with force and accuracy, and it is, consider putting this action alongside *rueda* or step aerobics or any other form of dancing. These movement forms must be done on demand coordinated to a beat in ambient music that has, say, 150 beats a minute (relatively slow). Beats are coming at 0.4 second inter-vals so that five beats will elapse in two seconds. Thus a dancer may well take five or even more steps in the same length of time it takes for a single male-style throw. Furthermore, these dancings may involve the execu-tion of a large number (as in hundreds of distinct named moves) of move-ment combinations, each involving various step patterns coordinated with musical beats or combinations of step patterns, some on half counts and some with pause counts (thus coordination with music), turns, pos-sible interconnection with other dancers and the movement of many oth-er body parts (arms, hands, hips, head, and so on) with precision and in a constant flow of improvised on-demand self-movement and done both to the right and the left (ambidextrous). Furthermore, there is as much affer-ent (muscle to brain) information flow as efferent (brain to muscle) flow. The constant integration of muscles, skeleton, and brain is essential to this form of movement. This comparison shows that this sort of move-ment, a movement much more closely associated with women/girls than with men/boys is highly complex and remarkably sophisticated and, when compared to the overhead throw, seems of an entirely higher order of sophistication.

What kinds of activities, functions, demands, professions, values, meanings might be well served by this on-demand improvisational self-movement style, this "dancing like a girl" movement? The answers span virtually everything in our culture today and the trends of movement are clearly in that direction, that is, away from heavy strength whole bodied force of construction, war, manufacturing, but, of course, not away from professional sports. The potential effect across culture of the spiraling influences of the image schemas correlating with styles/forms of throwing is simply astounding.

So a good case can be made for the title I have chosen for this section because I would rather "throw like a girl than dance like a guy." In a section in a later chapter I will return to this topic and consider the role of dancing in the threatened survival of men.

PLASTICITY AND LIFE CYCLE

The ubiquity of mobile phones worldwide has enabled studies that reveal interesting insights. While we may be worried or not about privacy given the popularity of Facebook, I understand that these studies examine billions of bits of information generated by mobile phones and that no one is ever identified. Sure. I recently heard about one study that asked, "What is the predictability of our physical location at any given time?" Apparently our phones leave tracks like GPS maps as we move around throughout our days and lives. I have no idea how this study was able to establish this, but the results were that our quotidian movements are over 90% predictable. At first I was incredulous, but then I reluctantly accepted the results. I get my schedule set and pretty much keep to it. I go to the university on a schedule. I go to the gym on a schedule. I go to the dance studio on a schedule. I almost never shop for anything other than food, but I do that on a fairly regular schedule usually on my way home from some scheduled activity. So when I look at all this evidence, I realize that, at least so far as where I might be found at any given time, I am pretty close to 100% predictable.

It seems to me that human movement across our life cycle gradually changes both in style as well as in quantity. I was thinking about this this morning while doing a Zumba class (one of the few classes I take that isn't so demanding, so that I can actually reflect in this way about what I am doing). I noticed that while I could do all of the dance steps fairly well, I had trouble with movement that required me to bend down extensively and especially rapidly. I noticed that other dancers close to being my chronological peers experienced similar restrictions. Even for someone as active as I am, there are types of movement that are more difficult.

It is also rather obvious that in early childhood movement is typically constant and full. I find it delightful to see that most little kids run everywhere they go. They simply love to run. When they get in school however they are usually told to sit down and shut up so they can learn. Then they are given "recess" to burn off all that kid energy, that is, the seem-

ingly innate love to move lots and rapidly. By middle school recess becomes "physical education" and kids begin to change their attitudes
about moving. Some like it but lots do not. By the high school years many
kids find themselves almost immobile. In teaching dance to high school
kids I find that a rather large percentage seem to feel physically exhausted most of the time. I have learned to keep them constantly moving,
and I mean constantly, because the shortest pause results in about half
the kids instantly sitting down. In my experience high school kids beg for
breaks so they can sit or lie down.

The higher the level of education, the greater time commitment to
sitting while reading and writing and attending class. College students
elect majors and this often means that most of their classes are in the
same building. Most colleges have given up any physical education re-
quirements, however most have recreation centers for physical activities.

By the time young people are first employed, most find that their jobs
require confinement to small cubicles with extensive periods sitting, often at computers whose screens cannot be adequately seen without
hunching over, which results in the kyphotic posture that is the emblem
posture of our age. Weekends become our respite for physical movement
activities, yet television and other forms of entertainment often are done
in a sitting position. Consider the body concepts and even moods that
correlate with such restricted mobility and with kyphotic posture.

It is a given expectation in our culture that we decrease mobility as we
age, yet interestingly we often attribute this increasing inability to move
to chronological aging. I am frankly embarrassed at how often I hear
people in their 50s talk of the many things they physically can no longer
do and how willing they seem to be to attribute their decline simply to
their chronology. We identify aging with increasingly bent posture, increasingly reduced and restricted mobility, reduced physical flexibility,
and decreasing travel or increasing difficulty traveling.

The patterns of our culture have strong tendencies to progressively
decrease self-movement beginning at a shockingly young age. Given that
life is inseparable from self-movement, a reasonable question is this: Is it
possible that many of the physical signs of aging, the seeming steady
decline of acuity, are the result of a culturally encouraged lifestyle that
practices a progressing decrease of movement corresponding to an increase in chronology? I think there is much evidence that the answer to
this question is a resounding "yes."

This is the age of plasticity. In the last several decades neuroscientists
have discovered that, while it was thought that our brains were physically complete at around age seven, they in fact continue with periods of
rapid growth (termed exuberance) through the teens and into the early
twenties and that neuroplasticity is possible throughout life.[53] Stroke vic-
tims who were formerly thought to be "permanently" damaged were not
given much physical therapy. It is now widely accepted that to an amaz-

ing degree the neurobiological system has considerable capacity to repair itself, to undergo change and growth. There are many theories of neuroplasty and all of them connect changes in the brain with bodily movement. As infants we discovered ourselves in self-movement; yet, one of the major points I want to make is that the same process continues throughout life. Moving, self-moving, demanding self-movement, are essential to vitality, health, longevity, acuity. Cultural patterns that result in progressively decreasing mobility are as great a contributor to physical and mental decline as is the biological aging process.

Philosophy draws inspiration from neuroscience in turning towards plasticity as a cutting-edge issue.[54]

DANCING

"I'm dancin' in the rain" is the lyric that marks the moment of the "break into" dancing for Gene Kelly in that wonderful scene from the film *I'm Singin' in the Rain*. Kelly moves rhythmically for more than a minute before he starts dancing. I began this chapter with this example noting that all dancing is moving, but not all moving is dancing. Dancing is an important form of movement in all cultures and most religions. Exploring movement, self-movement, living movement, offers not only insight to dancing as moving, but also important insights about how to most fully understand and appreciate what distinguishes dancing as a form of movement.

I have shown the primacy of movement to our very being as animate organisms, to the perceptual processes by which we encounter and construct ourselves and the worlds we live in, the inseparability of movement and perception, the fundamental role movement plays in establishing and shaping body concepts/image schemas that are foundational to our construction of meaning, and I have also explored the ontogenetics of movement itself. I have considered the importance and relevance of movement to gender roles, to health as acuity of organism, and to cultural lifestyle and lifecycle expectations.

At this point I am experiencing a complex of emotions related to self-movement. Here is what I feel. Amazement and delight at how remarkably fundamental movement is to human life. I feel surprise and concern that movement is given so little attention in our daily thoughts and discourses on human development, health, and lifestyle. I'm also disturbed that the academic studies of all of these human concerns as well as studies of religion and culture rarely include movement, much less dancing, as important. I feel excited and rewarded at every moment to be exploring self-movement both in my own moving as well as by observing and analyzing moving practices and ideas as performed and expressed in cultures, but also to continue the rich and promising academic research on self-movement and dancing. Since dancing is often intimately connected with religion even in traditions that forbid it, there is much promise for religion and dance studies. And finally this particular approach to dancing may inspire expansion of the way we understand religion and the way we study religion.

This chapter has focused on movement because all dancing is moving. As we have come to appreciate and understand some aspects of moving, we can see that these same insights all apply to dancing. Yet, while I have constantly reminded that dancing is moving and while I have frequently called on dance examples to illustrate movement, I have held from the beginning that not all moving is or should be understood as dancing. This means that I must attempt to carefully articulate what distinguishes dancing among other forms of moving.

I want to begin this task by making a distinction between the consideration of dances, choreographers, and dance traditions and the effort to understand the "dancing" that is what is implicated in all of these manifestations of dancing. This distinction is parallel to that made by Bergson, in his analysis of Zeno's paradox, between movement backfilled, that is, movement as trajectory or grid, and the moving itself. This is a most important advancement in understanding movement because it returns the moving to the movement, that is, it emphasizes the dynamic and energetic and ontogenetic quality of movement even as moving is in this elusive process more a virtuality than an actuality. Dancing is made visible, performable, in some sense objectified as dances, yet dancing itself, like moving itself, is not form but process, a virtual. This does not mean that we cannot comprehend it in some sense despite its ungraspability; most certainly we can consider, as we did with movement, the character of its virtuality, processuality, and ontogenetics. We certainly should expect a language of paradox, of gaps, of negativity, of synapse. But, if we have gained any insight so far, it is that we must put the dancing back in the dance.

Moving is vitality, moving is life in process; to imagine or posit the cessation of movement is to designate the stillborn, the lifeless, the dead. A decline of movement, postures such as reclining that inhibit movement, the slowing of the pace of movement are all associated with the decline of vitality. It is the life force that animates. Movement is not something that we acquire; it is what is always already there as life.

Yet, dancing differs from moving with respect to primacy. It is not already always there. It is not the moving force that is ontogenetic to our self, life, perception, and world. This is a most important point with many implications. For example, a focus on movement joins humans with all other animate beings. I have frequently and purposefully used Husserl's phrase "animate organism" to keep humans connected with other animals throughout the consideration of movement. Yet, now, dancing is largely an acquired form of movement, distinctive largely to humans.[55] This is surely why dancing is often considered to be an art. Dancing is artifice, a clever skill. Dancing is ontogenetic process using self-movement as its fundamental constituency, manifesting and showing self-movement in process. To understand dancing promises insight into what distinguishes humans among animate organisms. Humans dance.

Dancing comes into being as an ontogenetic force, in the creation or emergence of a structurality that includes a dynamic separation of, or distance between, dancer and dance, dance manifesting. This is the sort of virtual distance explored by Barbaras related to movement. It is transcendence in its creation of a virtuality beyond the dancer's body, opening the space or distance that generates dancing movement. Yet this virtuality is of the dancer's dancing body. It is a distance that is also a desire to close this paradoxical gap, this distance which gives the dancing its movement. Yet the structurality of the separation is such that the realization of this desire is elusive and always present as the space that continuously allows and draws forth dancing self-movement, at least until the intentional collapse of this structurality which amounts to the end of the dancing. The dancing movement continues only so long as this paradoxical multiplicity, distance, desire is maintained. Dancing is this paradoxical identity/separation. There is also a kind of fear of the negativity of the gap of this virtual space or distance. Dancing is constantly moving to close the space between dancer and dance, all the while fearing that should this closing happen the dance structurality will collapse, ending the dancing. Since the dancing structurality is so compelling through repetition and pattern and the seduction of the almost, there is perhaps also the fear (as in awe) that the structurality will not allow the dancing to end. Dancing involves the constantly energizing tension or force of the dancing in order to both open the space for dancing as well as attempt to close it. This is the paradox that is dancing.

José Gil discusses something of this aspect of dancing in similar terms which he referred to as the "paradoxical body" and describes it this way. "The dancer's body unfolds in the dancing body-agent and in the body-space where it dances, or rather, the body-space that movement traverses and occupies."[56] Gil well understands that this distance arising from multiplicity and separation (in virtuality) is key to comprehending the moving of dancing, as he writes

> Complicity and distance of the actual body in relation to all virtual bodies are thus accompanied by a contemplation of the movement that simultaneously partakes of that movement and distance itself from it, in order to acquire a consistent perspective at the interior of movement itself.[57]

Gil's reference to multiple virtual bodies draws on Rudolf von Laban's analysis of movement of the body in space in the shape of an icosahedron, that is, a polyhedron with twenty faces, each one seen by Gil as potentially a virtual body, the same yet different than the actual dancer's body. This approach applies certainly to an analysis of all human movement. I'm interested here in keeping the focus on the simpler structurality of dancer/dance. Perhaps Gil says it best when he says it most directly, "To dance is to produce dancing doubles."[58]

Dancing has the same qualities of incipience and process as does moving itself, yet it is of a different order of reality, one that is not itself inseparable from vitality, one that does not have primacy in the same sense of being inseparable from life itself. I want to suggest that dancing is a virtuality of a second order. Dancing is a virtuality whose object is the virtuality of self-movement in its identity with vitality. It lifts out of quotidian life the dynamics and energetics of self-movement/vitality, placing these dynamics in a self-constructed context which allows us to experience and manipulate and objectify the ontogenetics of human self-movement. Dancing is about the energetics of living movement.

Movement recedes from our awareness in its naturalness, its identity with life itself. Movement, like the physical body itself, as shown by Drew Leder,[59] becomes hidden behind goals articulated, beneath backfilled trajectories and grids, behind the traces or stories of journeys of distances conquered, gaps closed. Dancing too recedes behind dances done, choreographers' works, dance traditions described, yet owes its distinction to its ability to make artifice of the energetics and dynamics of living movement, of self-movement, that is, of the virtuality that is movement itself. Dancing is an artificial made-up virtuality that draws for its apparent life on the very thing it helps us comprehend, living self-movement.

Babaras understands self-movement as living movement, but dancing movement is a kind of movement that abstracts (objectifies) the dynamic vitalizing energizing qualities of living movement as art, that is, for display, and as culture, that is, for the manipulation of these energetics in constructed forms for the purposes related to the human creation and continuation of cultural and religious identity and history. Dancing is a technique of culture distinguished by its capacity to harness and use the structurality of self-movement including its sense of primacy, to engage the most core energetics and values of culture, religion, and art and their enactment.

My efforts to say what distinguishes dancing as a distinctively human form of movement, and how to appreciate its dynamic ungraspable character as both the same yet distinct from living movement or life, are slippery and elusive. My belief is that clarity is gained little by little through iterative explorations of this structurality, each seeking alternative yet related terms and images, paradoxes, and contradictions. Each of the remaining chapters will bring into conversation the insights gained from the consideration of a specific dance tradition with ideas from a body of theoretical or philosophical work. The intended results are hopefully an expanding spiral that deepens, enriches, and clarifies dancing.

NOTES

1. Maxine Sheets-Johnstone, *Primacy of Movement* (Amsterdam: John Benjamins Publishing Co., 1999), 136.
2. Sheets-Johnstone, *Primacy*, 134.
3. Sheets-Johnstone, *Primacy*, 135.
4. Sheets-Johnstone, *Primacy*, 136-7.
5. Renaud Barbaras, "Life and Exteriority" in *Enaction: Toward a New Paradigm for Cognitive Science*, eds. John Stewart, Olivier Gapenne, and Ezequiel A. DiPaolo (Cambridge: MIT Press, 2010), 109.
6. Barbaras, "Life and Exteriority,"110.
7. As in Manuel A. Vásquez's *More than Belief: A Materialist Theory of Religion* (Oxford: Oxford University Press, 2011).
8. See John Stewart, "Foundational Issues in Enaction as a Paradigm for Cognitive Science: From the Origin of Life to Consciousness and Writing," in *Enaction: Toward a New Paradigm for Cognitive Science*, eds. John Stewart, Olivier Gapenne, and Ezequiel A. DiPaolo, (Cambridge: MIT Press, 2010), 1.
9. Renaud Barbaras, "Life, Movement, and Desire," *Research in Phenomenology* 38 (2008), 14.
10. These terms are not actually synonymous. I will develop a fuller discussion of proprioception later, yet at this introductory point I will not overly complicate.
11. The study of movement spanning neurology, biology, cognitive science, and phenomenology is, I believe, the core of the future of academic studies of culture and religion.
12. Francisco Varela, Evan Thompson, and Eleanor Rosch, *The Embodied Mind* (Cambridge: MIT Press, 1991), 175.
13. A sophisticated phenomenological argument for movement being perception is made by Renaud Barbaras in his *Desire and Distance: Introduction to a Phenemonology of Perception* (Stanford: Stanford University Press, 2006), 81-107.
14. Reported in Alva Noë, *Out of Our Heads: Why You Are Not Your Brain, and Other Lessons from the Biology of Consciousness* (New York: Hill and Wang, 2009), 55.
15. Beginning with C. S. Peirce, William James, and Henri Bergson.
16. Barbaras argues that the basis for a definitive or complete theory of perception and movement was established in Chapter 1 of Bergson's *Matter and Memory* (London: Swan Sonnenschein, 1911, English Edition Zone Books, 1990), ed. Barbaras, *Desire and Distance*, 97.
17. Barbaras, *Desire and Distance*, 87.
18. Barbaras, *Desire and Distance*, 88.
19. Brian Massumi, *Semblance and Event: Activist Philosophy and the Occurrent Arts* (Cambridge: MIT Press, 2011), 95.
20. "Event" is a key concept in Massumi's activist philosophy.
21. Barbaras, *Desire and Distance*, 88-9.
22. Barbaras, "Life, Movement, and Desire," 14.
23. Barbaras, "Life, Movement, and Desire," 15.
24. Barbaras, "Life, Movement, and Desire," 15.
25. Barbaras, "Life, Movement, and Desire," 17.
26. See also Pierce Howard, *Owner's Manual for the Brain*, 3rd ed. (Austin: Bard Press, 2006), 122-3 and 221-32.
27. Howard, *Owner's Manual*, 226-7.
28. "Grasping" is often a movement action used to discuss the character of movement. See Barbaras, *Desire and Distance*, 88.

29. Brian Massumi, *Parables for the Virtual: Movement, Affect, Sensation* (Durham: Duke University Press, 2002), 6.

30. Massumi, *Parables*, 1.

31. Barbaras, *Desire and Distance*, 86.

32. Barbaras, "Life, Movement, and Desire," 14.

33. Renaud Barbaras, "Life and Exteriority," 107.

34. Barbaras, "Life, Movement, and Desire," 11.

35. Massumi, *Parables*, 5.

36. Massumi, *Parables*, 30-31.

37. See Massumi, *Parables*, 58-62.

38. Massumi, *Parables*, 58-59. Massumi does not fully engage the neurobiological descriptions of the functioning of proprioceptors.

39. A term associated with Leroi-Gourhan; see Carrie Noland, *Agency & Embodiment: Performing Gestures/Producing Culture* (Cambridge: Harvard University Press, 2009), 102.

40. Noland, *Agency*, 59.

41. Noland, *Agency*, 59.

42. Jonathan Cole & Barbara Montero, "Affective Proprioception," *Janus Head* 9:2 (2007), 299-317; and Barbara Montero, "Proprioception as an Aesthetic Sense," *The Journal of Aesthetics and Art Criticism* 64:2 (Spring 2006), 231-242.

43. Mark Johnson, *The Meaning of the Body: Aesthetics of Human Understanding* (Chicago: University of Chicago Press, 2008), 20 (italics in original).

44. Daniel N. Stern, *Forms of Vitality: Exploring Dynamic Experience in Psychology, the Arts, Psychotherapy, and Development* (Oxford: Oxford University Press, 2010).

45. Johnson, *Meaning*, 25 (italics in original).

46. Maxine Sheets-Johnstone, "Thinking in Movement: Further Analyses and Validations," in *Enaction: Toward a New Paradigm for Cognitive Science*, eds. John Stewart, Olivier Gapenne, and Ezequiel A. DiPaolo (Cambridge: MIT Press, 2010), 167.

47. George Lakoff, *Women, Fire, and Dangerous Things: What Categories Reveal about the Mind* (Chicago, University of Chicago Press, 1987).

48. Johnson, *Meaning*, 154.

49. Iris Marion Young, "Throwing Like a Girl: A Phenomenology of Feminine Body Comportment, Motility, and Spatiality," in *Throwing Like a Girl and Other Essays in Feminist Philosophy and Social Theory* (Bloomington: Indiana University Press, 1990).

50. Young, "Throwing Like a Girl," 30.

51. Young, "Throwing Like a Girl," 42.

52. Greg Downey "Throwing like a girl('s brain)," Internet, February 1, 2009 http://neuroanthropology.net/2009/02/01/throwing-like-a-girls-brain/ (accessed December 2010).

53. Norman Doidge, *The Brain that Changes Itself: Stories of Personal Triumph from the Frontiers of Brain Science* (New York: Viking, 2007).

54. See, for example, Catherine Malabou, *What Should We Do with Our Brain?* 3rd ed. (Bronx: Fordham University Press, 2008) and Catherine Malabou, *Plasticity at the Dusk of Writing: Dialectic, Destruction, Deconstruction* (New York: Columbia University Press, 2009).

55. Surely many will immediately appeal to animal dances such as the "mating dances" of birds. Others may think of the "dancing" done by very young children and suggest that they have not learned this behavior nor do they perform it intentionally. Both concerns are worthy of consideration and indeed the perspective I am developing offers an important vantage for understanding both anew.

56. José Gil, "Paradoxical Body," *TDR: The Drama Review* 50:4 (T192) (Winter 2006), 23.

57. Gil, "Paradoxical Body," 25.

58. Gil, "Paradoxical Body," 25.

59. Drew Leder, *The Absent Body* (Chicago: University of Chicago Press, 1990).

TWO

Gesturing

UNDERSTANDING GESTURE

Bharata natyam, a South Indian Hindu form of dance that dates from antiquity, is often invoked when dancing is considered in terms of gesturing. A distinctive feature of *bharata natyam* is the extensive use throughout the dance of *mudras* or hand gestures/positions, particularly in the aspect of the dance known as *abhinaya* that focuses on the dance corresponding with stories from classical Indian literature, the Mahabharata and the Ramayana. There are 32 single-hand *mudras* which are taught independent of the other aspects of the dance as essential to *bharata natyam* training. These can be combined in a great many gestures using one or both hands.

Abhinaya is often referred to as the "storytelling" aspect of the dance with an understanding that the dancer, through posture and gesture, tells the classic stories. While I do not actually agree with this understanding of the dance, let's go on a bit to allow ourselves to understand that this view correlates with one of the persistent and most common understandings of gesturing. In his 2004 book *Gesture: Visible Action as Utterance* Adam Kendon articulates gesturing as *visible actions that have the features of manifest deliberate expressiveness*. Such visible actions often substitute for language and often occur where language would not suffice. For example, if I am standing roadside wanting a ride from passing motorists, it is not effective to yell at them as they pass, "Hey, buddy, how about a ride?" Rather I use the visible action of extending my arm, making a fist with my thumb fully extended, and rotate my forearm back and forth in the plane parallel to the road with my thumb pointing in the direction I wish to travel or, put simply, I "thumb a ride." The visible actions clearly have the features of manifest deliberate expressiveness. I do not do these

61

actions accidentally. This understanding pairs gesture with expressed meaning and sees gesture as primarily an act of communication. Studies of such gestures from era to era and culture to culture have occurred since antiquity. The common result of these studies is often the production of a chart illustrating gestures and what they mean.

From the perspective of this common view of gesture, we would approach *bharata natyam* asking what these *mudras* mean as manifest deliberate visible actions. So *bharata natyam* has a fixed number of one- and two-hand *mudras*, each with a name. The value or meaning of each *mudra* becomes specific only in the context of the body in motion in conjunction with facial expressions and the accompanying story being sung. The question is "do the *mudras* tell the story as would be expected of the sequence of words might in an utterance?" Clearly they do not bear meaning in this lexical sense. *Mudra*-based gesturing often becomes stylized illustrations of the physical actions of the characters in the stories being told explicitly in the song lyrics, for example, birds flying, the shooting of an arrow, a horned bull, shyness, giving a gift, or bees on a flower. Or they may have no literal connection with the actions of the story at all. Here *mudras* seem to be specifiable decorative elements of movement. Clearly it is the dancing, the sequence of movements in the context of music that allows the *mudra* to take on any delimiting of reference or value or meaning rather than the other way round. One cannot simply look at a *mudra*, as one would a word in a dictionary, and indicate the possible meanings it might convey. This is backwards to the way it works.

Returning to my objection of understanding the *abhinaya* aspect of *bharata natyam* as storytelling, it is important for us to understand that *bharata natyam* gesturing is not adequately understood if we narrowly limit our understanding of gesturing to visible actions that have the features of manifest deliberate expressiveness. *Bharata natyam* gesturing is much richer than this view allows. Furthermore, it is important that we reject this limited understanding of gesturing as adequate for the appreciation of any dancing. We have to seek a richer understanding of gesturing to help us more fully appreciate dancing.

To consider dancing in terms of this "poor" understanding of gesture is to limit it to being a language or an act of expression or communication. Though it is common to think of dancing as a language, such an understanding is a modern Western perspective that is, in any strict sense, untenable. So we need a "rich" understanding of gesturing if it is to be of value to the study of dancing.

Carrie Noland's 2009 book, *Agency & Embodiment: Performing Gestures/ Producing Culture*,[1] is an important introduction to the richness of gesture. Noland develops an understanding of gesture that I think is provocative and has great potential, especially for the study of dancing and religion. This is obvious from her observations of a graffiti writer which she describes in the opening paragraph of her book. Perhaps we would not even think of the sweeping fluid movements of the graffiti writer as gesturing, yet, once we allow this movement to be recognized as gesture, we can clearly recognize that there are techniques born in the muscles and neurons that distinguish this action. Noland has this to say:

> In the magnified scope of the graffiti gesture, writing affords the writer an opportunity to impress the individual shape and vitality of the body's motor power onto the contours of the cultural sign. Yet if the writer performs the motion repeatedly, his own body will eventually be inscribed, the muscles and ligaments physiologically altered, by the gestural routine that expresses and confines his body at the very same time.[2]

Noland shifts our attention away from the message communicated by gesturing to the very act of creating the gesture. She holds that the gesturing affords the writer a way of impressing his own body's movement onto a cultural sign, the resulting tag. The gesture mediates the body of the writer and the tag produced, and this connecting movement is about something other than intentionally communicating a message by producing a visible action. The tag is a sign of the action of graffiti writing more than the communication of some message.

Noland goes on to turn the gesturing back onto the body of the graffiti writer. Through his high repetition of these gestural routines, that is, the repetitious actions of physically writing, the writer's body becomes physiologically—that is, muscles and ligaments and sensorimotor programs—altered. The repetitions of performing the gesturing patterns of graffiti writing remake the body of the writer into a graffiti writer. Gesturing, she shows, goes both ways as the expression of body and in confining and remaking the body. The first paragraph of her book, read carefully, introduces a rich understanding of gesture, a daunting, provocative, and altogether amazingly interesting topic.

Noland might just as well have been observing a dancer as an exemplar of gesturing. Dancers of any particular dance form are trained in patterns of movement that are recognized as distinguishing the particular dance genre or form. It might be anything from the frame and walking conventions that designate tango to the contractions specific to Martha Graham's dance technique to the upright posture of dancing ballet *en pointe.* What we attend to in identifying specific dances are the gestural patterns of the dance. These gestural conventions are elements of the virtual dance that call forth the movement we recognize as dancing. And, like the graffiti writer, the continual repetition of these gestural/postural performances literally remakes the body of the dancer in the very terms of the gestures.

However, unlike the graffiti writer who leaves a tag or a piece of art,[3] the dancer's gesturing is both the means and the object and product of the dancing. Thus in the gesturing of dancing, trace or mark is collapsed into or folded back onto the act of gesturing itself, onto the moving body of the dancer. This oscillatory effort to manifest that is always also a folding back illuminated by considering dancing as gesturing is at the core of dancing. If we, like Noland, have the opportunity to watch a graffiti writer we can see that the sweeping gesturings of graffiti writing may, in themselves, be something rather like dancing.

Gesturing has complexity and richness. For example, gesture is not a onetime movement, but rather an iteration of a movement pattern established as convention through high repetition. In this sense gesture is something like skill in one context and habit in another.[4] Repetitive gesturing creates sensorimotor patterns[5] that support the seemingly natural use of gestures. Without repetition the movement would not qualify as gesture, nor would it have a field in which to be active. While gesture emerges from repetition and is performed as in some sense automatic sensorimotor programs, it is also necessarily in a sense improvisational, or as Noland, a dancer herself, calls it "an improvisational dance." Here we learn something essential about improvisation. Improvisation cannot occur as a unique movement, that is, as a movement without context or expectation against which to grasp it. Improvisation depends on gesture, that is, on established or conventional movement patterns that are rule governed.

I have a North Indian friend who is a master *tabla* drummer. I once paired him with a Senegalese *kora* player for a concert and to make a recording. I know that *tabla* drumming is based on highly defined complex rhythm patterns. In playing with the *kora* I could see the extent to which he was improvising to play with the *kora*. I asked him how that worked in the context of the precise expectations of *tabla* tradition and he told me that once you become a *tabla* master the rhythms are there to provide a context and framework in which to make new patterns and rhythms without the traditional ones being violated. I've heard the same from flamenco guitarist friends. You can also see this in Latin American music where all the rhythm players are playing around the specific beat that distinguishes the rhythm of the music being played, but no one is actually playing the core rhythm itself.

Gesture is like this. One would think that repetition to the extent of the movement becoming automatic, rule-bound, conventional, would simply wring from it all possible creativity, yet the exact opposite is the case. This is an essential perspective we need in order to appreciate dancing which is necessarily highly repetitive, yet always creative and new.

Noland explicitly states her thesis this way: "that kinesthetic experience, produced by acts of embodied gesturing, places pressure on the conditioning a body receives, encouraging variations in performance that account for larger innovation in cultural practice that cannot otherwise be explained."[6] Gesturing always seems to pull in both directions: routinization and improvisation, expression of self or culture, and the impression-creating self and enculturation. It will be important to appreciate that we gain knowledge through acquired gestural routines, through our dancings; the gestural sequences of dancing are not limited to just expressing ourselves by means of these gestures, these dances. They are also always heuristic or interrogative and always shape the dances.

From here we may begin to appreciate how dancing can be and often is a powerful means by which society, normative culture, religious principles are tested and changed. Gestures are clearly learned and reiterated behaviors or as Noland says, gesturing is "a submission of the shared human anatomy to a set of bodily practices specific to one culture."[7] Yet, precisely because of this submissive aspect of cultural systems of gesturing, gesturing is a fundamental means by which these cultural values are tested and changed. Noland notes that "gesturing also affords an opportunity for interoceptive or kinesthetic awareness, the intensity of which may cause subjects to alter the very way they move." Thus, "kinesthetic experience, produced by acts of embodied gesturing, places pressure on the conditioning a body receives, encouraging variations in performance that account for larger innovations in cultural practice."[8] With this rich understanding of gesturing, we may more deeply appreciate why dancing is almost invariably found at the heart of major cultural change.

From this perspective we can appreciate the common trajectory of the development of dance forms. They often begin as street dances, unacceptable and usually considered offensive to the more established segments of society. We need think only of tango, capoeira, swing, breakin', modern dance, contact improvisation, and certainly rock 'n' roll to get an idea. Yet, with time these dances "catch on" in that the gesturing patterns of the dances are almost invariably taken up, codified, and conventionalized so they may be accessible to a larger population and, in time, insinuate themselves into the muscles and ligaments and neurology of the dancing members of the society. Society members literally start walking and running and comporting themselves with different bodies remade through these gestural patterns. And, in time, these dances are appropriated by the more formal structured members of society and they become studio dances and codified to be judged in formal dance competitions. I think immediately of those after-school dance television programs of the mid-twentieth century where kids everywhere learned dances from culturally acceptable "white" kids who learned the dances from a segregated group of "black" kids who enjoyed far less air time. The important point for us to understand here is that gesturing offers both the means by which culture insinuates itself on the bodies of its members, but also the means by which members of the culture can, through altering gestural practices, effect change on culture, society, and religion.

As we expand our appreciation of dancing in terms of gesturing, we will build on this idea that gesturing involves the body in a "double

process of active displacement (through contraction of muscles) and information gathering (through the neuro-receptors located along the muscles)."[9]

I want to clarify my approach here a bit. I presented a rather extensive
chapter on "moving." The issue now is "how does gesture differ from
movement?" Noland actually proposed the replacement of the term
"movement" with the term "gesture" because she believes that gesture
"encourages us to view all movements executed by the human body as
situated along a continuum—from ordinary iteration of a habit to the
most spectacular and self-conscious performance of choreography."[10] I
understand the importance of this perspective, yet I think that there remains considerable value in seeing gesturing as a subset of or type of
movement. Certainly as I showed in the first chapter, there is remarkable
insight in the consideration of self-movement to deepen the appreciation
and comprehension of ourselves as animate organisms. Moving in this
framework may certainly include gesturing, but it is principally concerned with movement as it is inseparable from perception, from the
construction of self and environment (worlding), and vitality. The emphasis on living movement is broader and more basic than should be a
study of gesturing. Gesturing is inseparable, as Noland shows, from cultural, psychological, and historical concerns. Whereas there is something
"natural" about movement that is worth considering, there is nothing
"natural" about gesturing other than as it is also considered living movement. Gesturing to me is important when considered as a specific type of
culturally and historically situated routinized sequences of movement,
that is, as techniques of culture. Movement, it has been argued, is inseparable from life and it is in this respect that we gain the greatest insight by
considering it as living movement or self-movement. While gesture may
enact these qualities of movement, I believe it is not only possible, but
even beneficial to consider gesture understood as culturally situated patterned movement. It is in the consideration of gesturing that we begin to
see how movement takes on specific cultural function. And to see gesturing in this perspective moves us in the direction of being able to understand how the gestural/postural patterned movement of dancing com-
prises a very special subset, one that I will show allows us to use gesturing to construct culturally situated movement patterns that both depend
on and are about living movement itself.

Noland, as others, seems to me to understand gesture as applicable to
every human movement. I am not ready to go this far, but the idea opens
our understanding of gesture well beyond limiting it to being a visible act
of utterance. In this broader view we should consider that gesture has an
agentive role to play. The poor view limits the agency of gesture to the act
of communication or cognition, yet even from the perspective of speech
act theory we would expand communication to include a performative
function, as in doing something by communicating or saying something.

Standing beside the road with one's thumb raised communicates the information "I need a ride," but it also performs the act of "getting that ride," that it, the agency performed by "thumbing a ride," is much more important and significant than is communicating a message or a bit of information.

So to sum up here, rich gesture must, as I am proposing it developed from Noland, be understood as having agentive force beyond communication or messaging. Our gestures create space. Our gestures correspond with affordances and thus with our makings. Our gestures enculturate. Our gestures actually remake the body of the one gesturing at the level of tissue. Our body movement, our postural attitudes, our actions; they all correspond with our gestural practices. We are our gestures in the literal sense of being evident at the level of tissue. Gestures are affective as well. They shape and determine our feelings as well as those of others that experience our gestures. So the rich view of gesture sees it as having an enormous range of agentive powers that serve to create and shape ourselves and our environments. This agentive aspect of gesture is an efferent arc that extends the body into the environment as well as into one's very flesh.

This reaching out, this extension, this expression, this agency is complemented by a corresponding afferent arc of gesture that typically goes unidentified, not discussed. There were hints of this effect in the discussion of agency above, in that agency is also always a reaching out to impact the environment with the expectation that it will return to also change the self, feeling and tissues. Gesture is always a reaching out to touch, to explore, to grope, to experience, to investigate, to feel. In this sense its function, its agency, is heuristic, probing, and affective. In gesture we discover ourselves and our environment; we explore possible meanings as we physically and mentally grope the world with our gestures. To appreciate gesturing in terms of this loop or double arc, as efferent and afferent, as agentive and heuristic, as touching and being touched, will serve well our continuing explorations of dancing as gesturing.

DANCING AS TECHNIQUES OF BODY: MARCEL MAUSS

Once when I was in Bali I found myself walking with a group of young Balinese men along a rural road up in the mountains. It was a ceremonial occasion and we were walking from one village to another to retrieve a set of masks that were stored in a temple. As we walked along chatting I noticed how distinctive their walk was. They walked like Balinese men! I had noticed it before, but on this occasion I decided to try to imitate their walk—see if I could become a Balinese man. They immediately noticed what I was doing and among peals of laughter they started coaching my walking. Try as I might I managed only to look increasingly ridiculous. My conclusion is that you have to be a Balinese man to walk like one. The implication is that the gesture of walking one's culture insinuates itself into the very tissue of one's body thus shaping one's walking. Walking is not simply something of a style one assumes, a style anyone could simply effect; in living a cultural life it becomes in a very neurobiological sense who one is.

I have a female friend who is Indian. She was born in India and spent her early years there, but came to America when her father took an academic position here. She has continued to wear traditional Indian clothing and hair and makeup styles throughout her life. She told me that as an adult when she went back to India to visit, Indian people identified her as American despite her being Indian and appearing Indian. My hunch is that she walks and comports herself somehow physically "like an American woman" and these gestural patterns have insinuated themselves into her body to the point apparent to people in India.

Dancing is distinguished in most societies by culture, era, and gender among other things. We know and identify the people of a culture or subculture by how they dance, but also by how they walk, run, swim, eat, and perform many other cultural actions. Dancing then can be understood as gesture especially if understood in the rich sense I am developing here.

In 1934 French sociologist Marcel Mauss wrote an important article titled "Techniques of the Body"[11] that focused on what was at that time and continues to be rather often sidelined and ignored in a category of the miscellaneous. As understood by Carrie Noland in her recent careful reading of this article, Mauss laid the foundation for a rich understanding of gesture. As Noland notes, he was not interested in the "perfection" of the body or somehow isolating the "natural" body. Rather Mauss was interested in the meaning-making aspects of motor movements, in the way these movement experiences support yet establish a culturally identifiable signification.[12] He understood that there are three elements intertwined in these techniques: the mechanical/physical, the psychological, and the social. There are no "natural" ways for humans to act, rather all the techniques they know to use and comport their bodies have a basis in these three inseparable elements.

Foundational to his understanding of gesturing, Mauss argued that "social conditioning reaches beyond ideas in the mind . . . to lodge itself in the very tissues of the body" and that "cultural subjects have a lived experience of such social conditioning, that is, a sensual apprehension, in those tissues, of socially organized kinesis."[13] Thus society imprints itself into the very tissue of its members' bodies through the performance and practice of gestural patternings, while the performing of these gestures is sensually experienced as being of the fabric of their society. Mauss held these techniques to be central to an understanding of culture even more important than are discursive performatives. Thus, for Mauss what people do is more important than what people say they do. Gesturing is central to the cultural construction of the body. [14] From birth a member of society is "the subject of unintentional or intentional dressage." [15]

Noland finds that Mauss understood gestures to exist in several registers: as chains of movements performed by individual bodies, as gesturing practices that shape the bodies that perform them, and as gesturing acts that play a role in the wider system of social organization.

There is thus a paradoxical structure to gesturing. Gesture imprints the values and distinctions of a society on the habitual bodily techniques of the individuals thus marking them as members of the society, but also actually making them of the society. Yet the manipulation of techniques of moving bodies is the mechanism by which societies transform. Gestures are the means by which individuals and groups present resistance and effect change to society.

Mauss's work established important beginnings to the development of the rich understanding of gesture that I am pursuing as important to the study of dancing.

DANCING THE OTHER, BODY AS INSTRUMENT: ANDRÉ LEROI-GOURHAN

Renowned choreographer Twyla Tharp says that when she goes to the studio to create a dance (i.e., to "make work" in the parlance of choreographers), she sets aside her mind to let her body do the work. For years I have had difficulty accepting her statement because it seemed to me to affirm the classic split and separation of the mind/brain and the body. At least she sets a primary role to the body seemingly acting first and in a fundamental way. It is also common to hear dancers refer to their bodies as their "instruments"; this too is a statement that has, for obvious reasons, not set well with me.

Over time I have come increasingly to understand dancing in terms of what I often refer to as "self-othering" by which I refer to that remarkable and paradoxical distinction of dancing in which the dancer becomes, in her dancing, something or someone other than who she is, and she does so in the most embodied possible way. Self-othering is the topic of Chapter Three. The dancer becomes the body of an other, yet with the other experienced as her own body in the fullest proprioceptive and experiential way. In the act of dancing, she is the other in the fullest sense, yet she also remains herself, the dancer, the one dancing. I introduced this sense of othering at the end of Chapter One and it is an implication of self-movement or living movement as I have discussed above.

I want to explore this notion in the context of the perspectives on gesture developed by the paleoethnographer André Leroi-Gourhan, particularly in his 1964 book *Gesture and Speech*. I will depend on the assistance of Carrie Noland's insightful analysis of his work. I believe that approaching dancing from Leroi-Gourhan's understanding of gesture will help me better understand Twyla Tharp's intended meaning, the common statement of dancers that their bodies are their instruments, and finally it will allow me to clarify and enrich my foundational notion of self-othering.

Leroi-Gourhan's work was paleoethnography, that is, one who writes about the significance of Paleolithic cultures based on an analysis of the surviving artifacts. The Paleolithic Era is prehistoric and is of interest especially because it is the period distinguished by the development of the first stone tools. Wow! How could this have anything at all to do with Twyla Tharp, a contemporary choreographer, or with dancing for that matter?

Leroi-Gourhan's approach to understanding prehistoric tools was distinguished by his remarkable focus on the gestures required to manipulate the tools; "the lived, somatic-kinesthetic experience of being a human body engaged in interaction with tools."[16] It is fitting, I think, that this approach is similar to the way basic level categories are distinguished as I described in Chapter One. Leroi-Gourhan believed that humans invented themselves as human beings by means of the techniques of body accompanying their invention of tools. This statement and our images of the spear-throwing prehistoric hunter may remind us of my earlier discussion of this form of throwing which remains today the exemplar of proper throwing and is still inseparable from prototypical male gender identity. Yet Leroi-Gourhan's insights are much greater. Beyond holding that tools are nothing without the gestures that manipulate them, he understood this gesturing in a sophisticated way as being also "evaluative, a form of perception, adaptation, and creation."[17] That is, the gestures by which tools are manipulated not only provide insight into the lived bodies of the tool makers/users as sensorimotor programs and operating chains of gestures, but these gestural patterns and chains must also be appreciated for their role in perception, for the part they play in understanding the world and oneself.[18] Tools then, from Leroi-Gourhan's perspective, are inseparable from movement, from gesture, both in having agency in the world in the simple sense of the obvious effects of the tool's impact (killing animals or obtaining food, for example), but also as the means by which humans come to create themselves and to understand and create, that is, perceive, the world around them. This latter aspect, clearly the most surprising and important I think, will require our further careful attention to Leroi-Gourhan's theory of gesturing.

Leroi-Gourhan focused on the human hand as the first tool, understanding "the hand as a gesture that produces kinesthetic, proprioceptive, and haptic knowledge."[19] Through evolution the eventual upright posture that coincided with the emergence of human beings permitted

emphasis on the hand and the face. Posture is linked to modes of movement and certainly to the distinction of hands and the predominance of
the face. Thus, he argued, "modes of motility and gesturing could thus be
taken as defining features of being human."[20] With the hand being
understood as the first tool, understandable in terms of the modes of
movement, that is, the gesturing that makes the hand a tool, we can begin
to see the relevance of Leroi-Gourhan's perspectives to dancing and self-
othering. When the hand becomes a tool it is in some sense set apart from
the integrity of the body as an *other*, as a tool used by and extending
beyond the body, yet it is at once also one's hand, an integral body part.
The hand as the first tool becomes the locus for the first act of self-othering; that which is me (my hand) is also something which is other (a tool),
yet they are proprioceptively and experientially identical and inseparable
from me. As the hand is the first tool, there is nothing that would prevent
the arm becoming a tool, or the leg, and eventually the entire body. So
here I am back to Tharp and dancers who, perhaps inspired by musicians, more commonly refer to their bodies as "instruments." Thus dance
technique can, in this sense, be understood as the gestural patternings by
which the body is used as tool, yet, while this is a separation of body
from dancer, it is also a self-othering of dancer, a transcendent construction of a virtual body comprised of techniques. However, this virtual
other body, a tool in some sense, is always also inseparable from the
proprioceptive and experiential body of the dancer. Dancing, as gesturing, as emerging moving techniques of body, then can be seen as self-
transcending in that the dancer becomes something "other," something
"not self," yet, as gesturing, this othering, this transcendence, creates the
space of the vitalizing moving self. Wow! How cool!

We can begin to comprehend Leroi-Gourhan's understanding of the
heuristic or exploratory aspects of gesturing, that is, in strong terms, that
gesturing is perceiving, as we follow his analysis of human evolution. He
argued that "gesture always seeks 'contact' or touch, that is, a progressively better accomplishment of the gestural intention. Gesture is in service to agency. Gesture is always developed through touch contact,
through sensation, especially interoception."[21] Leroi-Gourhan described
this aspect of gesturing as *tâtonnement*, a French word that means "trial
and error," but which Noland translates delightfully as "groping." There
is an innate primacy of movement, as I have shown, that is characterized
in early life as "groping," a dynamism akin to play, by which through
contact with the world in self-movement we come to discover and create
ourselves and the world in which we live. This groping is, Leroi-Gourhan
argues, a distinctive characteristic of all gesturing. As we are discussing
throughout this chapter on gesturing and dancing, Leroi-Gourhan understands that "gestures connect muscles with mind" in the creation of a
skillset, in the use of skillsets which then develop and are used to alter
skillsets. Or in more neurobiological terms, gestures engage sensorimotor

patterns that require complex systemic interaction among the nervous system, the interoceptors (the proprioceptors in the muscles and ligaments), and the muscle fibers that is constitutive of being an animate organism. For gesturing, as with any self-movement, distinctions made between the nervous and muscle systems are products of territorialization as post-gestural analysis. And, further, as gesturing is always seeking contact it must always be understood as relational, as the body in relation to the other, to the environment on which its own existence depends, which is always being explored, contacted, engaged in the gesturing. Gesturing can be understood as culturally, historically, and psychologically shaped forms of living movement, effecting self-othering, the transcendence of the body by the body in the perception and realization of self and world. Gesturing is a cultural register for playing out natural self-othering.

Leroi-Gourhan discussed the acquisition of gestures. He understood that movements become gestural programs through not only groping, but also in apprenticeship through mime and by verbal instruction. We well know that we learn most movement behavior through simply imitating others. Often this is unconscious, but in dancing it is frequently quite deliberate. We are familiar with dancers arranged in lines across a dance floor imitating a teacher's movements as she performs them in front of us. We use mirrors to self-assess the accomplishment of mimetic similarity. I well remember trying to find a location on the dance floor where I could see not only the teacher but also my own reflection close to hers so that I could align my movements with hers for comparison. Verbal instruction is common as well both inside and outside of dancing. We are told to straighten an arm, to lift the head, to curve the spine, and so on. In some cultures—I saw this in Thailand and Java—dancers are instructed by the teacher who, rather than saying anything, actually physically repositions the bodies of the dancers while they are moving. We also understand that practice (high repetitions of self-conscious self-movement) is essential to building the sensorimotor programming that gives us ownership of and identified with these gestures. And, clearly, extensive repetition actually changes bodily tissues as demanded for execution of the gestural patterns. We become our gestures in a quite literal sense.

Leroi-Gourhan also understood gestures as occurring in "complex operating chains." As we move through our lives isolated gestures are rare. Indeed, isolated gestures usually occur as the result of an insistent application of the "poor" or narrow understanding of gesturing. In early human developmental an example of operating gestural chains is the related skills of toddlers lifting a spoon, retaining a horizontal position to avoid spilling, so as to finally hit their mouths with food. In child development this is a marvelous achievement. It requires much attention, assistance, verbal instruction, and seemingly endless exemplification and repetition. Yet, this gestural pattern becomes the base for increasingly complex operating chains that are involved simply in preparing food and eating it. The use of a spoon can eventuate in the culinary arts, complex operating chains of gestural patterns building on one another seemingly endlessly in not only the art of eating using many tools and skilled movements, but also extending into the preparation of food with endless possibilities of gestural patternings engaging a host of tools. Such gestural chains are obviously stamped with cultural identity as well.

Dancing is obviously similar. There are basic gestural patterns that underlie the distinctive features of each dance form. In sports we refer to these as the "fundamentals" and they are routinely practiced and endlessly repeated. One thinks of the countless hours of the ballet dancer throughout her career doing *barre* exercises with constant critique from her dance teacher.

The acquisition of gestures and the building of them into complex chains create super skills. If we are learning our first form of dance, for example, every aspect of the technique is new and often requires persistence through a long stage of awkwardness, discomfort, self-consciousness, sore muscles, and overtaxed brains. Yet, if we are accomplished in one dance form, learning another allows us to not only borrow from the gestural patterns built for the first dance form, it also actually allows us to develop a super skill set which makes other dance gestural patterns easier to acquire. We are all familiar with the common notion that ballet is foundational to all dancing. While it is possible to take some exception to this claim, it certainly is widely correct. Thus, ballet "training," an important notion itself, offers the acquisition of these building block gestural patterns that can then be drawn upon in the practice of many other dance forms. This super skill set (engram) is what in other contexts I talk about as the acuity gained through demanding self-movement. Interestingly, highly developed complex gestural chains support adeptness at improvisation and the groping aspects by which these movements enable us to explore ourselves and our relationship to the environment.

Leroi-Gourhan's consideration of the distinction between humans and animals is fascinating and provides us further insights about dancing. Leroi-Gourhan did not look for the distinction between humans and animals in the more common terms of instinct versus intelligence. Rather, he suggested that animals depend exclusively on the internal storage of memory and sensorimotor programming; whereas humans add to this internal memory a second mode of programming that relies on external supports for memory such as writing, art, video technology, and so on. He argued that external supports to memory cannot develop without gestural skills such as writing with a pen or using a brush to paint. The hand as a tool then is the first externalization of memory. "The hand is not born but made through its interactions with the external matter—the hand thus becomes a kind of prosthesis rendering it external to itself."[22]

The external othering is accomplished through gesturing, gesturing with the hand that renders the hand at once both hand and tool, prosthesis and body. It is this hinge, the othering of the hand as tool through gesture, which initiates external support for memory that eventuates in the great sophistication of writing and books and literacy. And it seems clear that this exact action of self-othering is essential to such distinctively human tropes as symbol, metaphor, art, language and so on each depending on the same structurality as self-othering, that is, that paradoxical interrelationship of something being both what it is and something other, both experienced through the sensorimotor loop that includes brain and muscle/bone.

Dancing, as I am trying to comprehend it as the actions of dancing or as dancing itself, is similar to this self-othering that occurs with the gestural act in which hand (or body) becomes tool both connecting to and constructing the environment, discovering and creating the self, and enacting the human distinction of external support to memory. Dancing however, I argue, stands at the threshold of this human capacity and distinctiveness of the paradox of self-othering. It uniquely provides fully bodied experiential affirmation of the structurality that underlies the whole distinctly human experience. This is the experience of that which is other than oneself, yet experienced in the identical neurobiological means by which one experiences self. External support to memory simply cannot exist, I contend, without this foundational experience, gained quintessentially in dancing, that allows the assured acceptance, because it is lived and felt, of the paradox that is distinctive to external memory support and the appreciation that it levers us into the distinction of our humanity. It is only because we experience the other as self, knowing it as other, wholly other, that something external can be equated with something internal; that something virtual can be equated with something actual. The major importance here is that dancing as gesturing is the culturally, historically, psychologically stamped movement that is self-referential with respect to being principally about the living movement that is human vitality.

For a paleoethnographer tools are the trace for the gestural patterns of the earliest tool-makers who set forth the distinctively human. What is not evident in this process of early human development—because it was not associated with stone tools yet which, I would suggest, was essential—was the dancing of the earliest humans, those performances of chains of gestural patterns that initiated the paradoxical character of gesturing as coincidence of self and virtual other both proprioceptively experienced that was necessary even before the first stone tool could be imagined. The traces of the dances of emergent humans were left in their very tissues—in their neurons and muscles—rather than in stone. The self-othering gesturing of dancing focuses its movement on the potential for movement to become gesture, an exploration of the body as tool, a necessary stage prior to the first stone tool.

Leroi-Gourhan was concerned about the possibility that humans through their development of increasingly sophisticated tools would eventually render their current form of embodied existence obsolete. Here is what he wrote,

> Liberated from his tools, from his gestures, his muscles, the program-mation of his acts, his memory, liberated from his imagination by the perfection of tele-diffused means, liberated from the animal and vege-tal worlds, from the wind, from the cold, from bacteria, from the un-known of mountains and seas, the *homo sapiens* of zoology is probably at the end of his career.[23]

I suppose we would immediately think of the image of bodiless brain that has frequently occasioned our imagination. But another image might be that offered in the 2008 film *WALL-E*. Humans amidst unchecked technological development have polluted the earth to the point it will not support any life at all. Humans have escaped to off-planet space stations to await the return of the possibility of life on earth. In line of Leroi-Gourhan's discussion of the shifts in posture occurring during the course of evolution that lead to the emphasis of hand and face, I imagine the continuing trajectory leading to the blimp-like reclining humans who live in these space stations. They float about on chaise lounges barely capable of self-movement with their entire experiential life being delivered to them virtually via video screens and serving robots. I think of those pos-ters that show the stages of development moving from quadrapedal mo-bility to upright bipedal posture and then the succeeding stages tip the evolving figure on to his back reclining on a chaise. Yet, in this film, the lesson for the redemption is with the trash gathering and compacting robot WALL-E whose movement remains and seems self-directed. His leisure is spent watching dance numbers of classic mid-twentieth century musicals on cassette videos. The rescue of the off planet humans emerges from the love affair between WALL-E and the feminine robot EVA con-firmed in their spiraling cosmic dancing. The robots display vitality, hu-mor, and emotions far more exemplary of humanity than the humans on these space stations simply through their self-movement and the quality of their robotic sounds. Inspired by the videos of dancing and remember-ing that dancing is distinctive of earth humanity the blubber-bodied cap-tain of the off-planet station finally gains the courage to retake the ship from machine control and return to earth.

In his concern for the end of the human career, Leroi-Gourhan gets to the heart of the inseparability of gesturing and the distinctively human. As Noland put it

> Leroi-Gourhan . . . suggests that without opportunities for physical activity, without the ability to practice and develop a vast motor poten-

tial, humans may be unable to acquire and process the sensations afforded by gesturing. In the triangular (not binary) commerce of animation, these kinesthetic, tactile, and proprioceptive sensations are the very matter on which all differential symbolic orders and hermeneutic, perceptual operations depend.[24]

Dancing, I am proposing, is at the very heart of this triangular gestural structurality, necessarily coming before there is anything to do or say, fundamental to the very doing and saying that distinguishes cultural historical human being.

An interesting example that perhaps helps us grasp Leroi-Gourhan's understanding of gesture and my extension and inspiration of his work to help us more fully appreciate dancing is the Hindu figure of Nataraja, Shiva as Lord of Dance. We are all familiar with the South Indian copper sculptures of Nataraja that date from the thirteenth century. It seems these images are everywhere. Here is how Ananda Coomaraswamy describes this figure:

> The images . . . represent Shiva dancing, having four hands, with braided and jeweled hair of which the lower locks are whirling in the dance. In His hair may be seen a wreathing cobra, a skull, and the mermaid figure of Ganga; upon it rests the crescent moon, and it is crowned with a wreath of Cassia leaves. In His right ear He wears a man's earring, a woman's in the left; He is adorned with necklaces and armlets, a jeweled belt, anklets, bracelets, finger and toe rings. The chief part of His dress consists of tightly fitting breeches, and He wears also a fluttering scarf and a sacred thread. One right hand holds a drum, the other is uplifted in the sign of do not fear: one left hand holds fire, the other points down upon the demon *Muyalaka*, a dwarf holding a cobra; the left foot is raised. There is a lotus pedestal, from which springs an encircling glory (*tiruvasi*), fringed with flame, and touched within by the hands holding drum and fire.[25]

It is held that Shiva's dancing represents "His five activities (*Pancakritya*), viz.: *Shrishti* (overlooking, creation, evolution), *Sthiti* (preservation, support), *Samhara* (destruction, evolution), *Tirobhava* (veiling, embodiment, illusion, and also, giving rest), *Anugraha* (release, salvation, grace)."[26] The stationary image of the dancing Shiva then is in a remarkable position. His posture is teeming with the incipient energies of the culturally and historically informed gestural patterns that constitute the cosmic activities, separately the domains of the most powerful of the Hindu deities. Nataraja's dancing is not simply a dance that creates the cosmos; it is in an even more foundational position. It includes cosmic creation, but also cosmic destruction, as well as preservation, embodiment, and release from the entire cycle of becoming. The incipience of Nataraja's dancing is caught in the Shaivite text: "Our Lord in the Dancer, who, like the heat latent in firewood, diffuses His power in mind and matter, and makes them dance in their turn."[27] Perhaps the popularity of replicas of these images of Nataraja is connected in some unconscious way to a sense of what is being shown: the incipient energy of dancing itself as foundational to creation and destruction; as prior to, yet enabling, the possibility of meaning; as the gesturing that initiates the complex gestural chains that constitute life and culture and religion.

Maurice Merleau-Ponty's mid-twentieth century work that reshaped our current understandings of perception also contributed importantly to a rich understanding of gesture. He placed interoception, the kinesthetic experience, as essential to perception. Merleau-Ponty moved closer to the issues of neurology and philosophy that recognized that human agency could not exist without the input of kinesthetic-touch sensations produced in self-movement. This is a position argued much earlier by John Dewey and William James as well as foreshadowed by early neurologists C. S. Sherrington and Henry Head. While this proprioceptive or kinesthetic input is often considered by them in terms of "feedback," which has implications I do not accept, it at least shows that movement is essential to perception and to agency and to affect and that movement establishes the basis for understanding gesture in terms of a loop or a reciprocity between agency and inquiry, between expression and formation, between tradition and change.[28]

In the spring of 2010 Jonathan Smith presented a major lecture at the University of Colorado, "'Now you see it, now you won't': The Future of the Study of Religion over the Next 40 Years." We asked him to set forth his prospects on what will shape the future of the academic study of religion over the next generation. Given that Smith is well known for his sedentary isolated text-limited studies, I was more than a little surprised that he listed "gesture studies" as one of five major areas he believes will shape this period. Another he named is neuroscience; another cognitive science.

Taking Smith's prediction seriously, I have returned to my earlier research on Australian Aboriginal cultures with the intent of approaching some of the most difficult of issues experienced for over a century by scholars in their efforts to understand these cultures. My intent has been to focus principally on gestures and on the gestural aspect of some of their dancings. The following section I believe demonstrates the potential of this approach as well as hopefully extending our understanding of gesturing and the gestural aspects of dancing.

"THEY JUMP UP OF THEMSELVES": GESTURE AND IDENTITY IN CENTRAL AUSTRALIA

The Arrernte word "*altjira*" is the crossing point for a complex series of histories and stories that played out in Central Australia beginning in the late nineteenth century and continuing right up to this consideration.

Altjira has been rendered in many ways—dreamtime, ancestors, the Christian God, for starters—with results that have had widespread and deep impact. The Hermannsburg missionaries arriving in Central Australia in 1877 understood the importance of using local languages to present Christianity to Aboriginal peoples. A. L. Kempe acknowledged the extreme difficulty of learning Arrernte language with no common language bridge, yet by the mid-1880s he had identified what he believed were five Arrernte gods. He then wrote, "All of them, the good supernatural beings, they also call 'altgiva,' [later standardized as *altjira*] . . . the word . . . signifies that these had an everlasting existence."[29] Kempe adapted this adjectival term for the missionaries to use as the word for God. These early difficult years exhausted the several missionaries who finally abandoned the station in 1891. In 1894 Carl Strehlow arrived to resume the work and quickly began a major ethnographic study of these aboriginal cultures, though he never attended any of their cultural or ritual functions. His multi-volume work published in German, *Die Aranda* (1907-1920), began with a section titled *"Altjira"* in which he reported that the Arrernte have "a being, called Altjira, who embodies the highest good (*mara*),"[30] showing no awareness that this figure had likely arisen in the vocabularies of his informants at the instigation of his predecessor Kempe.

Baldwin Spencer, a young London biologist who had been appointed by the University of Melbourne to establish the study of biology in Australia, was hired by the Horn Expedition (1894), the first great scientific expedition to explore and document life in Central Australia. Spencer saw little if any difference between the human and the plant and animal life and soon became an ethnographer contributing one of the most influential ethnographies of the late nineteenth century, *Native Tribes in Central Australia* (1899).[31] His coauthor was Francis (Frank) Gillen, a telegraph operator and station manager at Alice Springs. During this crucial period from 1894 into the first several years of the twentieth century, Spencer was in regular contact with Sir James George Frazer in London who was embroiled in the controversies that would establish the basis for twentieth century anthropology. One of the major areas of debate at this time was the presence of the "high god" among "primitive people" because of its decisive role in determining when religion appeared in the evolution of culture. Strehlow's identification of Altjira as the Arrernte high god was not welcome to Frazer's view on cultural evolution which placed magic as a stage prior to the development of religion. Writing to Frazer in 1903, Spencer reflects his obvious sympathy and support,

> Twenty years ago a man named Kempe, one of the first missionaries, seized upon the word Altjira (= our [i.e., Spencer and Gillen's] Alcheri) and adopted it as the word for "God." He knew nothing of its significance to the natives, or of its association with the word "Alchiringa"

(*Acheri*=dream; *ringa*=of, belonging to) but he saw that it had some special and sacred significance. Now after these twenty years (when the station has not been closed or the missionaries away) of endeavouring to teach the poor natives that Altjira means "God", Strehlow comes forward with the momentous discovery that in the Arunta, "*there is a Being of the highest order called Altjira or Altjira mara (mara=*good); . . . "that Altjira is the highest divinity; he is the creator of the world and maker of men" . . . The paper . . . has more utter misleading nonsense packed into a small space than I recollect having come across before.[32]

The connection made between the term *altjira* and dreams and dreaming which Spencer refers to in this letter was expanded by Frank Gillen to the term "Dreamtime" which has, despite many deconstructions and criticisms, entered the vocabulary of twentieth century Aboriginal self-understanding and remains today a distinctive marker of self-identity to many Aboriginals. Kempe later confirmed in a 1910 letter to Spencer that he remained well aware that *altjira*

is not "God" in that sense in which we use the word—namely, as a personal being—but it has a meaning of old, very old, something that has no origin, mysterious, something that has always been so, also always. . . . We adopted the word [*Altjira* for] "God" because we could find no better and because it comes nearest to the idea of "eternal."[33]

Spencer himself was not innocent of such manipulations. In *Native Tribes* he relied on two sets of Frank Gillen's field notes to describe the "Origin of the Alcheringa Ancestors." Comparing Spencer's text as it represented Gillen's unpublished notes I found that his selection, combination, and presentation of Gillen's notes almost wholly construct the results. Of most relevance here, Spencer combines different figures from Gillen's notes and attributes them with the origin of ancestors. He renders the Arrernte word *ungambikula*, an adjective meaning something like "they jump up of themselves" or "out of nothing" or "self-existing" as the class name *Ungambikula* designating these figures.[34]

Then, in Spencer's 1927 revised edition of *Native Tribes*, which he completed years after Gillen's 1912 death, published under the title *The Arunta*, the same sort of text manipulation reoccurs. Spencer, still bitterly hostile to Carl Strehlow's constructive ethnography, ended up repeating the same maneuver that seems the common thread in all these stories of observers of Aboriginal cultures, the rendering of an adjectival term into a noun and then allowing that to be used as a proper noun. Spencer's principal aboriginal consultant for his extensive field study in 1926 was an English-speaking tracker with the English name Charlie Cooper. During their conversations, Cooper told Spencer a creation story for the *tjilpa* or wildcat people, a division of the Arrernte, which featured the figure Numbukulla as a creator; Numbukulla now a proper noun based on the adjective *ungambikula*. This story features, among other things, Numbukulla erecting a pole, painting it with blood, climbing the pole and telling the *tjilpa* man to follow. The man tried to climb the pole but slipped down and then Numbukulla drew the pole up after him and was never seen again. Spencer added a whole new chapter to *The Arunta* that was not in *Native Tribes* presenting this material and, unwittingly it seems, offering his own evidence of an aboriginal "high god." There are a number of concerns about the credibility of Cooper. Theodor Strehlow, the son of Carl Strehlow and himself a noted scholar, later reported that Charlie Cooper had told him that he had contrived the story for Spencer's benefit. Theodor Strehlow was about as critical of Spencer's work as Spencer was of his father's, that is, Carl Strehlow's. Still, it is relatively clear that Numbukulla is a transformation that occurred during the first forty years of European contact with Aboriginals rendering the adjective *ungambikula* that describes the non-origination feature of figures known to the Arrernte into a class noun and eventually into a proper noun naming a creator figure, that is, Numbukulla.

The term *numbukulla* eventually enters the field of the academic study of religion mid-twentieth century when Mircea Eliade began to regularly use an example formalized in a narrative I call "Numbukulla and the Sacred Pole," which he took wholly from Spencer's *The Arunta*, as the prime and often single example by which to establish his understanding of religion, which turned on the valuation of a world axis that connected humans with deities and that held that myths of origination offered the pristine religious condition. The study of religion once again turned on Jonathan Z. Smith's critique of Eliade's use of this example and Smith then offered his own understanding, developed upon his careful reading of the story traditions of the *tjilpa,* or wildcat people, as the basis for establishing an alternative theory of religion. Thus, since mid-twentieth century this example has played a significant role in the defining discussions of the study of religion.

In the recording of the Arrernte story traditions, less contested but no less divisive, was to use the term *altjira*, which was an adjective describing something about the figures in these stories, as the noun rendered in English "ancestors" used to name this class of figures. The term *ungambikula* could also describe them. Géza Róheim reports that Aboriginal elders assured him the term *altjira* means "the eternal ones from the dream" or "the eternal people who come from dreams."[35]

This stream of Europeans performing the magic of turning adjectives into nouns, even proper nouns, makes for an engaging story of which I have given the barest outline.[36] My discerning the events and telling the story shows, however uncomfortably, that the academic study of other cultures, other people, is an interactive process in which certain projections, effected by theories, classifications, translations, and expectations, occur that result not only in the creative construction of the other on paper, but also in reality. Spencer indignantly recognized the process a century ago when he accused Carl Strehlow of discovering the "high god" only because his own missionary predecessor had introduced the idea years before as part of their process of proselytization. Géza Róheim recognized this process when he went to Australia to do fieldwork in 1929. His objective was to establish the subfield of "psychoanalytic anthropology" in which extensive psychoanalysis would be part of the preparation of an ethnographer for fieldwork because, Róheim argued, most of what occurs is "projection" anyway, so best to know what is being projected.

What I am doing here certainly does not escape this loop and accepting the implications of this process, in the spirit if certainly not the categories of Róheim, is how I hope to remain responsible.

First, I want to note that the ontological core value for all of the non-aboriginal renderings of *altjira* is time. From Kempe's "eternal" and "everlasting existence" to Gillen's "dreamtime" to Spencer's concern with cultural evolution (interestingly the term religion does not appear in the index of any of Spencer's books), to Eliade's *in illo tempore*, to Smith's event/memorial; all of these perspectives are based in an ontology that holds time sovereign.

In his 1993 book, *A Place for Strangers*, Tony Swain offered an alternative to this assumption of the appropriateness for Aboriginals of temporal ontology by presenting evidence and argument that at least at the time of contact, the Aboriginal ontology was based fundamentally on space, rather than time. While he noted that Aboriginals experienced time, he believes it held no sovereignty for them. Swain proposed that it is more appropriate to understand "dreamings" as *abiding events* which "are characterized by the fact that they take shape and are maintained as world-form."[37] He calls upon the work of Nancy Munn to articulate the basic tenet of abiding events as

> that something came out of, moved across, and went into, the earth. . . .
> Graphically, Desert societies render this by employing two basic iconic elements: the concentric circle representing sites and lines standing for tracks between sites. In the boldest of terms, Aboriginal ontology rests upon the maxim that a place-being emerged, moved, and established an abode.[38]

While I am convinced by Swain's argument, I empathize with the difficulty he has had trying to describe a space-based ontology against the established language of ancestor, mythology, and dreamtime, all evoking a strong temporal dimension. The term "abiding" denotes qualities like permanent, unshakable, and steadfast as well as long-lasting, enduring, and surviving, all of which have a temporal implication.

I want to return to several aspects of Arrernte culture for another look. I want to reconsider the stories that are associated with the land, the stories that provide identity to the tracks of land by which Arrernte identify themselves. Contemporary Aborigines commonly refer to these tracks as their "dreamings," but alternatively as "songlines," "country," and "track." I want also to look briefly at the Arrernte understanding of how this land-based identity is bestowed upon a human being. And finally I want to look at the distinctive features of Aboriginal ritual dancing, here finding only contemporary examples available.

I am inspired by the phrase "they jump up of themselves" which is used to describe some aspect of the figures in the stories. I think the phrase likely to be an Aboriginal-inspired casual description of an aspect of these story figures that I believe to be equivalent to the term *ungambi-kula* and also related to the term *altjira*. This homely phrase has similarities to the adjectival understandings of these terms as they have been understood since Kempe, "something that has no origin, mysterious, something that has always been so, also always." What is for me so interesting about the insights suggested by this English language phrase is that it points to an action distinctive of these figures, a type of movement, a gesture that is distinctive to them. To me this attention to movement inspires the consideration of an interestingly different approach to these stories than has yet been taken, to the cultural practices associated with identity, and more. My approach here is to focus on gesture as inseparable from agency and identity. It is to focus on the living bodies rather than a territorialization, a fixing in time and space that necessarily requires the removal of living movement and gesture.

I want to reconsider the terms *ungambikula* and *altjira*, not as the names of the figures in these stories or any class of beings, but rather as designating a gestural movement that distinguishes these figures. As I have said, it is difficult for us to avoid introducing temporal reference, yet the rendering of these terms as "they jump up of themselves" suggests that there are no predecessors, no others directing their movement, that they are "it." I'll return to this a bit later, but here I want to ask, what do these figures do once they are about? In other words, what other gestures do they practice? Following Jonathan Smith's critique of Eliade, I have carefully analyzed the body of stories that are associated with *tjilpa* identity (the wildcat people). In this series of stories there are 90 places designated, most by name. The basic gestural patterns are these. Once the figures in the story are present, having "jumped up of themselves," they travel as groups from one geographically designated location to another. The names used to designate these places are known geographical locations. The 90 story segments track the movement of four different groups. The gestures or gestural patterns that designate what occurs at these locations are notable. At all 90 locations they erect a pole. They perform ceremonies of various types at 54 locations. Circumcision as part of initiation is done at 21 locations. Other gestures that were performed at but a few locations include changing language, drinking blood, sexual intercourse, and painting bodies. While not obviously gestural the presence of sexually transmitted disease was indicated for a few locations. The sequence or itinerary of these locations becomes tracks across the geographical landscape identified with the traveling figures. The travels are often referred to in ethnographic accounts as "wandering" without adequate justification for the implications of randomness. The travels are on some few occasions indicated as occurring underground.

Now before doing some additional analysis of these gestural patterns and movements, I want to briefly discuss what has long been a controversy in anthropology, the sex education of Aboriginals at the time of contact. While much ink has been shed over this matter, it is not the sex education matter that interests me here, but rather the cultural practices that motivated the anthropological discussion. I am much more interested in the gestural aspect associated with how aborigines acquired identity with specific land tracks, countries, or ritual organizations. I am carefully avoiding calling these "totems" because this term too has been the subject of an energetic discourse in anthropology that is not relevant here.

The gestural practice I am referring to is that identity is bestowed *in utero* when the Aboriginal woman first feels herself pregnant. Here is how it works: as the woman travels about the landscape gathering, when she feels herself to be pregnant, she considers that a *karuna*, usually understood as a spirit child, residing in the land associated with those who "jump up of themselves" selects her and jumps up into her, thus impregnating her. The land identity of the *karuna* gives an essential identity to the fetus. I suggest that we might well be justified in removing the temporal marker that indicates that these *karuna* were at some time before left behind by those beings that are identified with the land and simply settle ourselves to be comfortable with a non-temporal understanding that identity is gesturally connected with the land, specifically the gesture is described as a "jump up without preparation or motivation." So there is a gestural homology between the stories of the identification of particular tracks of land and the beliefs of how individual Aboriginals gain identity in terms of the land. There is nothing I see as essential to adding any sort of temporal markers to these events.[39]

Okay, leaving this idea regarding acquisition of individual identity hanging for a bit along with its obvious connection to the *ungambikula* "jumping up" gesture, I want to return to those other gestural practices that occur at the various locations as described in the stories: the gestures of erecting a pole, performing ceremonies, performing circumcision (the practice is actually subincision), and so on. As Erin Manning has shown, gesture is a means of creating space and time, that is, creating a world.[40] This certainly aligns with the motivation that was pursued by the early missionaries, the ethnographers, and the students of religion. Yet, there is an important difference. Gesture is not a creator of space and time and world on a single one-time basis performed by deities *in illo tempore* or by deities at the *axis mundi* who then disappear into the sky. Rather gesture is by its nature a repeated and repeating chain of actions, a looping or reciprocation that delimits space and time but is also constantly reaching out to contact the given environment to adjust and respond to exigencies. Gestural patterns are then the means by which identity and value and meaning are constructed through interaction with features of the environment, yet they always are also a reaching out to adjust and respond to the exigencies in the changing environment.

The gestures that are described in the stories that give identity to the land share attributes with the gestures practiced in Aboriginal ritual. Aboriginal rituals are performed at these locations enacting the identity-creating gestures of the location by the people who share identity with the land-track identified with these places. It is supposed that both the stories and the rituals change through the repetition of gestural practices. These gestures then constitute an important agentive aspect of Aboriginal culture as they constitute techniques of body that are the basis for identity, that constitute identity.

I want now to circle back to pick up the gestural designation as *ungambikula* of the story characters, the jumping up of the *karuna*, and add to that the distinctions of Aboriginal ritual dancing. This analysis is based on contemporary examples of Aboriginal dancing. A few years ago Jiri Kylian, choreographer from The Netherlands, observed Aboriginal dancing and he describes the remarkable way in which these dancers jump. He says "they jump without preparation" a gesture that he finds quite remarkable, so remarkable indeed that he says it may take a lifetime for him to understand it. Aboriginal dance movement inspired his acclaimed dance, "Sinfonietta, Symphony in D, Stamping Ground." Looking at a wide variety of contemporary Aboriginal dancing, while this jumping up without preparation is certainly not present in all dances, a common and distinctive style of Aboriginal dance movement is a whole bodied forward jump or a sudden bringing together of open knees. These movements are characteristically done rapidly seemingly without preparation; they just suddenly occur.

Gestural practice as I have shown actually insinuates itself on the tissues of the practitioner. To jump without preparation, to snap one's knees together without preparation, is not simply a movement that one learns to do, although it is learned in the process of enculturation, it becomes a technique of body inscribed by cultural practice onto the very tissues of the person. One's identity is, through gestural practice, literally bodied at the level of muscle tissue and sensorimotor neurological loops that connect neurons, muscle, skeleton in ways that shape movement and posture. Physical identity, movement, posture are constructed gesturally based on cultural, historical, and psychological environmental factors.

Now I want to think more about the implications and valuations of this gestural patterning. To understand the gesturing that we refer to as "they jump up of themselves" or "they jump without preparation" we need to understand that this movement is not about accomplishing some results, as in designating space. Perhaps other gestures do so such as erecting a pole. Nor is this jumping gesture about the trajectory of the movement on a grid, as in moving from one location to another through a designated path. Rather, I think we must understand that "they jump of themselves" is more about the movement itself. It is about incipience, movement about to happen, living movement. It is about potential, or better, potential energy. It is about the vitality factor of self-movement. It is about movement that is always process, always on the brink of moving elsewhere, engaged but at the point of not quite yet. These qualities correlate with life-force or vitality and thus seem entirely appropriate for understanding both the figures active in stories associated with tracks of land, as well as the *karuna* that vitalize new life in a woman, as well as the enactment of ritual and ritual dancing. This gesture is about the quality we can identify as vitality.

To understand the Arrernte in terms of gesture has a number of advantages.[41] We no longer need attempt to negotiate that unfortunate and uncomfortable placement of "ancestors" in some mythic past, indeed, in any time at all. We can understand that the ritual performances are characterized by the same gestural patternings with the same vitality affects as are the story figures. We can avoid the Eliadian understanding that perfection and order were established by the gods in the beginning at the center of the world and that all movement since is somehow a descent into chaos, a loss of order, a degradation by history; that ritual is primarily a method of eternal return. The study of religion exemplified by Eliade, on the one hand, and Smith, on the other, is at stark tension in most respects, yet the both share the importance of "place." To know the character of the place on which one stands is to know that person's religion. Smith frequently invoked Archimedes' dictum, "Give me a place to stand on and I will move the world." Interestingly, we have all heard this but we, like Smith, have devoted ourselves to territorializing the place rather than recognizing that Archimedes was focused on movement. I will return to this concern in the final chapter. Smith often cited Levi-Strauss making a similar point that meaning correlates with having a place and being in it. In contrast to this emphasis on place, a concern with gesture and movement and dancing places emphasis on self-movement, on incipience, on dynamics and energetics, on change and it does so without dismissing the momentary importance of place in either time or space. Gesture joins the visible and invisible, the real and virtual, in an intertwining paradoxical unity that is chiasmatic. Gesture, like dancing, as dancing, opens the gap for movement. The space/time distinction is significant only in that they are negotiated in the gestural and postural patterns that both express personal and group identity and that also offer the forms in which change can be absorbed and initiated.

GESTURING AND TOUCHING

I clearly remember the exact moment when it finally dawned on me, although I'd known it for a long time. It was December 2007. Elise Butler, my former salsa student and frequent dance partner, was home for the winter holidays from New York University, where she was a student. During the holiday we had only an hour or so to meet, catch up, and dance a little. We chatted a bit over coffee and then turned on the music to dance salsa. As we danced I immediately felt the familiar joy and ease of dancing together. I never fail to be amazed at how great it is to really dance with another person and dancing with Elise is really fun. The moment came when in the middle of leading Elise in a simple right turn I was suddenly inspired to change it into a left turn. I was astounded that Elise followed this without a hitch or jerk. She smiled to show her pleasure at seamlessly following this surprise lead. We were truly connected in our dancing; we had what I now call *the salsa connection* and what has become the center piece of what distinguishes my approach to teaching salsa.

As I teach it, salsa dancing is comprised of a set of ten basic foot patterns and a range of hand, arm, and upper body gestures that create the connection between lead and follow. In my teaching I have replaced the notion that leads lead and follows *just* follow along, with a notion that, through touch, the lead and follow are inseparable through their interactive gestures. Anyone who has gained a bit of competence in partner dancing understands how through mastery of the gestural patterns and the skillful active connection through touching, the results are that two people become one, each experiences her/his body extended into the movement/gesturing of the other. This too is a way, in dancing, of experiencing what I refer to as self-othering. José Gil suggests a relationship between partner dancing and the replication of multiple bodies that constitute dance structurality.[42]

Building on Noland's rich understanding of gesturing, by analyzing the gestural processes of salsa partner dancing, something I would/could never do on the dance floor, we gain some insights into gesture. In learning to dance salsa, or any partner contact dance, the cultural/social/psychological values insinuate themselves through high repetition training into the muscles, ligaments, and neurons of the dancers. The person dancing becomes a salsa dancer in that literal sense that muscle fibers and neurons are shaped by the skills and movement patterns that distinguish the dance. In the act of salsa dancing, the gestural patterns express the values sutured to them by society, but these same acts of gesturing are also exploratory in that they are the means by which one comes to know one's partner. The socially prescribed gestural methods of touching another person serve to collect and absorb at the level of the tissues remarkable amounts of information about one's dance partner. There is inevitably also an emotional component, an affect, to this information, this contact through gesture. One feels and experiences the connection and the information absorbed often through the lightest physical touch.

I want to explore especially the notion that gesturing is inseparable from touch and to further pursue that gesturing is also a way of exploring the world, acquiring knowledge of the environment, and effecting the world not only by offering an expression and transmission of tradition, but by incorporating change.

We can declare that gesturing is inextricably linked with touch. Erin Manning's 2007 book *Politics of Touch: Sense, Movement, Sovereignty*[43] offers insights. Her chapter "Negotiating Influence: Touch and Tango" is a discussion of touch as an essential aspect of gesture (however metaphoric and virtual) illustrated through occasional examples clearly inspired by her experience as a tango dancer.

Let me begin to explore how Manning associates touch and gesture starting with her tango example. As in salsa dancing, in tango gestural conventions define the dance form. These are acquired as one learns the dance and they are shared among and abided by all tango dancers; they constitute something of what I think she is pointing to as a politic. These rules and conventions establish and order the group. The rules and conventions become gesture through repetition and performance, that is, through taking tango lessons, receiving tango instruction and critique, and dancing tango with partners. The result is that the rules and conventions that define the basic movement elements become gestures, sensorimotor programs, engrams, that amount to the acquisition of tango skill by the dancer.

Tango dancing is not done by oneself (well, with some exceptions and those surely aren't much fun) but with a partner. The connection through touch is fundamental to the relationship and thus to the dance. Manning explores the touching aspect of tango as a way of illuminating the touch aspect of gesture. Touching evokes of gesture a condition of being multiple, that is, the touching aspect of tango gesturing (and gesturing itself) is an interaction, a reaching toward an other, a connection and identity with an other yet with the simultaneous assurance that the other is different, and never fully touchable or reachable. The reaching forth that is gesturing carries the potentiality of connection, while implying something tenuous and ephemeral. Manning holds that the touch aspect of gesture redirects away from that simplistic understanding of gesture as trace or as visible act of communication. Touch directs us to a much richer understanding of gesturing as potentiality-in-movement. Touch, in terms I have mentioned before, is the inherent reversibility, interactivity, unrealizability, potentiality aspect of gesturing. Touch opens gesture to its movement. Touch always is a reaching out, implying a negativity of self; that is, that the self cannot be without the moving out, the reaching out, to some other. There are always two bodies as Manning says. Further, she states it this way,

> As a movement reaching toward, a gesture evokes an instance in which nothing is absolutely maintained. A gesture explores the medium—be it the movement, the touch, the word—as a means not of transforming potentiality into actuality, but as a way of eclipsing actuality by placing the emphasis on the movement itself, on the exchange. . . . Gesture as such has nothing to say. It is only relationally that gestures create the possibility for exchange. Gestures negotiate both transgression and understanding. [44]

Touch then is the aspect that reminds us that all gestures are incomplete or in process.

The touch aspect of gesture is associated with knowing and constructing self and environment. As Manning writes, "it is through touching you that my body is a body, for my body cannot be otherwise than singular and plural." [45] This reminds us of Maxine Sheets-Johnstone's notion that we discover ourselves in movement a process that, with reference to gesture, we can articulate in more precise terms.

Touch is also the aspect of gesturing that points to the perhaps unexpected spontaneity and improvisational aspects of gesture. While it is easy for us to see gesture as routinized behavior, it may be more difficult to see that despite its identity with sensorimotor programming, it has the possibility for change. Here is how Manning puts it,

> This play between transgression and cohesion takes place in the weaving of tango's complex webs, webs entwined around tango's implicit desire to communicate, through the body, with an other. A dance that must be re-encountered with every new dancer, tango appeals to the senses. It does so through microperceptual movements initiated through improvisation and spontaneity that requires an adequate response yet suggest, always, the possibility of subverting the unexpected. [46]

However, at base the tango is a gestural pattern through which two dancers touching are at once expressing themselves in various dimensions from the intention to move in a specified way to the expression of desire which, according to the conventions of the dance, will remain unfulfilled (at least during the dance). Barbaras identifies desire with movement itself. Yet, through the touch connection of the gestural patternings, the dancers are learning about one another, are improvising movement patterns (seemingly seamlessly), and actually creating space and time.

Now the tango as a dance where the partners hold one another in close embrace is an example that serves well to assure us that touch is an aspect of tango gesturing, yet clearly only perhaps a minor portion of all gesturing involves physically touching another body. How then, we need ask, is touch relevant to those gesturings where there is no physical touching of an other? As a sensorimotor programmed bodily movement, gesture always requires interoception or "inner touch" for the movement to be identifiable as gestural. Thus there is always touch even if it is virtual or inner or self. Gesturing also involves *tonus*, that neurobiological readiness for encounter that folds touching back into the body.

Dancing is an exemplary gestural act in its style of gesturing which always evokes an other in a gestural act that identifies dancing as a bodily exploration of gesturing itself, a reflexive act of reaching without grasping, an interaction, yet that has no message. Dancing is gesturing that is the incomplete reversibility of self-othering.

My salsa connection dancing with Elise told me something about her, but the affect of the dance touching gesturing was almost totally about the gestural/touching/self-movement itself.

THE NEUROSCIENCE OF TOUCHING AND GESTURING

In his 2011 book *Out of Our Heads: Why You Are Not Your Brain, and Other Lessons from the Biology of Consciousness* Alva Noë quotes the late Nobel laureate co-discoverer of the structure of DNA, Francis Crick, who proposed an "astonishing hypothesis," in a book by this name, that hypothesis being "you, your joys and your sorrows; your memories and your ambitions, your sense of personal identity and free will, are in fact no more than the behavior of a vast assembly of nerve cells and their associated molecules."[47] Noë responded that what he finds interesting is how astonishing this view isn't! And he turns to show how common are views that "there is a thing inside each of us that thinks and feels and wants and decides."[48] He acknowledges, as clearly we would protest, that Crick is proposing something quite different than a spirit or soul or even a mind, yet his point is really that it has been common, if not the exclusive approach in the West for a good long time, to understand consciousness by looking within. Recently neuroscientists have sought consciousness in the "brain in the skull," as I have come to call it, and Noë recounts this tendency for us as well.

Noë then turns to what he considers to be a "really astonishing hypothesis" and he states it this way,

> we must look not inward, into the recesses of our insides; rather, we need to look to the ways in which each of us, as a whole animal, carries on the processes of living in and with and in response to the world around us. The subject of experience is not a bit of your body. You are not your brain. The brain, rather, is part of what you are.[49]

Well, I must say that I was immediately perked up by the phrase "the processes of living in and with and in response to the world around us" because to me this refers to nothing other than gesturing in the rich sense as I have been trying to develop it. Yet, Noë never mentions the word gesture in his book. He has a chapter on "Habits" that borders on a discussion of gesture something on the order of Pierre Bourdieu's notion of *habitus*.[50] Noë discusses perception somewhat, yet even here he focuses on vision. And he gives little more than a mention to the extensive philosophical work on perception by Merleau-Ponty and others.

Still, I find Noë's book of interest in its unacknowledged affirmation of the essential role that gesture (though unnamed) plays in the formation and existence of consciousness. It powerfully affirms, from a perspective of neuroscience and biology, that our study of gesturing, especially if understood in its richness, will, as Jonathan Smith predicts, be central in the era of the study of culture and religion that is just beginning.

I want to briefly reflect on movement/gesture/touch from the perspective of neurobiology. As I have just indicated neuroscience tends to focus on the brain, the central nervous system. Even when the sensorimotor system is invoked it is often the sensorimotor cortex that is the implied reference, the part of the brain that "controls" movement. When the proprioceptive and other interoceptive aspects of the nervous system are included, rare enough, they are usually referred to as providing "feedback" for the benefit of the central nervous system.

Yet, our persistent inquiries and reflections on the role of movement/gesture/touch/posture suggest that a revised valuation of the sensorimotor system is necessary; especially important as background for building a deeper and richer appreciation of dancing.

Leroi-Gourhan's understanding of gesture as both agentive and heuristic or exploratory is essential to our revised position. Groping (*tâttonements*) is the gestural patterning of reaching out to the world. Touch is the way we articulate this connection or interaction be it encounter with some physical other or the inner touch of proprioception, motion/body awareness relative to the environment. We have come to see that gestural patterns create what are variously understood as body concepts, image schemas, basic level categories. All of these are the foundation for and the building blocks of conceptual thought and constructions of meaning. These are the foundations by which we have a sense of self and the world. They are all based in movement/gesture/touch which have a primacy, a firstness in the sense Charles Sanders Peirce articulated, to our sense of self, identity, environment, meaning, consciousness, thought.

Movement is not simply the result of commands from the central nervous system; movement has a place of inseparability from the development of the sensorimotor cortex and the sensorimotor system. These neurological systems develop and take shape under the tutelage of movement and operate as much in response to proprioceptive stimulus as they direct physical movement by stimulating muscle cells.

It is essential that we understand that the sensorimotor system, an emphasis on movement/gesture/touch, obviates any need to make reference to the pesky issues that accompany the separation of brain (central nervous system, sensorimotor cortex) from body (proprioceptive, muscular, skeletal). Anything short of the whole system distributed throughout the body is just dead tissue.

In the midst of this recent discussion arguing over the location of prime territory, I find the following description of the nervous system most interesting. It is from the 1977 book *The Anatomy of the Human Body*. "The nervous system is merely a [part of a] mechanism by which a muscular movement can be initiated by some change in the peripheral sensation, say an object touching the skin."[51]

DANCING AND THE SURVIVAL OF MEN

A friend of mine teaches special education in a grammar school and she told me that all of the students in her "special ed" program are boys. I got an email from another friend who told me that of her six grandchildren, four boys and two girls, "the girls are easier to enjoy but I miss all of them." My daughter recently volunteered among a group of parents to do special programs for small groups of second graders. She was assigned three boys and two girls and the teacher told her that if the boys were impossible to manage she would reassign them. They were making films. On the second meeting the boys did need to be reported to the teacher because they were so rambunctious that nothing could be accomplished and the teacher responded by taking strong disciplinary measures. My daughter also reported that the boys were obsessed with including violent acts in the films and described these acts in graphic detail. I saw the two movies that the kids produced and the boys were great and creative and contributed enthusiastically. My daughter enjoyed working with them. My sister reported to me that her grandson loves ice hockey and is very good at it, but he struggles with reading. Another friend who has a boy reports the same. Okay, these are just comments I've heard in the last month and notably I didn't seek any of this information. All these reports came from women. All but one of the boys who were reported as having problems were being educated by and cared for by women. In the same timeframe I heard these anecdotes I didn't have a single male say anything to me about his experience with or care of children or boys. The comments the women made about these boys had no counterpart of women talking in largely positive terms about the accomplishments and behaviors of the boys they know. I don't think these anecdotes vary much from national trends and practices. Women take care of and educate male children and there is both expectation (which is significant) and experience that boys are "hard to manage" and are more likely to have academic and behavioral problems than their girl peers.

So here are some sobering facts as summarized in the *New York Times* (March 28, 2010):

- High school GPA for boys is 2.86 compared to girls' 3.09
- Girls now score equal to boys in math (but boys more often score extremely high or extremely low)
- Girls outscore boys in verbal
- Girls appear to make more effort
- 64% of National Honor Society members are girls
- In many colleges, boys are now given "special consideration" so ratios won't become out of balance (i.e., affirmative action for boys)
- Girls are out-reading boys at all age/grade levels in all states, with the number of girls achieving proficiency level at 79%, boys at 72%.
- Boys are two times more likely to repeat a grade than are girls, two times more likely to be suspended, and three times more likely to be expelled
- 25% more boys are dropouts in comparison to girls
- 57% of master's degrees awarded to whites go to females, and 62% of doctorates go to females
- 66% of master's degrees awarded to blacks go to females, and 72% of doctorates go to females
- In the national writing exam, 32% of girls are proficient, but only 16% of boys

Guy Garcia in his 2008 book *The Decline of Men* predicted that in eight years women would hold as many jobs in America as men. In an early 2010 National Public Radio interview Garcia expressed surprise that this had already been achieved. Of course, this does not mean that women yet make a combined wage equal to that of men, although that is predicted to occur by 2028 and will surely happen before 2020, or that discrimination against women does not still exist in the workplace.

There has recently been a rapid increase in the number of women CEOs and women in politics at every level, both areas almost exclusively controlled by men until recently. Few would even question the likelihood that one day a woman might well be President of the United States. Women have long outnumbered men as voters. Increasingly women are heads of households and do not think that they need a man to have a family. There are increasing numbers of relationships where the female earns more than the male. In hard economic times, women get jobs more readily than men.

That boys/males are lagging behind girls/females is not really news because it has been occurring for 25 years at least, yet it has not been widely acknowledged among the general populace. It is not just in the education and rearing of boys that this is occurring; the rebalancing of gender positioning is working its way throughout society—the work-force, politics, leadership positions—and it is taking place at a remark-ably rapid pace. This trend is being accompanied by a shift in the way women look at their relationship to men and, increasingly, in men's self-image and self-esteem. As alarming numbers of men simply do not finish high school, do not go on to college, do not compete with women for jobs, the question is becoming "Where are the men?"

It is not just the United States that is experiencing this shift, this re-alignment. As Hanna Rosin points out in her August 2010 *The Atlantic* article titled "The End of Men,"

> Up to a point, the reasons behind this shift are obvious. As thinking and communicating have come to eclipse physical strength and stami-na as the keys to economic success, those societies that take advantage of the talents of all their adults, not just half of them, have pulled away from the rest.[52]

Rosin cites the dramatic shift and attitude towards a preference for girls in South Korea and concludes that "with few exceptions the greater the power of women, the greater the country's economic success." So this isn't simply about an overpowering Western feminist movement, it is deeply entwined with economics.

Now for some of the solutions that are being posed for this situation as it relates to boys. In his 2007 book, *Boys Adrift*, physician and psycholo-gist Leonard Sax offers five underlying causes:

- The current way schools do business does not typically permit boys to be boys.
- When they do try to be boys, they tend to get (falsely) diagnosed with ADHD and (over) medicated, leading to an unmotivated, al-ienated anomie.
- Meanwhile, years of consuming foods and beverages poisoned by estrogen-mimicking phthalates from plastic containers has led to endocrine imbalances and anomalies.
- This triple-whammy has nudged many boys into the "safe" virtual reality of video games and pornography, where they can have thrills without responsibilities.
- The family and society have allowed negative cultural role models (epitomized by Homer Simpson) to reinforce an image of boys and men as lazy, unambitious, and lacking in courage, with too few positive role models demanding that young boys exhibit courage and service in approaching manhood (epitomized by the scouting movement)—what is known as "rites of passage."

Okay, so the fault is schools, Homer Simpson, plastic containers that give off estrogenic chemicals, and the scarcity of "real" manly models. I don't even dare follow out the implications of these silly positions.

Christina Hoff Sommers's 2000 book *The War Against Boys: How Misguided Feminism is Harming Our Young Men* is an ax-grinding often, to me anyway, annoying book that also argues a "naturalness" base for the solution. Repeatedly she returns to the position that "boys will be boys" after all and nothing is about to change that, indeed, it has been an unfortunate product of twentieth century feminism that boys have increasingly been treated like girls—expecting them to be able to learn to read and to sit quietly and so on. Sommers ends her book by citing a number of espoused feminists who have discovered the "misguidedness" of their feminist perspective when confronted with their own sons' behavior. And, indeed, Sommers is the mother of two sons and one would suspect the book was her own way of trying to realign herself, being utterly obnoxious about every influential feminist who has promoted female-friendly education, most particularly Carol Gilligan, and ends her book with these words, "If you are a mother, as I am, you know that one of the most agreeable facts of life is that boys will be boys."[53] I understand this statement about as well as the rest of her book. She has shown that it is overwhelmingly recognized that boys being boys is rarely agreeable to anyone who is anywhere near them. If she means that mothers agree that they can't do a damned thing about the way their sons behave, and thus this "boys will be boys" view finds some consensus among mothers, that's another face of the same sad valence. It is incredible to me that the same argument would be admitted for girls, as I discussed in Chapter One, and that "girls will be girls," that is, that they throw awkwardly with all the subtle and not so subtle associated pejoratives. Yet, if it is of boy nature to be a certain way, then it has to hold that there is also a girl nature that one must simply accept and do one's best to cope with.

But, while the intention to support the more meaningful and successful education of boys is obviously well intended, the whole set of premises on which Sommers's argument is based is flawed and the recommendations it produces are highly distasteful, to me anyway. She recommends that boys be isolated, rigorously disciplined, punished for misbehaving, taught morality (although who determines what is moral is not discussed), and placed in environments of competition.

What is missing, among many things actually, is that, however natural boy behavior appears it is in significant measure a product of history and culture. One should set this whole "naturalness" argument even in the context of the history of the child in the West to recognize that the behavior identified among boys that seems to be natural to maleness today was not there in such universal ways not that long ago. What is missing is an adequately sophisticated means of understanding what creates and maintains the seemingly natural boy behavior. Many observers hold that since boys-will-be-boys-behavior appears soon after birth it must be naturally male.

We have yet to understand and appreciate the extent to which gestural and movement patterns and touching behaviors that are insinuated by adults on infant bodies are themselves gendered and reflect gestural and movement patterns deeply bodied. We have been less than aware of the impact of adult gendered gestures on infants. We must recognize that infants can imitate and respond to gesture within the first hour of their lives and thus, right from the start, their pliable tissues (muscles and neurons) are being shaped in gendered movement patternings. We surely do not recognize that adult gestural and movement and touching patterns unconsciously enacted when an infant reaches for a toy—truck or baby doll—scream gender expectations in the ways babies understand deeply; that is, adult facial expressions and movements even at the micro-level are inputs to the groping movements of infants. We do not adequately appreciate that the way we move, hold, and touch infants, the voice qualities we use with them, everything we do in the vicinity of infants all insinuate on them gendered identities. Before they can speak these gestural patterns enculturate the infant with gender identity in ways deeply set in the tissues of their muscles and neurons. Then when they are schoolchildren, we sigh in resignation to what now seems innate that "boys will be boys" while, increasingly in recent decades, also being secretly thankful that "girls will be girls." The apparent naturalness is that human identity arises in a rich complex of genetic potentialities shaped by experience of the environment. And, while there is not so much we can do about the genetic part, the amount we can do about the experiential part is far greater than we likely have imagined.

Appropriate to the principal subject of this book and to my personal interests we must ask the question, "So what does dancing have to do with this messy situation about the decline or possible even disappearance of men?" I have been waiting and waiting to write this section and I have not quite known why. Last night I went to Denver to see the musical version of "Billy Elliot." As today I think of this musical and reflect on how it deals with the gender/dancing issue compared with the movie version. I really needed to see and experience "Billy Elliot" the musical to give me some of the terms and perspectives valuable to communicating what I want to say. So here goes.

I've been eager to experience the musical *Billy Elliot*, because I knew I would enjoy it, but also because I wanted to compare its treatment of gender roles and dancing with the film treatment. Okay, first, I have to say that I loved this musical with its great music by Elton John and amazing dance numbers. Generally, I found that the musical correlates closely with the movie in the treatment of gender roles related to dancing. One slight yet comical twist is the treatment of Billy's friend Michael "the puff." Michael is a cross-dresser and he does so with amazing flair for a pre-teen, yet he finds Billy's ballet dancing far the greater candidate to be interpreted as weird or queer than his own dressing in women's clothing. He tells Billy, "Dad does it all the time."

The entire male mining community eventually comes round to support Billy's audition for admission to the Royal Academy of Ballet in London, although retaining a clear identity of ballet dancing with femininity. Billy is accepted to the academy, but, in contrast with the film version which ends with Billy as an adult dancer frozen in mid-leap, in the musical the only sense of Billy as an accomplished adult dancer comes in a mid-second act Christmas fantasy in which young Billy performs with his older self-to-be a boy-man *pas de deux* of Swan Lake. In this breath-taking dance the young Billy dances (and flies) with himself as he is to become, a wonderful explicit example of the self-othering so distinctive of dancing structurality. This dance is, for me anyway, the artistic climax of the show, but the final dance scene featuring the entire cast is done with all cast members wearing tutus. The adult men, miners and policemen, wear bulky coveralls with white tutus. During the dance young Billy is given a tutu which he steps into over his long pants and joins all the tutu-clad others.

So what is the message here? Surely it is, in at least the not so subtle register of costume, that dancing is feminine. Feminine, as I will discuss in the chapter "Seducing," in a more interesting way than simply that it is done by girls. Dancing produces nothing; it says nothing; it is done for its own sake; it is the play of signs that transforms and transcends (that is, others) the dancer.

At his audition Billy is asked "how do you feel when you dance?" His response is Elton John's "Electricity" whose lyrics capture this understanding of dancing. Elton John gets just right, I think, the self-othering freeing electric flying transcending paradoxical conflicted feeling; the loss of self that makes you whole, the bursting open, the burning inside.

Let me take this discussion a bit further and try to address the dancing and the decline of men in terms of the "Billy Elliot" musical. In the very scene in which Billy learns he has been accepted by the Royal Academy of Ballet, the coal miners learn that the union, after a year on strike, has caved in and the miners must go back to work under the old conditions. There is a powerful dance done by the miners wearing hard hats with lights atop them raging against Margaret Thatcher's government and the coal industry because they recognize that their union's loss is the loss of their entire way of life as lived by coal mining men for generations. In the face of the crisis Billy declares that he won't go to the ballet school; he'll stay home and work with the men. But he is forcefully told to leave because their way of life is over and will soon be gone forever. One miner tells Billy "Go, we can't all be dancers." And the men grouped together in the dark at the back of the stage seen only in silhouette with their lights shining out on the audience appear to descend into the mine, yet the feeling is that they are descending into a grave.

So this musical also bears the message that this male work of producing coal, working at brute labor, doing crude dirty dangerous male work is done, over; yet, the tutu-wearing, thus feminine, occupations—here exemplified by dancing—remain on stage at the end of the show celebrating vitality and joy. The conjunction between dance and the feminine (even when danced by so many males including the star of the show, Billy) marks, it seems to me in the musical version of this show, the way to the future and that way is gesturally iconized as dancing.

I do not want to suggest that the solution to the crisis of the decline of men is to enroll all boys in ballet and hand out tutus to all men. But I do want to suggest that there is something gestural in dancing that is fundamental to understanding this issue.

We can say that "boys will be boys" and argue that since the dawn of "man" (surely this word says much) the male gender has been physically strong and distinguished by broad forceful thrusting aggressive whole body gesturing as needed to provide shelter, food, and protection for their families. Perhaps because men have been so successful over the long haul, the developments afforded by having these basic survival needs met, this has allowed the development of tools of increasing sophistication and complexity, tools that have been accompanied by gesturing that has needed to be increasingly refined, subtle, and sophisticated; gestures that correspond more closely with the long evolutionary history of women's activities of preparing food, making home, child-rearing, making clothing, multi-tasking, simultaneously using multiple body parts, throwing objects in a variety of ways, and so on. The gestural patterns associated with gender images, especially the male image, have persisted more than the gestural patterns associated with the development of tools and, I would argue, there has come a tipping point (and this has occurred only recently and arisen in such a short period as to have little impact on the evolution of gendered gesturing) where women's gesturing prepares them far better for the tools and practices of the contemporary world. Doesn't this make sense?

I strongly avoid the "by nature" or "essentialist" view that "boys will be boys" because that leads us to have expectations captured in such phrases as "throw like a girl" and "men can't dance" both of which are sexist and crude and simply stupid. The contemporary period will surely be understood above all else, if we survive, as the period of plasticity, that is, the period in human history when we understand that we are amazingly malleable, that we can change ourselves in fundamental ways and do so without awaiting the eons it takes for evolution to do it for us. And one of the major forces and hopefully deep insights I want to present is that movement, gesture, dance do something more than reflect gender, history, culture, upbringing that has been inherited in the composition of our bodies. Much more importantly I believe movement, gesture, dancing actually transform the very tissue, muscles, and neurons that comprise our identities, our basis for meaning, our vitality or life-force.

Rather than holding that "boys will be boys" and finding ways of coping and somehow surpassing the negatives of "boyness" we imagine to be innate, we need look to the construction of gestural practices that, through endless repetition and imitation, will permit boys to do more than measure up a bit better to girls, but rather to actually take their places in the world that is emerging from the male and female efforts of eons. Human roles are changing, including gender roles. Both males and females need to create themselves, at the very level of tissue, in ways that will seem "natural" in that they feel easy and obvious, so that all have a meaningful and rightful gendered place in the emerging and rapidly changing world.

The challenge is to imagine, create, and construct distinctly male gestural movement patterns that shape the male human organism in such a way that it is prepared for the emerging world. One of the lessons of "Billy Elliot" is the very old and culturally very widely practiced notion that dancing is one of these movement gestural forms in which such issues are worked out or it represents something essential to the gestural forms to be created. And dancing is now being embraced in some clearly male-friendly environments like hip hop and break dancing. Still, as studies have shown, as reported by Garcia, "beginning early in childhood, girls as a group are more coordinated than boys and are better at tasks that require fast and nuanced physical movement. Girls also tend to be more articulate and have better communications skills than boys."[54] This means that parents and anyone around children must understand that from the first moments of life children are deeply influenced, including the markers of gender, by the tiniest gestures they observe.

My point is that we (and I can't even imagine who will constitute this "we" and I'm feeling remarkably gender lonely at this moment) need to boldly invent male movement/gesture/posture/dance that will directly reshape maleness in such a way as to create men that are equal to, yet complement in a decidedly masculine way, women so that men will contribute powerfully and confidently to the emerging society.

NOTES

1. Carrie Noland, *Agency & Embodiment: Performing Gestures/Producing Culture* (Cambridge: Harvard University Press, 2009).

2. Noland, *Agency & Embodiment*, 1.

3. While it is common now to understand some graffiti as works of "art," the term graffiti seems to belie the possibility that it could be art in the usual sense in which we think of it.

4. See Alva Noë, *Out of Our Heads: Why You Are Not Your Brain, and Other Lessons from the Biology of Consciousness* (New York: Hill and Wang, 2009), see Chapter 5 "Habits."

5. On engrams: "each discrete sensory record of a particular gesture or series of gestures is called a sensory engram, and once the feeling of it is firmly established as a clear recallable memory, this 'engram' works something like the templates which produce the stitching patterns in a sewing machine. ... The translation of an engram into motion involves the entire collection of sensory and motor apparata." Deane Juhan, *Job's Body: A Handbook for Bodywork* (Barrytown, NY: Station Hill Press, 2003), 267.

6. Noland, *Agency & Embodiment*, 2-3.

7. Noland, *Agency & Embodiment*, 2.

8. Noland, *Agency & Embodiment*, 2.

9. Noland, *Agency & Embodiment*, 15.

10. Noland, *Agency & Embodiment*, 6.

11. Marcel Mauss, "Techniques of Body." Originally published as "Les techniques du corps," *Journal de Psychologie*, XXXII, 1936.

12. Noland, *Agency & Embodiment*, 20.

13. Noland, *Agency & Embodiment*, 21.

14. Noland, *Agency & Embodiment*, 22.

15. Noland, *Agency & Embodiment*, 26.

16. Noland, *Agency & Embodiment*, 94.

17. Noland, *Agency & Embodiment*, 95.

18. Barbaras's discussion of movement in *Desire and Distance* is essential.

19. Noland, *Agency & Embodiment*, 98.

20. Noland, *Agency & Embodiment*, 99.

21. Noland, *Agency & Embodiment*, 109.

22. Noland, *Agency & Embodiment*, 108.

23. Andre Leroi-Gourhan, *Gesture and Speech* II, 266, quoted in Noland, *Agency & Embodiment*, 118.

24. Noland, *Agency & Embodiment*, 118.

25. Ananda K. Coomaraswamy, "The Dance of Shiva," (New York: Sunwise Turn, 1924), 69-70.

26. Coomaraswamy, "Dance of Shiva," 70.

27. Coomaraswamy, "Dance of Shiva," 70.

28. It would be appropriate to develop these ideas in terms of works by Henri Bergson, Pierre Bourdieu, Erin Manning, and others and developed in various fields from neuroscience to child development to perception.

29. F. E. H. W. Krichauff, "The Customs, Religious Ceremonies, etc. of the 'Aldolinga' or 'Mbenderinga' Tribe of Aboriginies in Krichauff Ranges, South Australia," *Royal Geographical Society of South Australia* 2 (1886-88): 33-37. Quoted in Sam D. Gill, *Storytracking: Texts, Stories, & Histories in Central Australia* (Oxford: Oxford University Press, 1998), 87.

30. Carl Strehlow, *Die Aranda und Loritja-Stämme in Zentral Australia*, edited by Moritz Freiherr von Leonharde, translated by Hans D. Oberscheidt (Frankfurt am Main: Joseph Baer, 1907-15), vol. I, part I, p. 1. Quoted in Gill, *Storytracking*, 98.

31. W. Baldwin Spencer and Francis J. Gillen, *Native Tribes of Central Australia* (London, Macmillan, 1899).

32. W. Baldwin Spencer, *Spencer's Scientific Correspondence with Sir J. G. Frazer and Others*, ed. R. R. Marrett and T. K. Penniman (London: Oxford University Press, 1932), 95-97. Quoted in Gill, *Storytracking*, 99.

33. W. Baldwin Spencer and Francis Gillen, *The Arunta: A Study of a Stone Age People* (London: Macmillan, 1927), 596. Quoted in *Storytracking*, 100.

34. See discussion in *Storytracking*, p. 13.

35. Géza Róheim, *The Eternal Ones of the Dream: Psychoanalytic Interpretation of Australian Myth and Ritual* (New York: International Universities Press, 1945), 211. Quoted in Gill, *Storytracking*, 105.

36. I dealt with these matters as exhaustively as I possibly could in Gill, *Storytracking*.

37. Tony Swain, *A Place for Strangers: Towards a History of Australian Aboriginal Being* (Cambridge, MA: Cambridge University Press, 1993), 28.

38. Swain, *A Place for Strangers*, 32.

39. I am aware that "without preparation" suggests an awareness of a causal sequential and thus a possible temporal reference. This may be introduced in the rendering of Aboriginal concepts and terms into English where temporal references are extremely hard to avoid. It may reflect some aspect of Arrernte perspective. My guess is that we likely no longer have the means to determine decisively which.

40. Erin Manning, *Relationscapes: Movement, Art, and Philosophy* (Cambridge: MIT Press, 2009), 15.

41. Brian Massumi offered insights into this shift in his provocative 2002 book, *Parables for the Virtual: Movement, Affect, Sensation* (Durham: Duke University Press, 2002). His book explores the "implications for cultural theory of this simple conceptual displacement: body—(movement/sensation)—change." He shows that cultural theory has tended to bracket the middle term—that is, movement/sensation—and thus it "has significantly missed the two outside terms," that is, body and change. His work is to add movement itself back into the picture, yet it must be movement as "qualitative transformation" rather than simply "displacement." While Massumi does not identify his exploration of movement in these terms as gesture, it is clearly consistent with the notion I have been exploring. And the implications of this perspective which he develops in some detail are clearly important.

42. José Gil, "Paradoxical Body," *TDR: The Drama Review* 50:4 (T192) (Winter 2006): 25.

43. Erin Manning, *Politics of Touch: Sense, Movement, Sovereignty* (Minneapolis: University of Minnesota, 2007).

44. Manning, *Politics of Touch*, 8.

45. Manning, *Politics of Touch*, 10.

46. Manning, *Politics of Touch*, 3.

47. Noë, *Out of Our Heads*, 5.

48. Noë, *Out of Our Heads*, 5.

49. Noë, *Out of Our Heads*, 7.

50. See Bourdieu, Pierre, *Outline of a Theory of Practice* (Cambridge: Cambridge University Press, 1977).

51. Robert D. Lockhart, Gilbert F. Hamilton, and Forest W. Fyfe, *The Anatomy of the Human Body* (Philidelphia, PA: J. B. Lippincott Co., 1977), 267.

52. Hanna Rosin, "The End of Men," *The Atlantic* (August 2010): 58.

53. Christina Hoff Sommers, *The War Against Boys: How Misguided Feminism is Harming Our Young Men* (New York: Simon & Schuster, 2000), 213.

54. Guy Garcia, *The Decline of Men: How the American Male Is Getting Axed, Giving Up, and Flipping Off His Future* (San Francisco: Harper, 2009), 5.

THREE

Self-Othering

Dancing is the interplay among dancer-self and danced-other; at once separate and the same. The dancing movement is in the dynamic of the two. While self-movement is primary to animate organisms, to anything that has the capacity for movement, dancing as acquired gestural/postural patterned movement is of another order distinctive to humans. In the culturally, historically, personally shaped techniques that contour and interrelate this paradoxical relationship of self and other, dancing has a primacy to human life. The contribution of dancing is to forge the human capacity to harness the energetics of animate self-movement for cultural and personal ontogenesis. Dancing is the deep experience, and thus the embracing with certainty, of the structurality I call self-othering; the experience that something completely other than self can be experienced as self. Dancing offers the experiential grounding that makes it possible to know the other, to be aware of the other, to represent the other, to name the other, to comment on the other. Dancing is to experience the creative ontogenetic energetics of the paradox of the separation of self and other that is also their identity. Thus dancing shares in the vital enabling of external memory and language and art and symbolism and ritual and mythology, all things human.

In this chapter I turn to a powerful cultural example, Javanese *wayang kulit* (shadow theater) and classical dancing (*wayang wong*), as well as to the insights of one of the most important figures that reshaped the modern understanding of perception, Maurice Merleau-Ponty. While Merleau-Ponty did not include dancing in his discourse, I want to show the importance of Merleau-Ponty's philosophy to the self-othering understanding of dancing I have been developing and I want also to show that dancing is an important way of exemplifying and understanding the flesh ontology that Merleau-Ponty developed.

JAVANESE *WAYANG KULIT*

There is nothing to a shadow; its being is in its nothingness. A shadow is an absence. Yet we can see it as surely as we can feel the wind.

Java, in the heart of Indonesia, has a fascinating complex of cultures whose ancient shadow play, *wayang kulit*, is the prototype for its life and arts including court-supported classical dancing. Dancing and shadow theatre are based on and illustrate Javanese philosophy.

Java was populated for thousands of years by tribal peoples before Indian influence began to be felt in the eighth and ninth centuries of this era. The extent of Indian influence is evident in the grandness of the religious structures that were built in south central Java during that time. Near present day Yogyakarta, the Hindu Sanjaya dynasty built the vast temple complex, Prambanan, comprised of one hundred fifty-six shrines around eight major temples, the dominant structure being the temple of Shiva. At roughly the same time, only thirty kilometers away, the Mahayana Buddhist Sailendra dynasty built the magnificent stupa, Borobudur, including hundreds of Buddha statues and thousands of bas-reliefs illustrating Buddhist literature and stories.[1] Both structures had been long abandoned, buried under ash and dirt, when discovered in the nineteenth century. Since then both have been restored, resurrected from the jungle, by archaeologists and cultural preservationists. Indian influence has remained strong in Java despite half a millennium of Islamic influence. Remarkably, Java has the largest concentration of Muslims in the world. The stories of classical Indian literature, found in the Mahabharata and Ramayana, adapted to the Javanese world are the foremost influence on popular culture, art and the heritage and identity of the Javanese.

Wayang kulit,[2] the shadow puppet theatre found throughout Southeast Asia, plays a powerful role in maintaining this vital heritage and in applying it to ongoing life. *Wayang kulit* is in many ways the prototype for the arts, including Javanese classical[3] dancing. The *dalang* or puppet master sits on one side of an opaque screen. Hundreds of puppets, leaning against the screen with their supporting rods stuck in green banana logs, flank the *dalang* to both his right and left. The *dalang* casts the shadows on the screen by manipulating the chosen puppets in the light from a lamp that hangs above him. Members of the *gamelan*, the Javanese musical orchestra, sit behind the *dalang* accompanying him[4] as he sings and chants the stories he enacts by manipulating the puppets. Formerly the women and the invited guests sat on the side of the screen opposite the *dalang* where only the shadows cast on the opaque material can be seen. The men sat on the same side as the *dalang* where they could see not only the partial shadows but also the puppets, the *dalang*, and the musicians. Today, generally, all guests have the freedom to watch the theatre from wherever they like.

Shadow is a double, a doubling. It is a play of puppet and shadow, of light and darkness, of substance and insubstantiality, of visibility and invisibility, of radiance and occlusion. Shadow play is fascinating. Why? The Javanese puppets, like most puppets in Southeast Asia, are elaborately painted. They are objects of beauty and are often displayed as works of art. The identity of the hundreds of figures is interconnected with not only the outline shape but also the clothing, facial features, and accessories that are painted on the puppet. Indeed, puppet design involves a remarkably complex system of defined shapes and characteristics. But, as importantly, indeed even more so to shadow theatre, the puppet is created and used as an occlusion, as a mass to block the light. It is only with the puppet as an occlusion blocking the light that we can see the shadow figure.

Shadow puppetry is the play of the visible and the invisible. The light, both in its quality of radiance and in its location or position, is vitally important. Shadow cannot exist without light. But the light, in itself, is sheer radiance and lacks distinction apart from the occlusion of the puppet. Only when paired with the shadows whose creation it enables, the dark nothings that are nonetheless present, does light take shape. The shadow is always different from the puppet and cannot exist except in its separation from the puppet. As soon as the puppet is moved away from the scrim enough for a shadow to be cast, the shadow cannot possibly exactly replicate the shape of the puppet. Thus the puppet and the shadow can never be simply duplicates. Among the fascinating characteristics of shadow play is that a broad array of shadow effects are created by moving the puppet closer and farther from the screen, tipping and turning the flat puppet in relation to the plane of the screen. These effects produce the illusion of dimension, that is, depth and life, which is all the more fascinating given that the shadow itself is an absence rather than a presence. While electric light bulbs now often replace the oil lamp as a source of light, the Javanese still indicate a preference for the live flame which they say causes the shadow figures to appear to breathe. Where the light is located with respect to the puppet and the screen determines not only the location of the shadow, but also its qualities and character.

Drawing on our experience of making shadow figures by our occluding hands, we are reminded that, in some sense, we lose our hands in the forms we create. Our hand manipulations become tacit as we *attend to* the shadow forms. Philosopher of science Michael Polanyi's notion of the tacit dimension[5] is relevant. He holds that we know more than we can say. That is, when we focus on some object about which we seek knowledge we are attending to that object. However, at the same time and inevitable to the process is that we must also *attend from* a whole body of tacit knowledge and assumptions–all our former experience, our image schemas, our array of categories, the tacit rules that underlie grammar and a vast embodied experience of gesture. We cannot articulate all that is known in this tacit dimension—it is hidden to us though we know it is there and certainly depend upon it. Our hands, or the puppets, become tools we use to effect the world. Yet, as Leroi-Gourhan showed us, while the hands or puppets themselves tend to disappear in the puppet shows, it is their gestural patterns that create the illusion of presence and life for the figures who have no physical reality at all, who exist as gestural illusions. The revelation here is that the world is known only through a process of doubling, through the pairing of the known and the tacit, the visible and the invisible, the conscious and the unconscious, the real and the virtual. Understanding this relationship shows the folly of attempting to reduce the world to singularity, to truth or reality, a common Western strategy. The metaphor, the analogy, of shadow play, both our innocent playing and the formal Javanese shadow theater, powerfully articulate and illustrate that the interactivity of gesture, even the hiddenness that is inherent to it, must be embraced and celebrated.

While our bodies are seemingly lost in the menagerie of shadows we create, there is a hinge in the making of these shadows that allows us to experience our own aliveness. The doubling is no simple mutually exclusive dualism. The making and perception of these shadow figures is inseparable from the gestural movement of our bodies or the bodies of the puppets. Occlusion reveals depth or distance and suggests that life is inseparable from movement. The shadows dance and come to life, become of interest to us, as our bodies move and gesture to make them. Our oddly entwined hands look like nothing but a knot of fingers until we see the moving shadow they cast. The doubling is the key. The play of the two is what intrigues. The play depends on gestural movement. What we see is not a simple literal presentation; it is a seduction—an appearance, a promise of something always unfulfilled—that invites comparison to facets of our distinctly human existence. For centuries the Javanese have offered a profound exemplar.

The Javanese recognize a gradient of values delineating the range of possibilities of the human character.[6] The ideal of refinement, *alus* (*halus*), has its origins in the *prijaji* or gentry who, in pre-Muslim days, were royalty. *Kasar*, designating the crude or rough, is the opposite of *alus*. Refinement is exemplified in the ubiquitous arts of dancing, poetry, batik, and shadow puppetry. The refined demeanor of royalty sets the etiquette of much of city culture in Yogyakarta.[7] Following the royal example, the general citizenry routinely practices politeness and civility in its speech, dress, and actions. Poor and homeless bicycle rickshaw drivers, shopkeepers, and waiters are reserved and polite. Even street touts are refined. One common scam is for them to encourage tourists to visit what they say is an exhibit of fine batiks. They insist that it is a show of Javanese batik master artists and that, not to worry, nothing is for sale. Invariably the show is closing that very day, so you learn that this is your last chance to see it. If you go, and of course you do, they treat you to a cup of tea and chat about the last time they visited your home country or about an uncle that lives in your home state. They show you the batiks and introduce you to one of the artists. They leave you alone to enjoy the "fine art" and allow you to eventually, and we always do, ask if anything is for sale. This request seems to take them by surprise, actors they are, and they appear reluctant to suggest a price. The art is not for sale, they will remind you. Yet, for the sake of the opportunity to share their art with people in other parts of the world, they agree to consider selling it. They ask which your favorite piece is and promptly hang it over the door, the better light to see it, yet also effectively blocking the exit. They suggest a price. When you try to bargain for a better price, as we know we are supposed to do, they do rapid calculations on a notebook that has suddenly appeared. They assure you that any reduction of price would be inappropriate to the quality of the art, yet, because it is the last day of the show and it would save them effort in transporting the works to another city, they agree to make some adjustments. Only later, of course, do you learn that the whole thing is a scam and that the vendors would have been thrilled to get a small fraction of what you paid. Though you rationalize the price as including a cultural experience, it is still difficult to see quite as much beauty in a work of art that is now a folded-up piece of cloth fitting neatly in a shirt pocket.

Javanese philosophy is intertwined with this valuation of the human character. The body is distinguished in terms of an inner (*batin*) and an outer (*lahir*) aspect. *Lahir* is the bodily realm of human behavior including self-movement, posture, and speech. *Batin* is the inner realm of experience including feelings, emotions, and imagination. Both are conceived as aspects of the body; they are, like the inner and outer sides of flesh itself, interdependent and inseparable. The Javanese consider *lahir*, the outer aspect or behavior, the more easily directed and controlled, that is, the more easily refined. By practicing *alus* behavior one comes to experience refined feelings and emotions; in other words, refining *lahir* is accompanied by the refinement of *batin*. Put simply, how one moves affects how one feels; and, of course, the opposite also pertains. Javanese culture is defined in terms of highly prescribed gesture and posture.

Wayang kulit is a complex representation and enactment of Javanese philosophy. The shadow, in its insubstantiality may be considered—this is my construct not explicitly put this way by the Javanese—to represent *batin*, the inner body, while the puppet in its physical substantiality represents *lahir*, the outer body. The characters in the stories portray the full range of values from *alus* to *kasar* in both their physical forms and in their gestural/postural behaviors. The refinement of the characters of the dramas played in puppets and shadows is easily recognized by their physical appearance (posture) and movement patterns (gestures). The stories (*lakons*) drawn from the Javanese versions of classical Indian literature reinforce the character valuations in the consequences they enjoy or suffer resulting from their actions. Illustrating that the outer affects the inner, the *dalang* moves the physical puppet, the correspondent of *lahir*, the outer body. The *dalang* cannot manipulate the shadow except by moving the puppet. Yet, the *dalang's* attention is primarily on the shadow effect, corresponding to the inner body, as he manipulates the substantive puppet. The shadow is at once completely separate and yet inseparable from the puppet; it cannot be without there being both.

The Javanese understanding of the Indian *rasa* is consistent with this interpretation of *wayang kulit*.[8] In Sanskrit *rasa* has two roots, one referring to hidden significance or ultimate meaning,[9] the other referring to tactile sensations or taste. For the Javanese, the five senses are seeing, hearing, talking, smelling, and feeling. As feeling, *rasa* is a sense that includes touch on the body, taste on the tongue, and emotional feelings like sadness and happiness. It refers to feeling from without as well as within. As meaning, *rasa* refers to something like deep significance, subtle or elusive meaning. The Javanese have a fondness for the artful use of language, for poetry, and for verbal etiquette. They both blend and hold separate the two meanings of *rasa* resulting in the distinction, identification, and interplay of the inside feeling with outside sensation and with meaning, the subjective and objective, one's behavior in the world and one's character. Refinement is directed toward achieving the ultimate *rasa*, the fullest realization[10] of this complex relationship, though it is often expressed as the union of inner feeling with outer action, the full concert of feeling and meaning. The Javanese believe that happiness and unhappiness are interlinked, allowing one to move beyond the distinction between them, to experience a certain tranquility in the midst of intense polarity. Evidence of this tranquility can be seen and experienced in human countenance and comportment, a kind of remote or detached presence, of the royal family and members of court. It can also be experienced in the court's dance pavilion, considered the still center of the universe, quickened by the presence of dancing.

JAVANESE CLASSICAL DANCING

Wayang kulit has been performed in Java for over a thousand years. There is debate as to whether its origins are Indian or indigenous,[11] yet it is clear that it is an important model for Javanese dance and theater.[12] *Wayang topeng* refers to masked dancing. *Topeng* means mask. There is remarkable resemblance of *wayang kulit* and *wayang topeng*. This masked dance theater form, performed in Java for perhaps as long as shadow theater, preserves the doubling, the intertwining I discussed related to shadow puppetry, yet it is not shadow play, but masked dancing.

One of the fascinating things about masks is that they are so apparently artificial and unlifelike.[13] This quality is observable in the rigidity of mask construction, its tendency toward exaggeration of features and design, its simple and crude mechanics, its incompatibility with nature. A mask is not a disguise. A mask is like a puppet manipulated by the dancing masker. Whereas in *wayang kulit* the puppet representing the outer body (*lahir*) and the shadow representing the inner body (*batin*), in *wayang topeng* this model is turned inside out while keeping with the structurality of intermingling and inter-positioning. The mask, like the puppet, is the rigid form, but it is given life, animated, by the sentient human dancer who, behind the mask, is the partially hidden inner animate body. The identity of the dancer is usually obscured (or partially so), being occluded by the mask; yet, like the puppet, the mask gains its aliveness by its being a distinctive gestural self-moving occlusion. The virtual entity identified with the mask, rather than the personal identity of the dancer, comes to life by being moved and manipulated in its distinctive gestural patterns danced by the dancer.[14] The intent is not complete disguise, a total absence of the masker. The power of the masking is in its doubling, in its reversibility; an *incomplete* reversibility as I will explain later. Indeed, the most distinctive aspect of mask is that it hides as it reveals, that it is lifeless yet alive. I'll return to consider masked dancing again in the next chapter, *Playing*.

Javanese trance dancing has likely even more ancient roots in Java and it continues to be practiced today in village culture. In trance dancing, the dancer is understood as being possessed by a spiritual entity. The dancer gives presence and life, that is, reality, to this otherwise virtual being. We see the same doublings here—the spirit outside the dancer possesses or entrances the dancer, a process usually depicted as the spirit entering the body of the dancer. Yet the dancer's body, in some sense, is inside the manifestation of the spirit who takes physical form by means of the body of the dancer. The two intertwine; the two are reversible, yet incompletely so.

Javanese classical dancing (*wayang wong*) does not employ masks yet retains the structure in the mask-like appearance of the dancer's face and the puppet-like movement style of the dancer's technique. We commonly consider the face itself a mask especially when it is rigidly set, held in a fixed expression. Javanese classical dancers are trained in this technique. This dancing takes the doubling, appropriately called "self-othering," to greater sophistication. The dancer is no longer hidden by the danced character in any literal sense, yet she or he remains doubled with the character or the dance performed. A spectacular form of dancing that does not use masks is *wayang wong*, or human puppets.[15] Dating from ancient times this form of dance-drama became highly popular in the eighteenth century and has since received royal support. These dances are direct adaptations of *wayang kulit* to the realm of human dancing. The characters are the same and the costuming and makeup serve to make them appear similar to the puppets, especially when seen in profile. In a

fascinating and effective way, classical Javanese dancing applies the Javanese principles and relationships articulated in shadow puppet theater.
The presence of the Sultan during the performance has suggested to the
Javanese the idea that the Sultan is the *dalang* or puppeteer of the performance.[16]

The philosophy of Javanese court dancing was codified under the
reign of Sri Sultan Hamengku Buwana I who reigned from 1755 to 1792.
But it was not until 1976 when dance master B. P. H. Suryobrongto delivered public lectures on dancing that this philosophy was known outside the succession of dance masters. The philosophy is complex and
intricate beyond adequate presentation here, yet it is important to mention several fundamental elements because they all are consistent with
self-othering structurality. While dancing provides aesthetic pleasure or
entertainment, it also, and perhaps more importantly, provides the dancer, and in turn audiences, with models for appropriate behavior (*lahir*)
and inner growth (*batin*). Javanese court dancing is characterized by total
concentration that does not cause inner tenseness (*sewiji*). There must be
an inner dynamic that gives life to the dancer's presence, but which must
be carefully controlled to avoid coarseness of expression (*greged*). Dancers
must be self-confident yet without arrogance or conceit (*sengguh*). And
the dancers must experience freedom, which is understood as the courage to face difficulties, total dedication, and a full sense of responsibility
(*ora mingkuh*).[17] What is particularly notable in light of this discussion of
Javanese arts and philosophy is that each of these key principles requires
opposing values or traits to be co-present and in concert. We begin to
appreciate how fully the Javanese have developed this very specific
structural dynamic of joining oppositions without resolution to produce
clearly identifiable results, a distinctive quality they often refer to as
"profound tranquility" that stands at the center of the Javanese character.

MERLEAU-PONTY'S "FLESH ONTOLOGY"

While it may seem that twentieth century French philosophy is at a distance relative to Javanese dancing on the same order as the great physical
distance between France and Java, I believe the distance calls forth creative movement. I will return to Java after a French interlude to make this
point.

Maurice Merleau-Ponty was a French existential phenomenologist
whose understanding of human perception reshaped traditional philosophical positions. He denied the body-mind split that has for centuries
shaped the way the West has understood not only perception and body,
but also what it means to be human. His conjunctive constructions of the
lived-body and the minded-body seek acknowledgment of the traditional

distinction without the radical separation.[18] He defined the mind as "the *other* side of the body" holding that

> we have no idea of a mind that would not be *doubled* with a body. . . .
> The "other side" means that the body, inasmuch as it has this other
> side, is not describable in *objective* terms, in terms of the in itself—that
> this other side is really the other side of *the body, overflows* into it (*Ue-
> berschreiten*), encroaches upon it, is hidden in it—and at the same time
> needs it, terminates in it, is *anchored* in it.[19]

There can be no mind without body. At the time of Merleau-Ponty's
death in 1961 he was working on a manuscript that was to broadly expand his earlier ideas, specifically through his development of what has
come to be termed "ontology of flesh." The manuscript was edited and
posthumously published as *The Visible and the Invisible* and the ontology
of flesh is developed most fully in the complex often-opaque essay "The
Intertwining—The Chiasm."[20]

Merleau-Ponty does not limit his understanding of flesh to skin and
meat, nor are these its primary reference, yet his most enduring and
inspiring analogy and example of what he termed flesh[21] is developed in
his reflections on our experience of touching one hand with our other
hand.

> If my hand, while it is felt from within, is also accessible from without,
> itself tangible, for my other hand, for example, if it takes its place
> among things it touches, is in a sense one of them, opens finally upon a
> tangible being of which it is also a part. Through this crisscrossing
> within it of the touching and the tangible, its own movements incorpo-
> rate themselves into the universe they interrogate, are recorded on the
> same map as it; the two systems are applied upon one another, as the
> two halves of an orange.[22]

There are at least two things here: a hand touching an object and a sentient object being touched, but in this case the object touched is the other
hand of the person, the subject, doing the touching. There is a complexity
here, as Merleau-Ponty shows, that denies the simple division between
object and subject, between the perceived and perceiver. What is doing
the touching is also being touched and vice versa. Merleau-Ponty points
out the crisscrossing in which the touching and the tangible are but two
sides of the same thing as are the two halves of an orange. The unifying
structure of two hands touching is the inarguable singularity due to both
being of the same human body. As Merleau-Ponty writes, "My two
hands touch the same things because they are the hands of one same
body."[23] "The body unites us directly with the things through its own
ontogenesis, by welding to one another the two outlines of which it is
made, its two laps: the sensible mass it is and the mass of the sensible
within it is born by segregation and upon which, as seer, it remains
open."[24] "Our body is a being of two leaves, from one side a thing among

things and otherwise what sees them and touches them; we say, because it is evident, that it unites these two properties within itself, and its double belongingness to the order of the 'object' and to the order of the 'subject' reveals to us quite unexpected relations between the two orders."[25]

This image of the body that is two yet one is clarified with Merleau-Ponty's discussion of chiasm (a cross piece, crossing place, or to mark with the letter *chi*), that is, a crisscrossing, intertwining, folding that he calls "flesh." Flesh is not stagnant or inanimate matter, but rather it is on the order of an element (in the same sense as fire, air, earth and water) in the sense of being constitutive of reality.[26] I might prefer the term "structurality" to indicate a dynamic relationality. It is a texture, he says, (a woven fabric) that expresses the fundamental unity and continuity, yet allowing diversity, division, and opposition, that permeates all interrelated and interwoven pairings. It is no thing, but the formative medium of the subject and object. As a skin or fabric, flesh is two-sided — the sensitive and the sensed — yet where the two are not entirely separable from one another. The hand being touched is also capable of touching. The sides are reversible as are the insides and outsides of a jacket or glove or, to suggest a metaphor Merleau-Ponty did not use, the windings of a Möbius strip. A Möbius strip is a single-sided geometrical structure. It can be modeled by taking a thin strip of paper, twisting it a half turn, and joining the ends together. At any point on the strip one can turn it over to confirm that it has a second side. By holding the paper between one's finger and thumb it is clear that the finger is on one side, the thumb on the other. Yet, when one traces the extent of one side, say by marking a line along the length of the strip, it is continuous and single; the line meets itself without any break to move from one side to the other. The endless conjunction and continuity of inside and outside is also captured by the infinity sign this form takes as a three-dimensional object.[27]

For Merleau-Ponty, the essential feature of flesh is its reversibility (a description of a structurality), the exchange between the inside and outside, the subjective and objective, the touching and the touched, the seeing and the seen, and so on. Which hand is touching; which is being touched? Which side of the Möbius strip is the outside? The structurality that Merleau-Ponty calls flesh is characterized by reversibility, a capacity to fold in on itself, a reflexivity, a fundamental gap or dehiscence that is also continuity and connection of being that Merleau-Ponty shows is the operative relationality that makes possible perception, language, and thought. Merleau-Ponty did not explicitly give primacy to movement in his discussion, but there are plenty of signs he recognized it. And, of course, Renaud Barbaras, the leading authority on Merleau-Ponty, has written much on movement clearly developed from Merleau-Ponty. It is in the separation and division that perception, language, and thought occur; but were there not also a unity or interdependence among the parts, there would be no connection, no passage, no access from one part of a structure to the other. It is the reversibility of flesh—"a texture that returns to itself and conforms to itself,"[28]—that offers the separation that is also continuity and therefore motivates movement and makes life possible.

As perception is the intertwining of the percipient and the perceptibles, Merleau-Ponty extends his notion beyond the boundaries of the human body in his understanding of what he called the "flesh of the world." Merleau-Ponty attacks the self-other distinction that usually survives even those philosophies that interrelate or identify mind and body. He sees that to allow this radical separation, this dichotomy, would be to stop too soon. "Is my body a thing, is it an idea? It is neither, being the measurant of the things. We will therefore have to recognize an ideality that is not alien to the flesh that gives it its axes, its depth, its dimensions."[29] Merleau-Ponty expands the understanding of body to extend beyond that space displaced by the physical body. The flesh of the world extends perception beyond the physical body, but as importantly, it reconceptualizes the body as extending into the world. As the inner and outer are continuous (separable, but unified), as the body and mind, subject and object fit the same pattern, so too do the physical body and the world beyond it.

This development is fundamental to Merleau-Ponty's understanding of perception. Perception, as usually understood, bifurcates the perceiver and world perceived, yet, for Merleau-Ponty, they are of the same fabric; they are both of the flesh of the world. He writes,

> If the body is one sole body in its two phases, it incorporates into itself the whole of the sensible and with the same movement incorporates itself into a "Sensible in itself." We have to reject the age-old assumptions that put the body in the world and the seer in the body, or, conversely, the world and the body in the seer as in a box. Where are we to put the limit between the body and the world, since the world is flesh?[30]

Otherwise, Merleau-Ponty argues, we would be in a world he finds impossible, a world divided into discontinuous paired members isolated from one another. The flesh of the world is the fabric that at once divides us from and unites us with the world in which we live, the world beyond the bounds of our physical bodies, the world that we perceive and experience. Here our sentient bodies are understood by Merleau-Ponty as belonging to the same flesh as non-self-sentient sensibility, as those things outside the body that we perceive as objects sensed. Merleau-Ponty argues that we are able to perceive that which is beyond us because our bodies share the same fabric, a fabric he calls the flesh of the world.[31]

Merleau-Ponty investigates the bond that he calls flesh between the physical and the idea or internal image, the issue addressed by the title

given his book, the bond between the visible and the invisible. He writes,
ideas

> could not be given to us *as ideas* except in the carnal experience. It is not
> only that we would find in that carnal experience the *occasion* to think
> them; it is that they owe their authority, their fascinating, indestructible
> power, precisely to the fact that they are in transparency behind the
> sensible, or in its heart.[32]

He says further,

> The idea is this level, this dimension. It is therefore not a *de facto* invis-
> ible, like an object hidden behind another, and not an absolute invis-
> ible, which would have nothing to do with the visible. Rather it is the
> invisible *of* this world, that which inhabits the world, sustains it, and
> renders it visible, its own and interior possibility, the Being of this
> being.[33]

Merleau-Ponty's flesh ontology addresses the current most engaging cultural and intellectual problem: is there intrinsic order in the world? Merleau-Ponty articulates his understanding of this intrinsic order in the
terms of this doubling structurality, this intertwining, this reversibility,
this reciprocity, this flesh that makes possible, that grounds, that both
distinguishes and unifies self and other. For Merleau-Ponty the reversibility of flesh constitutes "the ultimate truth."[34]

JAVANESE-FRENCH CONNECTION

Javanese philosophy as exemplified in shadow puppetry and classical
dancing has provocative and tantalizing parallels to Merleau-Ponty's
flesh ontology. It exhibits in the concrete terms of these artistic and cultural forms many of the attributes that Merleau-Ponty developed as an
abstract discussion of flesh and in the Javanese examples we can perhaps
more clearly see the intertwining, the reversibility, of the body and the
body with that which is beyond the body; or turned inward, the body
physical and the body of ideas and emotions, the outward body and the
inward body. Interrelating the Javanese philosophical principles of distinctive human structuralities exemplified in shadow theater and classical dancing with Merleau-Ponty's flesh ontology develops and clarifies
the way I am approaching dancing, here in terms I call self-othering.

Classical Javanese dancing exhibits the same self-othering structurality I have shown as basic to shadow theater, yet interpreted for dancing.
In Javanese dancing, the thing seen is the dance presenting the characters
of the *lakon* as though projected on the bodies of the dancers. But where is
the light? Where is the puppet? What is manipulated to present the appearance that is nothing, that is only because of some occlusion? What in
shadow puppetry is so neatly and unambiguously distinguished—pup-

pet and shadow—are collapsed and seem inseparable in dancing, yet the fundamental structurality remains. The dancer and the dance, corresponding with puppet and shadow, are bound in unity in being the same body. Amazingly, and distinctive to dancing, the thing made by the body never leaves the body because it exists only in the body's self-movement, yet in some sense this thing made, the dance or a character danced, seems to transcend both the body and the dancer; it is identified as other. While dancer and dance are one, indeed identical, they are also separable. The self-movement of dancing is possible only as an aspect of the virtual distance that separates. Dancer and dance, as puppet and shadow in *wayang kulit*, are clearly and easily distinguishable, yet utterly inseparable.

Dancing, as exemplified by Javanese classical dancing, corresponds with Merleau-Ponty's much-studied example of one hand touching the other, in that object touched (perceptible) and subject touching (percipient) are at once distinct and the same. This is the interdependence and inseparability of self and other that I have been developing throughout this book as self-othering. Dancer and dance are separate, yet intertwined in the dancing, as are toucher and thing touched in the touching. Yet, the dancer-dance example is, to my mind, richer in that it shares the distinction of the puppet-shadow example in exhibiting two entirely different orders of things—one immanent the other transcendent—rather than one order as in Merleau-Ponty's example, that is, the one hand touching another where both hands are of the same order. And the identity of dancer and dance realized in the self-movement, the self-othering, of dancing is also more powerful than simply two body parts (hands) connected by being of the same body as in Merleau-Ponty's example. Thus dancer-dancing is itself in a chiasmatic relation with Merleau-Ponty's principle flesh analogy in that it offers clarification and extension to his ontology of flesh, while in turn, his flesh ontology deepens our understanding of dancing as self-othering, the structurality most primary to humans. Indeed, even this peek at dancing in light of the ontology of flesh causes a bursting open, a flowering that puts a smile on the face of our understanding of dancing because it contrasts so sharply with the common Western marginalization of dancing. Let me continue to show how dancing—comprised of the intertwining of dance and dancer, dancing and being danced—exhibits and is more deeply apprehended when understood, when seen, in the terms of self-othering.

Dancing is chiasm. Dancing is flesh. Dancing is self-othering. There is a Christian theological chiasm. The Christian cross is a chiasm exhibiting the transcendence of verticality and the immanence of horizontality. Christian theology is exemplified in Christ and the Christ event. As God the Father he is transcendent; as Jesus he is immanent. The two are distinct and radically separate, yet one, even identical. This chiasm is at the core of the story of Christianity. One would suppose that this paradoxical core of Christian theology would have been what created the distance, the desire (in Barbaras's terms) that has fueled the movement of Christian history. It is confounding to me that Christianity has throughout its history abandoned what seems a central aspect of the chiasm that is Christ by its devaluing the immanent aspect of the structurality and radically separating it from the transcendent aspect. To deny the visible or to make it suspect, as exemplified by the Christian attitude toward dancing, surely closes or denies the gap that energizes the movement that is vitality. The gap or distance that calls forth movement, that is movement, then would need to be created by other strategies as in negatively valuing what is unavoidable, the immanent, the body, the dancing. Dancing is often referred to as spiritual. One reading of this reference in the Christian context is that dancing can be valued only to the extent there is a corresponding devaluing of the body. How else can this be understood when the contextual system of values radically separates body and spirit, and holds the body suspect? Dancing is accepted to the extent that it is not bodied.

The dancing body is always a sentient body; a living, feeling body. Dancing is flesh, dancing is the play of the double, the möbiatic play of multiple bodies that are yet one body. The dancer—the named human being with distinctive personal history and physical appearance—imagines or knows a dance. The imagined or known dance is of the interior of the dancer as invisibles, ideas or emotions. The danced body—that is, an often costumed moving sentient form—physically manifests the ideas as the dance, the actual or the visible. The dancing is the virtual self-moving, self-othering structurality that emerges in the gap that both separates and unites dancer and dance.

Dancing, the dancer manifesting the dance, can be seen as a movement from inside to outside, a projection of what is inwardly felt and imagined outward onto the body as a dance, but with the powerful effect of extending the sentience of the body throughout the real and imagined world. Dancing effects a realization of body that not only gives continuity between inside and outside, but also extends the body by the projection of its imagination and sentience into the world beyond the limits of the skin to the flesh of the world.

The inside-to-outside movement of dancing is doubled and reversed, that is, dancing is not simply expressing a movement from inside to outside, it also moves from outside in. This looping aspect of dancing is easily demonstrated in a number of ways. At the psychobiological level we know that dancing changes the way we feel. This is a principle of dance therapy. The rote embodying of fictional forms of movement has predictable effects on feelings. Whirling movements tend to entrance; jumping and bounding movements tend to quicken, brighten, and energize.

This outside to inside movement must also be understood in the broader frame beyond individual expression by recognizing that the dancing body is a construct of its historical and cultural experience. Moving gesturing bodies are always historical cultural bodies. The Javanese hold that comporting the outer body or *lahir* in culturally defined movements of refinement (*alus*) results in the refinement of one's inner body or *batin*. That is, the dancing body is one way Javanese culture makes itself and provides an ongoing evolving reference to its cultural identity born as gestural and postural traits and values.

MERLEAU-PONTY AND "PURE DEPTH"

As we contemplate the distinction between the clear physical separation between puppet and shadow in *wayang kulit* and the seeming collapse of that distinction in the physical identity of dancer and dance in *wayang wong*, Merleau-Ponty may inspire us further. In some sense this condition was his constant concern. How is it that self and other are separated yet inseparable? How can the perceptible and perceiver at once be at a distance but inseparable, of the same flesh? As we have been considering dancing as self-othering we have found that it is a structurality where distance is at the core of the very movement of dancing (Barbaras), yet that distance has no dimension. It is precisely in this respect that dancing is a distinctive human activity that can provide us insight into this most fundamental issue.

One way that Merleau-Ponty approached these most fundamental concerns is by a consideration of depth. How do we perceive depth? This is a basic issue for psychology, philosophy, and any studies of perception. Distance is key, however distance must be understood relationally, and this suggests depth. The concern with how we perceive depth is an old one, usually understood as "a line endwise to the eye,"[35] and was thought as derivatively perceived, added to an otherwise flat and static image produced by a two-dimensional array of radiant energy on the retinal surface. Maurice Merleau-Ponty and James Gibson (among others) rejected the classical explanation. Notably, Merleau-Ponty's ways of resolving the issue of distance and depth then become fundamental to his flesh ontology. Depth comes to be understood as that which both allows difference and distinctness while creating a bond or connection or identity between perceiver and perceived. The exploration of depth is necessarily complex, yet it leads to profound insight.

James Gibson's approach[36] is environmental. For Gibson distance is an intrinsically dynamic concept that requires movement. We do not actually see depth but rather we see one thing behind another. Movement reveals the occluding edges of objects that are separated and connected along the dimension of depth. Gibson formulates depth in terms of para-

dox, a "unity through disparity." The environmental aspect of his approach is articulated in terms of *affordance,* as he termed it. Affordance is
the value and meaning of things in the environment, and value and
meaning are always understood in terms of the relationship to the perceiver. Thus depth is the dimension that points both to the object and to
the perceiving subject. Depth is the significance of surfaces in relation to
the body.[37]

Merleau-Ponty held that an essential aspect of every meaningful perception is a spatial orientation. It is always already there because it must
be presupposed in the body holding some place in the world as the locale
for perception. Depth is then a primordial spatial orientation. Merleau-
Ponty holds that we come into the world as perceptible bodily beings; we
belong to the flesh of the world. The body is already oriented by being a
perceiving body inseparable from the perceiving-perceptible world.

The body has in its structure and behavior examples of distance and
separation that are also unities. One hand touching the other hand is a
favored example often contemplated by Merleau-Ponty. Another example is stereopsis, seeing a single image yet with two eyes. We, in fact, see
the singular world clearly, under normal circumstances, through two
eyes that *see* separate images. We can test this easily by closing first one
eye then the other in a variety of situations. Difference, separation, is
easily confirmed. Yet, so thankfully also is the unity of the visual image.
Even vision situations in which there is a distinct disparity between the
images separately seen by our two eyes get reconciled; they appear as a
unified image that is nearly impossible to willfully separate. This separation yet unity is fundamental to Merleau-Ponty's consideration of depth
and, interestingly, in the crossing of the optic nerves in which the left eye
is connected with the right brain and vice versa offers a rather literal
example of Merleau-Ponty's chiasm.

Depth at this naïve level then is understood as that dimension by
which we see something from *here* that is at its place *there.* The *here* and
there are contemporary in our experience. Here and there are joined in
time through their visibility and this is *depth,* a space of "copresent implication." Depth is inseparable from movement. Gibson appreciated movement for the discernment of occluding edges. Merleau-Ponty appreciates
depth as a "sensitive space," as "living movement," as "lived distance."[38]
Barbaras, in the lineage of Merleau-Ponty, understands living movement
as fundamental. Depth, in this progressive consideration, becomes increasingly profound. It is that dimension that contemporaneously unites
and separates; it is the condition of living movement, vitality. It is "a
thick view of time." Depth is the "most existential dimension."[39]

Depth, we might call it more properly *pure depth,* when taken in this
most profound sense, is a dimension that is primordial, allowing the
perception of distance and the value of the distant. Primordial depth, in
itself, does not yet operate between objects, between perceiver and per-

cipient. *Pure depth* is depth without distance from here.[40] In its thickness, depth preceding perception is perhaps difficult to grasp. Merleau-Ponty offers an analogy that both depends on vision and also foils vision to the point of replacing it with touch, with feeling. This lever is *dark space*, the visual experience of night or darkness. In darkness seeing is thwarted, yet seeing into the darkness elicits a feeling of thickness, a density, a materiality, a tangibility, an intimacy. In dark space everything is obscure and mysterious. Eugene Minkowski, an early twentieth century psychiatrist who offered the idea of *dark space*, held that "the essence of dark space is mystery."[41] The experience of dark space provides a means of trying to grasp pure depth. Pure depth is depth without foreground or background, without surfaces and without any distances separating it from me. Menkowski understood dark space, which Merleau-Ponty identifies with pure depth, as "the depth of our being," as "the true source of our life."[42]

Pure depth is key to understanding flesh which, like pure depth, as pure depth, is always already there as *precessive*, that is, "the formative medium of the subject and object" and as *progenitive*, the "inauguration of the where and when."[43] The moving body is fundamental to flesh, because through movement flesh begins to understand itself or become aware of itself.[44] Flesh, without the moving body, is not yet even possibility in that percipience is disconnected from perception. The body in living movement is then, as Merleau-Ponty termed it, a *percipient-perceptible*, that is, an entity possessing the potential to perceive while also being capable of being perceived. The living movement is an intertwining of two sides, the adherence of a self-sentient side to a sensible side. The moving body blurs the boundary between the flesh of the world (depth) and our own bodily flesh. The body as the environment (the world) comes to exist then in an ambience, a primordial given, of depth, the hidden dimension behind everything.[45]

This doubling is for Merleau-Ponty a *reversibility*. Reversibility is a way he expresses the interconnection among distinctions. A subject requires an object and vice versa; they are reversible; as vital movement they oscillate back and forth among themselves. Movement is an essential quality of reversibility; movement is necessary to occlusion, for perception to take place. Yet, this reversibility is never complete. This is a fascinating phase in this argument, I think. Complete reversibility would result in identity among the distinctions and a collapse of perception through the collapse of movement. Without a negativity or incompleteness there is no desire (to use Barbaras's term) as movement. Were the touching of one hand with the other to be completely reversible it would not be possible to distinguish one hand from the other, the touching from the touched. The images provided by each eye would be the same and there would be no negotiation and reconciliation between the two, no vision. The term *chiasm* here identifies this gap or crossover space; chiasm is always also chasm. There must remain this undetectable, in itself, and unbridgeable space or gap or hiddenness for reversibility to be incomplete. Incomplete reversibility is not some flaw to be overcome in perception, it is rather the very motor that drives the movement of reversibility that allows for simultaneous interdependence and distance. Since the chiasm is hidden, since chiasm precedes and makes possible reversibility, it can be thought of as depth or better as pure depth as analogized by dark space, but equally and I think more powerfully by dancing. Chiasm, pure depth, this incompleteness is the source or condition of percipience and at the same time unifies flesh ontology.

The Javanese usually say that *wayang kulit* is the foundation for all Javanese arts. Perhaps this is because it offers a powerful analogy by which to comprehend *pure depth* through dimension and actual distance. From our perspective outside of Java, the amazing experience of witnessing Javanese classical dancing is penetrating in its demonstration of pure depth through the self-othering structurality of dancing. Dancing is always creating a virtual other. The dancer is the corporeal aspect of the incorporeality of this virtual other. They are separated in some ways that can never be united; this is the negative that is living movement. They are united in their separateness as the living experience of pure depth. The self-othering that is dancing is living moving pure depth.

REFLECTIONS ON JAVA

As I approach Borobudur I know that I should circumambulate the temple, progressing through the levels, keeping the center on my right as is appropriate to the right-handed tantric method. I should study and decipher the many tales depicted in the thousands of bas-relief images on the inner and outer walls of the open air corridors that surround level after ascending level. Only after gaining this knowledge will it be appropriate for me to finally emerge at the upper open levels to suddenly experience the enlightenment of an open outward gaze. At this sunrise hour, my eagerness is uncontainable, I ignore the imagined tradition and, somewhat guiltily, bound quickly up the eastern steep stairs, noting the portals through which I pass. Exploding onto the open terraces atop the temple I find myself among the latticework stupas each containing a statue of the Buddha. Most of these Buddhas are without hands; all are looking outward across the expansive and varied landscape. This morning as we—the Buddhas and I—look, we contemplate, they more patiently than I, the forest of palms with the occasional majestic hardwood tree rising above. The forest is afloat this early morning in a sea of gray fog; soft, calm, mysterious. I feel that I am at the still center of the universe. I sit on the upper terrace behind a stupa left open by modern reconstructors so the sitting Buddha can more easily be seen and appreciated by me and my fellow tourists. Sitting here I think about the centuries this Buddha has patiently held his mudra and his gaze. I try to imagine myself a Buddha sitting here for a thousand years. Though it has countless moods, I doubt the landscape has changed all that much in this long time. The Buddha is calm, patient, confident. Perhaps he is telling me that life is transient—it comes, it passes away; that not even he is permanent; the best one can do is to be what one is, to be centered and calm and patient, to watch but also to be a part of the endless cycles in which one has a moment of existence; to be the stories that constitute one's existence.

Now in the sultan's palace, having made my way through a political protest carried on by a crowd of rowdy youths dressed in blood-red head bands and black tee shirts revving the engines of their smoky motor bikes and protesting through cheap crackling loud speakers, I observe the dancing. Dressed in immaculate costume, their faces utterly calm yet acutely attentive, the dancers approach the dance pavilion and squat to enter the floor using the waddling step that shows their respect for the sultan, though he is not present today. The dances are not irrelevant to the political actions just beyond the *kraton* walls, though I suspect the enthusiastic youths would have little interest in or see any relevance to these dances—at least not today. The dance is the *bedoyo*. The dance presents nine sea nymphs dressed as royal brides. They dance in perfect unison swaying gently like seaweed moved by water currents. Their palpable presence as sea nymphs is extraordinary self-othering; it takes considerable effort to find any presence of the human dancers. Yet the power of this presence is its uncanny otherness, an otherness that is wholly due to the dancers always also being there, at the occluded edges.

In their energized calmness, through their ability to control, in the fictions they dance, the dancers, like the Buddha at Borobudur, have created in their dancing the calm yet vital center of the whirling chaotic world of Javanese existence. As powerful as is the message of the great temple and as amazed as I am at the unfathomable inspiration and imagination of the temple's architects and builders, I am more deeply moved by this dancing. It is at once more accessible through the amazing skills of the dancers and the experience is even more powerful. The dancer is the live medium of her art and her product is nothing more, nor certainly less, than herself, her body danced, othered into anything imaginable. The dance is entirely ephemeral, passing away as it comes into being. As fragile as it is, by giving life to the gods, the stories, and the world, the dancing quickens even the cold stones of Borobudur.

NOTES

1. John Miksic, *Borobudur: Golden Tales of the Buddhas* (Singapore: Periplus Editions (HK) Ltd., 1990).

2. Ward Keeler, *Javanese Shadow Plays, Javanese Selves* (Princeton: Princeton University Press, 1987).

3. Terms such as "classical" need to be used with caution and suspicion. Here I intend only to indicate dance forms that are carefully codified, learned through formal and rigorous training, and that endure, certainly with some modification over time, in a culture for a period spanning multiple generations of dancers.

4. Javanese *dalangs* are male.

5. Michael Polanyi, *The Tacit Dimension* (Gloucester, MA: Peter Smith, 1983).

6. Clifford Geertz, *The Religion of Java* (Glencoe, IL: Free Press, 1960).

7. For example, the sultan, who lives with his family in the palace in Yogyakarta in southern Java, serves in the current times as an overseer of the city and surrounding areas. Far more important than his powers of governance is the example of refinement he sets for all in his domain. Not only does he present this example in his own physical appearance and demeanor, but in his sponsoring the daily performances of music and the arts (dance, gamelan, and *wayang kulit*) held in pavilions that exude the spirit of peace and tranquility.

8. See Geertz, *The Religion of Java*, 238.

9. It is of interest that ultimate meaning and hidden significance are equated with *rasa*, suggesting not only the importance of occlusion but also that in its inaccessibility, there is seduction involved with ultimate meaning.

10. There is the issue of what constitutes this fullness of realization. I think it best not to use the notion of union (though even in union separation may still be implied), but rather taking inspiration from Friedrich Schiller's *On the Aesthetic Education of Man* (Oxford: Clarendon Press, 1967 [1793]), I suggest the use of the word "concert."

11. Mantle Hood, "The Enduring Tradition: Music and Theatre in Java and Bali" in *Indonesia*, ed. Ruth T. McVey (New Haven, CT: Human Relations Area Files, 1963), 447.

12. This dependence on *wayang kulit* of dancing is clear in Javanese performance theory (*joged mataram*) where the dance must become the puppet. See Felicia Hughes-Freeland, "Consciousness in Performance: A Javanese Theory," *Social Anthropology* 5:1 (1997); 55-68 and Ben Suharto, "Transformation and Mystical Aspects of Javanese Dance," *UCLA Journal of Dance Ethnology* 14 (1990): 22-25.

13. The exception is the lifelike rubber masks—we think of gorillas, US presidents, and celebrities—whatever they might share. And even these are far from lifelike.

14. Kathy Foley, "The Dancer and the Danced: Trance Dance and Theatrical Performance in West Java," *Asian Theatre Journal* 2:1 (1985) 28-49, following Jane Belo, offers the idea that the dancer (as the puppet and mask) is an "empty vessel" awaiting "the vital energy of the other to fill it." Foley discusses that the dancer is trained not to reach within her/himself to find the resources for dancing, but to empty her/himself and to execute the movement as a puppet (see especially 37). What is important about this is not that the dancer disappears, but that she or he fully experiences otherness, rather than some expression or projection of the self.

15. Garrett Kam, "Wayang Wong in the Court of Yogyakarta: The Enduring Significance of Javanese Dance Drama," *Asian Theatre Journal*, 4:1 (1987): 29-51.

16. See Kam, "Wayang Wong," 32.

17. For dance philosophy see Hughes-Freeland, "Consciousness in Performance" and Suharto, "Transformation and Mystical Aspects of Javanese Dance."

18. In general ways these ideas are explored in terms of dancing by Sandra Fraleigh in her book *Dance and the Lived Body* (Pittsburgh: University of Pittsburgh Press, 1987).

19. Maurice Merleau-Ponty, *The Visible and the Invisible* (Evanston, IL: Northwestern University Press, 1968) 259. "In itself" or "being-in-itself" is a Sartrian term referring to nonconscious being. See Jean-Paul Sartre, *Being and Nothingness* (New York: Washington Square Press, 1966), especially the glossary by translator Hazel E. Barnes.

20. Merleau-Ponty, *Visible and the Invisible*, 130-55. The predecessors to this theory are found in "The Philosopher and his Shadow," trans. Richard C. McCleary, in *Signs* (Evanston, IL: Northwestern University Press, 1964).

21. I believe this example provides the "flesh" terminology Merleau-Ponty adopted. The difficulty with this terminology lies in its inevitable identity with substantive banal flesh, an identity we have constantly to deny even though it is the basic bodied experience we must always depend on as the basis for our understanding. There is a certain irony in the need to disembody, even dematerialize flesh, in order that it help us more fully understand our being lived-bodies.

22. Merleau-Ponty, *Visible and the Invisible*, 133.

23. Merleau-Ponty, *Visible and the Invisible*, 141.

24. Merleau-Ponty, *Visible and the Invisible*, 136.

25. Merleau-Ponty, *Visible and the Invisible*, 137. The leaves metaphor is interesting. Leaves, as of a tree, are all different yet all connected to the same species (we know a tree by the shape of its leaves) and even of one entity. Leaves of a book carry on the structurality and include a sense of the two sides, as in turning over a new leaf, meaning I suppose in the behavioral analogy that one side of a leaf differs from the other while still being the same.

26. The shift of flesh from the gross matter of the inspiring analogy, that is, two hands, to the elemental is a difficult one largely because of the gross physicality, the bloodiness that is almost inseparable from the word "flesh." Dancing, I'll suggest, is an important alternative.

27. Merleau-Ponty did not refer to the Möbius strip as a model. Elizabeth Grosz did apply it to his work. See *Volatile Bodies: Toward a Corporeal Feminism*, (Bloomington: Indiana University Press, 1994), 36. Merleau-Ponty used an analogy that was quite close, "If one wants metaphors, it would be better to say that the body sensed and the body sentient are as the obverse and the reverse, or again, as two segments of one sole circular course which goes above from left to right and below from right to left, but which is but one sole movement in its two phases. And everything is said about the sensed body pertains to the whole of the sensible of which it is a part, and to the world." *Visible and Invisible*, 138. His reference to one sole circular course is but a half twist from being a Möbius strip and clearly the Möbius strip would have served him as a better metaphor.

28. Merleau-Ponty, *Visible and Invisible*, 146.

29. Merleau-Ponty, *Visible and Invisible*, 152.

30. Merleau-Ponty, *Visible and Invisible*, 138.

31. This understanding of the body as extending beyond the skin into the world is not unknown beyond Merleau-Ponty. One thinks of Edward T. Hall's work *The Hidden Dimension* (New York: Anchor Books Doubleday, 1966) with proxemics, which explores how our physical bodies are surrounded by domains (bubbles) that can be characterized differently that extend us into the world seemingly outside of ourselves. However, Merleau-Ponty's work is far more radical. Rather than our bodies extending into the world beyond our physical boundaries, Merleau-Ponty argues that we are continuous with the world, of the same fabric, yet still distinct from it.

32. Merleau-Ponty, *Visible and Invisible*, 150.

33. Merleau-Ponty, *Visible and Invisible*, 151.

34. Merleau-Ponty, *Visible and Invisible*, 155.

35. From George Berkeley's *New Theory of Vision*, cited in Sue L. Cataldi, *Emotion, Depth, and Flesh: A Study of Sensitive Space* (Albany: State University of New York Press, 1993), 30.

36. James Gibson, *The Ecological Approach to Visual Perception* (Hillsdale, NJ: Lawrence Erlbaum Associates, 1986).

37. See Cataldi, *Emotion, Depth, and Flesh*, 31-34.

38. Erwin Straus clarifies, "Distance is a primal phenomenon . . . there is no distance without a sensing and mobile subject; there is no sentience without distance." Quoted from his *The Primary World of Senses* in Cataldi, *Emotion, Depth, and Flesh*, 45.

39. Cataldi, *Emotion, Depth, and Flesh*, 45.

40. Cataldi, *Emotion, Depth, and Flesh*, 48.

41. Eugene Minkowski, *Lived Time* (1933), 429, cited in Cataldi, *Emotion, Depth, and Flesh*, 49.

42. Cataldi, *Emotion, Depth, and Flesh*, quoting Minkowski, 50.

43. Merleau-Ponty, *The Visible and the Invisible*, 140, quoted in Cataldi, *Emotion, Depth, and Flesh*, 60.

44. Cataldi, *Emotion, Depth, and Flesh*, 61.

45. Cataldi, *Emotion, Depth, and Flesh*, 67.

FOUR

Playing

The word "play" labels one of the earliest basic level categories we acquire and it is important to human development. Ontologically play is closely aligned with self-movement and dancing; one simply cannot imagine play without movement. Paralleling the shifting Western attitudes toward movement in the progress of human development, participation in play also undergoes a rather radical shift around age seven. In the developmental period before school age, play is considered essential to both physical and mental development. Play is associated with that healthy groping that characterizes early development. It has a certain randomness and purposelessness (it is autotelic) that is encouraged in early childhood, but soon thereafter becomes increasingly marginalized and compartmentalized. Upon the advent of school a wedge is driven between the physical and the intellectual and, while play continues to be associated with physical and artistic development (as in playing sports, playing music), it is opposed to intellectual development. "Stop playing around and get serious about learning!" Play becomes leisure, sport, frivolous, extra-curricular. Eventually it starts taking on the connotation of the irresponsible and the irrelevant (playboy, player, playing around).

The autotelic quality of play and its inseparability from movement correlates importantly with my discussion of movement itself in Chapter One. Movement requires a distance that is not from here in any sense that can be traversed but rather in energizing the movement itself. Movement is ontogenetic, in process, moving. Play or playing, not to overdo it, is movement itself in this very sense. A central attribute of play is that it has little expectation for trajectory or destination or the satisfaction of need. It resists backfilling. Play inherently folds back on itself; it is looping, oscillatory. Play designates the groping qualities of the self-movement of perception that characterizes animate organisms. There is a certain playful quality in the vital self-movement of all animate beings. Play designates the repeating looping patterning self-movement of the dancing that emerges in the interplay between dancer and dance. Play is the coming-forth quality of dance movement, its incipience, its energetics, its vitality. The structurality of self-othering, of the distance/desire of movement discussed by Barbaras, of the dancing connection of dancer and dance, is a doubling, a gap, a separation, a chiasm that opens to movement that proceeds without dissipating the structurality. Play designates the openness, the ongoingness, the continuity of movement that is not backfilled grid or trajectory.

While play is dismissed as frivolous, as not serious, as even negative in popular Western cultural valuation, philosophers and anthropologists have maintained a steady interest in play for centuries. In this chapter I will present and discuss a few important contributions to the development of thinking about play by several select philosophers from Friedrich Schiller in the late eighteenth century to Jacques Derrida in the late twentieth century. Perhaps surprisingly play is a topic of fundamental importance both to the concern with aesthetics and to the issues distinctive to a postmodern perspective.

With the marginalization of play in Western cultures any association of play with religion would seem perhaps inappropriate. The Hindu concept of *lila* (play) is central as I will show and is identified with the dancing of Nataraja, Lord of Dance, that establishes a frameless framework in which to comprehend cosmic processes. The ancient Hindus saw a fundamental connection of playing and dancing. Further, based on my studies of Native American cultures in the American Southwest, I will consider how the philosophical views of play offer wonderful insight into aspects of these religious traditions. I will return to the topic of masking introduced in the consideration of Javanese *wayang topeng* and play will be valuable in my efforts to appreciate the self-othering aspects of Native American dancings.

NATARAJA: HINDU LORD OF DANCING

Replicas of the bronze figurines of Shiva as Nataraja "Lord of Dancing" dating from thirteenth century are popular today. I see them everywhere. Perhaps the popularity of this particular figure has something to do with Shiva's dancing, frozen in a moment. Maybe something about these figures hints of the religious importance of dancing ignored, if not actually opposed, in the West.

In this Hindu figurine Nataraja is depicted as dancing while holding in his hands symbols representing the five cosmic processes: creation, preservation, destruction, embodiment, and release. His dancing is not a part of these cosmic processes, but rather the primordial grounding, which of course is no thing, upon which all these cosmic processes become possible. His dancing is understood as *lila* or play and, as such, it is not done for any reason, but simply because it is his own nature to do so, to dance. I suggest that dancing is selected as the playful actions of Nataraja because the ancient Hindus comprehended the fundamental paradox of self-othering that distinguishes dancing; that they sensed what I will discuss in Chapter Five as its "seduction"; and that they understood something profound about play in identifying this dancing action of Shiva as *lila*. In their wisdom, they understood that dancing precedes and grounds ontology, that dancing is ontogenetic. We need to understand this figure more fully and then engage in a richer exploration of play as it has been understood in Western philosophy in order to appreciate how we might enhance and enrich our understanding of dancing by considering it as play.

This figurine of Nataraja depicts his Nadanta dance which is done in the golden hall of Chidambaram, the south Indian temple considered the center of the universe. The image is associated with a story. A number of heretical rishis lived in the forest of Taragam. Shiva went there to subdue these rishis accompanied by Vishnu disguised as a beautiful woman. The rishis turned on Shiva, attempting to destroy him with spells. A fierce tiger was created in sacrificial fires. Shiva easily subdued the tiger and removed its skin with one of his fingernails and wrapped the skin about himself. Next the rishis sent a snake against Shiva, yet he simply seized it and wrapped it about his neck as a garland. Finally, the rishis set an evil dwarf against Shiva and he stepped on the dwarf breaking its back. Vishnu, witnessing all this as the beautiful woman Ati-Sheshan, worshipped Shiva and asked to see the mystic Nadanta dance promising Shiva that he should dance in Chidambaram. Many elements of this story are represented in the popular figurine of Nataraja. Yet, this story has little to say about the significance of the dance itself.

Other aspects of the image are important in this respect. The dancing Shiva has four arms, braided and jeweled hair with the lower locks whirling in his dancing. The hair may contain a wreathing cobra, a skull, and the mermaid figure of the river Ganga. A crescent moon rests upon the head which is crowned with a wreath of cassia leaves. Shiva wears a man's earring in his right ear and a woman's in his left. Necklaces and armlets, a jeweled belt, anklets, bracelets, finger and toe rings adorn his body. Shiva wears tight pants and a fluttering scarf. He also wears a sacred thread. One right hand holds a drum, the other is lifted in a sign meaning "do not fear." One left hand holds fire and the other points to the subdued dwarf on whom Shiva stands. His left foot is raised. All is supported on a lotus pedestal and Shiva is surrounded by an encircling glory (*tiru-vasi*) fringed with flame.[1]

At this point it is important to understand that in its imagery the dancing figure represents all five cosmic activities, that all of them occur within the dancing of Nataraja. It is not that Shiva's dance is a creative force in the universe, that the universe proceeds from his dancing. Rather, and much more importantly, creation and destruction both occur within the context of the dancing Shiva. If we can grasp this we can begin to understand the importance of the sense that Shiva is dancing to accomplish nothing. It is not that he wants to create or destroy or enable or have any effect whatever. He dances only and simply because it is his nature to do so. It is play (*lila*); something done for the sake of just doing it, with no other intent or motive. I must take this autotelic aspect of dancing seriously because I believe that there is a close connection between play and dancing and that to develop our appreciation of this connection is to enhance our understanding of both. In the following sections I will examine several perspectives on play from the history of Western philosophy and then I will return to Nataraja for a fuller consideration.

One other thing important at this point is to think a bit about the motionless aspect of the figurines that present Nataraja. The representation of the contextualizing story to Shiva's dancing Nadanta in Chidambaram and of the cosmic activities it encompasses tends to set a boundary or an including perimeter to the entirety of cosmic space and time. Yet, the figurine depicts Nataraja, while clearly dancing, in a fixed moment in the dance. What is important I think is actually what the image suggests and implies, yet does not depict; and that is the dancing movement itself. The figure bears a sense of the incipience, the potential, the about to be released force that is fundamental to dancing and to playing. So it is not this figure itself that is key, but what the figure points to that cannot possibly be caught or depicted in any way, but that can be known. This sense is expressed in the text which reads, "Our Lord is the Dancer, who, like the heat latent in firewood, diffuses His power in mind and matter, and makes them dance in their turn."[2]

And, in the distinctive Hindu perspective of seeing the whole of the cosmos in the heart of the human, Ananda Coomaraswamy writes that the deepest significance of the dance is "felt when it is realized that it takes place within the heart and the self. Everywhere is God: that Everywhere is the heart." And he continues by quoting from a Hindu text:

> The dancing foot, the sound of the tinkling bells,
> The songs that are sung and the varying steps,
> The form assumed by our Dancing Gurupara—
> Find out these within yourself, then shall your fetters fall away.[3]

Thus, Nataraja's dancing is the vitality of the cosmos and the human being at once, one and the same. It seems that the fullest realization of this vitality depends on seeing beyond the frozen image of Nataraja to glimpse a sense of his dancing, his moving, his playing.

The dancing is described as spontaneous, indicating primarily that it is not motivated or planned or directed toward any goal or end. The playful aspect of Nataraja's dancing is suggested in Skryabin's *Poem of Ecstasy* which includes this passage.

> The Spirit (*purusha*) playing,
> The Spirit longing,
> The Spirit with fancy (*yoga-maya*) creating all,
> Surrenders himself to the bliss (*ananda*) of love . . .
> Amid the flowers of His creation (*prakriti*), He lingers in a kiss . . .
> Blinded by their beauty, He rushes, He frolics, He dances, He whirls . . .
> He is all rapture, all bliss, in his play (*lila*)
> Free, divine, in his love struggle
> In the marvelous grandeur of sheer aimlessness,
> And in the union of counter-aspirations (*dvandva*)
> In consciousness alone, in love alone,
> The Spirit learns the nature (*svabhava*) of his divine being . . .
> 'O, my world, my life, my blossoming my ecstasy!
> Your every moment I create
> By negation of all forms previously lived through:
> I am eternal negation (*neti, neti*). . . .
> Enjoying this dance, choking in this whirlwind,
> Into the domain of ecstasy, He takes swift flight.
> In the unceasing change (*samsara, nitya bhava*), in this flight, aimless (*nishkama*), divine
> The Spirit comprehends Himself,
> In the power of will, alone (*kevala*) free (*mukta*),
> Every-creating, all-irradiating, all vivifying,
> Divinely playing in the multiplicity of forms (*Prapancha*), He comprehends Himself. . . .
> 'I already dwell in thee, O, my world,
> Thy dream of me—'twas I coming into existence. . . .
> And thou art all—one wave of freedom and bliss . . .'
> By a general conflagration (*maha-pralaya*) the universe (*samsara*) is embraced
> The Spirit is at the height of being, and He feels the tide unending
> Of the divine power (*Shakti*) of free will. He is all-daring:
> What menaced, now is excitement,
> What terrified, is now delight. . . .
> And the universe resounds with the joyful cry I am.[4]

Hold these beautiful images now for a while.

PLAY: FRIEDRICH SCHILLER

That you are here—that life exists and identity,
That the powerful play goes on, and you may contribute a verse.
Walt Whitman

Man plays only when he is in the full sense of the word a human being,

and he is only fully a human being when he plays.
Friedrich Schiller

Play is a light and easy word, the natural activity of children and animals, especially young ones. Leisure and freedom. Commonly opposed to work and the serious. Surprisingly long the subject of philosophers, social scientists and artists, play is also a key to the topsy turvy world of postmodernity.

In many ways Friedrich Schiller's late eighteenth century discussion of play surprisingly anticipates the mid-twentieth century views of Hans-Georg Gadamer and Gregory Bateson and the late twentieth century consideration of play by Jacques Derrida and Jean Baudrillard. Rather than presenting a thorough history of the consideration of play, given the unbearable lightness of play, I will here consider but several significant contributions to this history. My objective is to explore these select writings/thinkers on play to expand our appreciation of the richness of play.

A curious thing happened in the course of a series of letters that Friedrich Schiller published in 1793 on the subject of aesthetic education. Well, it did not really originate with Schiller. He was influenced by Immanuel Kant and there were others before Kant. Still I find Schiller to be the most notable and interesting among them. Writing about aesthetics, Schiller began with a discussion of his understanding of the fundamental drives or impulses that make up the peculiarly human character, conflicting impulses, yet somehow both necessary. Beauty characterizes the situation in which these impulses are happily conjoined without either one losing its force. But how to understand this both-that-cannot-be conjunction? This is the curious thing. Schiller wrote of this conjunction in terms of play. Furthermore, since beauty characterizes this relationship of concert,[5] he wrote of beauty also in the terms of play. Schiller, I believe, anticipates twentieth century writings on play, particularly those of Hans-Georg Gadamer, Gregory Bateson, Jacques Derrida and Jean Baudrillard. And it must be remembered that Schiller's writing directly influenced Charles Sanders Peirce.

Though considered a notable work in the history of aesthetics, the collection of letters known by the title *On the Aesthetic Education of Man* is rarely referenced in considerations of play. There is an occasional reference to the Letters as contributing to one of the modern theories of play. Herbert Spencer, the nineteenth century psychologist, credits Schiller as the inspiration for his discussion of the surplus energy or exuberance theory of play. In the revised version of his *Principles of Psychology* (1870-2), Spencer cited Schiller for support, though indirectly since he could not remember his name, referring only to the influence of "a statement of a German author."[6] This exuberance theory has become prominent in its relevance to the modern correlation of play with leisure, in contrast to work, and with the modern sense of the value of psychological release.

The work most commonly cited since mid-twentieth century as the source or inspiration for contemporary studies of play is Johan Huizinga's *Homo Ludens: A Study of the Play Element in Culture* (1944). Huizinga cites Schiller only one time. In his chapter "Play-forms in Art," he equates Schiller's *Spieltrieb*, play drive, with the human propensity to ornament, which he exemplifies by a reference to doodling.[7] Huizinga gives no evidence of having read more than the Fourteenth Letter and he unfortunately misrepresents Schiller.[8]

Schiller's connection of play with art was likely influenced by Kant's discussion of art in his *Critique of Judgment* (1790). In distinguishing "art" from "handicraft" Kant holds that "the First is called *free*, the other may be called *industrial art*. We look on the former as something which could only prove final (be a success) as play, i.e., an occupation which is agreeable on its own account; but on the second as labor."[9] Art, like play, is autotelic as opposed to handicraft which works to produce something for a purpose other than the making.[10] Kant calls upon play to make clear what he means by soul (*Geist*) in his discussion of what constitutes artistic genius. Some works of art are deserving of being called art in their demonstration of taste, yet somehow they are soulless. Soul is the animating principle in the mind. Soul is "that which sets the mental powers into a swing that is final, i.e., into a play which is self-maintaining and which strengthens those powers for such activity."[11] In his discussion of the three divisions of the fine arts, Kant identifies one division as the "play of sensations" or the "beautiful play of sensations," by which he refers to music and the "art of color." By play Kant refers to "the *effect* of those vibrating movements upon the elastic parts of our body that can be evident to sense."[12] In Kant's usage, play is "agreeable on its own account," that is, it is autotelic, and it designates a self-maintaining swing or harmony of vibrating movements. The association of play with vibrating or oscillating movement will be developed by others. Play can scarcely be imagined apart from movement.

Schiller's *Aesthetic Letters* argue for the importance of aesthetic education, proposing that aesthetic education is essential to the realization of human potential. Foundational to his argument is Schiller's description of the two forces or impulses that drive human action, that define the human character. Schiller describes these two opposing forces in various ways. Analyzing the age in which he lived, heavily influenced by the French Revolution, Schiller felt that culture tended to bifurcate the individual, placing him or her at odds within him or herself, with detrimental results,

> either as savage, when feeling predominates over principle; or as barbarian when principle destroys feeling. The savage despises Civiliza-

tion, and acknowledges Nature as his sovereign mistress. The barbarian derides and dishonors Nature, but, more contemptible than the savage, as often as not continues to be the slave of his slave. (IV.6)[13]

Schiller felt that his "age is, in fact, moving along both these false roads, and has fallen prey, on the one hand, to coarseness, on the other, to enervation and perversity. From this twofold swaying it [the age] is to be brought back by means of beauty."(X.1)

These forces operate not only within culture, but within the individual in the terms of "person" and "condition," that is, the self and its determination or environment, being and becoming, endurance and change. These forces constitute

two contrary challenges to man, the two fundamental laws of his sensuo-rational nature. The first insists upon absolute reality: he is to turn everything which is mere form into world, and make all his potentialities fully manifest. The second insists upon absolute formality: he is to destroy everything in himself which is mere world, and bring harmony into his changes. In other words, he is to externalize all that is within him, and give form to all that is outside him. (XI.9)

Schiller formalizes these forces in terms of drives or impulses: the *sensuous* drive (*sinnliche Trieb*) and the *formal* drive (*Formtrieb*). The *sensuous* drive proceeds from the sensual and physical aspect of human existence. It is concerned with physical place in time and space. Whenever this drive acts exclusively, one is but "a unit of quantity, an occupied moment of time"(XII.2). There is no person, no enduring form, only the moment of sensation. The *formal* drive proceeds from the rational nature and strives to set the human at liberty from the flux of change and sensation. It strives to embrace the wholeness of time and space, seeking eternity to the annulment of temporal change, of determining event. Yet, when this impulse dominates, the human entity loses individuality, becoming an idea, a species. Humans are no more in time, they have become time. (XII) This is the bifurcated world Merleau-Ponty found to be impossible.

Schiller holds that neither impulse is dispensable, yet both require restriction and moderation. (XIII) Indeed, one reaches perfection through

a reciprocal action between the two drives, reciprocal action of such a kind that the activity of the one both gives rise to, and sets limits to, the activity of the other, and in which each in itself achieves its highest manifestation precisely by reason of the other being active. (XIV.1)

One cannot achieve this fullness so long as only one of these two impulses is exclusively satisfied or both alternately. Schiller argues that one gains a "complete intuition of his human nature," a "vision [that] would serve him as a symbol of his accomplished destiny," when these drives are conjoined in a third drive, that is, an experience in which "he were to be at once conscious of his freedom and sensible of his existence, were, at one and the same time, to feel himself matter and come to know himself as mind." (XIV.2) This view foreshadows Merleau-Ponty's entwining visible and invisible as chiasm.

Remarkably, in his attempt to give clarity to this combination of impulses, Schiller turns to the language of play, calling it "that drive . . . in which both the others work in concert" (XIV.3), the "play drive (*spieltrieb*)," begging his reader patience with the term until he might justify its appropriateness. This third drive is

> directed towards annulling time within time, reconciling becoming with absolute being and change with identity. . . . The play-drive, in consequence, as the one in which both the others act in concert, will exert upon the psyche at once a moral and a physical constraint; it will, therefore, since it annuls all contingency, annul all constraint too, and set man free both physically and morally. (XIV.3 and 5)

Whereas the object of the sense drive is "life" and the object of the form drive is "form," the object of the play drive, to Schiller's understanding, is "living form," a concept that denotes aesthetic qualities, that is, "Beauty."[14] Living form, beauty, is the consummation of humanity. Again Schiller anticipates Merleau-Ponty's conjunctive term minded-body and his valuation of the third thing "flesh" that conjoins yet separates that he understands to be "ultimate reality." Schiller pronounces: "With beauty man shall only play, and it is with beauty only that he shall play. . . . Man only plays when he is in the full sense of the word a human being, and he is only fully a human being when he plays." (XV.8 and 9)

Why "play"? By using the term play, does not Schiller risk trivializing both human perfection and aesthetic qualities? What is there of play that helps Schiller communicate these central concerns? He holds that his use of the word is fully warranted in terms of its usage in common speech, where play denotes "everything which is neither subjectively nor objectively contingent, and yet imposes no kind of constraint either from within or from without." (XV.5) In other words, Schiller appeals to the usage of the word play in common speech, where he holds that it is understood neither as a state of mind nor as class of objects,[15] where it is understood to be engaged without goal or necessity, that is, play contains its own satisfaction. Schiller, it seems, was not advancing a new theory of play, he was not advancing a theory of play at all. He was merely relying on what he considered common knowledge and experience of play.

Schiller avoids the trap of so many modern understandings of play by appealing to a common understanding that it is neither subjective nor objective, that is, play is not distinguished as state of mind or attitude, nor as a particular set of actions or objects. By calling it a drive or impulse, but even more by describing play as a certain kind of interaction among other drives or impulses, Schiller moves play to the level of the description of relationships between and principles of interaction among other things—here the formal and sensuous drives.

Taking inspiration from Schiller, we may suggest that play refers to the principles or grammars that characterize structures, a set of structuring principles, a metastructure. This, I believe, is what Derrida refers to as "structurality."[16] Play is akin to Merleau-Ponty's chiasm and my self-othering. Play denotes the principles in which structural oppositions, even structural anomalies, may at once be held together without reconciliation or reduction. It is not the simple alternation of taking turns, but a momentary focus on one structural element that reveals the power and dynamics of the opposing elements. Schiller thought of it in the dynamic terms of reciprocity and oscillation, even vibration. Play occurs in the virtual gap or space as movement; the movement exercising the energetics of the structurality; play is not movement to close the space or to stop the play.

A mere game may be thought of as a set of relationships and activities prescribed by a set of rules, often including the designation of a space and the definition of an objective. Games, in general, may be designated as a particular kind of activity. But one may also think of game as the designation of a state of mind, a mental strategy, or an attitude. The word "game" is sometimes even used as a verb, as in such phrases as "to game a situation." The play of a game is a result of a grammar of interaction as specified in the terms of rules and objectives. Common to the rules of a game is a description of "the play." A game "in play" subjugates its goal or objective to the holding together of opposing forces, an oscillation or back and forth movement among them, without resolution. There is no play when this principle fails or ceases to be operative; at that point the play of the game is over. Play is not game; game is not play. Game is played. There is the play of the game.

Considering game in terms of Schiller's form and sense drives, the rules to a game are at one polar position in this continuum. Here there is no play, only the potential for play. At the opposite pole, there are no rules, no boundaries, no definition, and therefore no game. Game play arises in the oscillating interaction between these poles.

A further clarification can be made to Schiller's understanding of the formal and sensuous drives. The rules and procedures that define a game may be thought of as their formal dimensions while the raw physical actions of the game, its sensual dimension. The play of the game is achieved in the way that the rules both make possible, yet also restrict, the sensual aspect of the game, that is, the range of allowable raw physical action, while at the same time, the physical actions (the sensual drive) give life and application to the rules. There is no play of the game if either the formal or sensual dimension is missing.

Play, for Schiller, was a third drive, yet unlike the other two, play exists as the oscillating interplay of the other two drives. Yet while it may appear that these drives arise from themselves and precede play, Schiller clearly sees that these two drives cannot exist alone, cannot have force other than when bound with, yet are distinguished from, one another by their interplay, that is, by the play drive. Various aspects of this characterization of play are present in the following quotations.

> the play-drive, in consequence, as the one in which both the others act in concert, will exert upon the psyche at once a moral and a physical constraint; (XIV.5)
>
> it is precisely play and play alone, which of all men's states and conditions is the one which makes him whole and unfolds both sides of his nature at once; (XV.7)
>
> the utmost that experience can achieve will consist of an oscillation between the two principles, in which now reality, now form, will predominate. Beauty as Idea, therefore, can never be other than one and indivisible, since there can never be more than one point of equilibrium; whereas beauty in experience will be eternally twofold, because oscillation can disturb the equilibrium in twofold fashion, including it now to the one side, now to the other. (XVI.1)

It is little surprise that Schiller would declare "With beauty man shall only play, and it is with beauty only that he shall play."

Understood in this way, Schiller, parting from Kant's view, does not base the aesthetic in the subjective. The aesthetic is articulated in terms of being "neither subjectively nor objectively contingent." Beauty, the valuation of play realizing human potentiality, is neither a state of mind nor a class of objects. However, as Anthony Savile shows,[17] Schiller discussed beauty primarily in terms of the achievement of the ideal human state and, by extension, that of society and the world. Beauty is necessary to the achievement of this state and characterizes its manifestations. Because of this concern with human ideals and his discussion of human impulses there is the general, but, I believe, incorrect, impression that Schiller held the aesthetic to be subjectively based.[18] This leaves open the determination of the ideal.

It must be asked whether there is any basis, as claimed by others, in Schiller's work for an exuberance theory of play. In the final letter, Schiller considers the universality of the aesthetic ideas he has presented, the possible perfection not only of individuals, but of societies and of the universe. Schiller considers the presence of play structurality in the natural world that is apart from humankind. He considers the question of the play of the world. "Nature has given even to creatures without reason more than the bare necessities of existence, and shed a glimmer of freedom even into the darkness of animal life." (XXVII.3) For example the lion, when "not gnawed by hunger . . . fills the echoing desert with a roaring that speaks defiance, and his exuberant energy enjoys itself in purposeless display."(XXVII.3) He sees the same spirit of joyousness expressed in the swarm of insects in the sunlight and in the melodious warbling of songbirds. Here in nature there is freedom apart from necessity, apart from external need.

> An animal may be said to be at work, when the stimulus to activity is some lack; it may be said to be at play, when the stimulus is sheer plenitude of vitality, when superabundance of life is its own incentive to action. Even inanimate nature exhibits a similar luxuriance of forces, coupled with a laxity of determination which, in that material sense, might well be called play. . . . Thus does Nature, even in her material kingdom, offer us a prelude of the illimitable, and even here remove in part the chains which, in the realm of form, she casts away entirely. From the compulsion of want, or physical earnestness, she makes the transition via the compulsion of superfluity, or physical play, to aesthetic play; and before she soars, in the sublime freedom of beauty, beyond the fetters of ends and purposes altogether, she makes some approach to this independence, at least from afar, in that kind of free activity which is at once its own end and its own means. (XXVII.3)

My understanding of this discussion suggests that Schiller was developing the necessity for play being self-actualizing and autotelic; that is, play is not done to accomplish anything or to mean anything or to do anything other than the exercise of its own energetics, its own oscillatory looping movement. This quality is why play is so important to assist in extending our understanding of the energetics and vitality and ontogenetics of movement, dancing, self-othering, gesturing. Exuberance is maybe one way of indicating this quality, yet it seems that exuberance with respect to play is to explain it, or better to explain it away, as the outlet for an overplus of energy.

Though, like Kant, Schiller opposes work and play, he describes an aesthetic hierarchy based essentially on the common presence of play. The expression of exuberance, the actions not accountable by any outward or inward necessity, is the product of play and thereby is linked, both hierarchically and developmentally, with the aesthetic in the human realm. It is quite in contrast to Schiller's stated understanding of play to credit him with a theory of play in which otherwise inexplicable actions and expressions—lion roars, bird warbles, insect swarms and a host of human actions—are thought to arise to meet the need to express exuberance or overabundance, for this is a need-based theory focused on a particular class of objects. To acknowledge that Schiller's advance was to identify play as metastructure,[19] or better as structurality, and to designate it as "neither subjectively nor objectively contingent, and yet imposes neither outward nor inward necessity" clarifies his aesthetics, and establishes a perspective on play that, while heretofore not adequately acknowledged, has played an important role in the development of modern thought.

Schiller's *Aesthetic Letters* have an iterative structure, their form corresponding with their theme, their author artfully engaged in the play of substitution.[20] Substituting one set of terms for the previous set, in supplementarity, Schiller moves from a concern for individual human potential all the way to the fulfillment of cultural potential in an "Aesthetic State." He uses some terms, like *Natur*, in many ways.[21] He uses many terms for the same referent—eight, for example, to refer to God.[22] Antithesis is preferred to synthesis. His translators proclaim dance as

> the most apposite of all metaphors for the form of his treatise. Not just for the rhythms of his periods . . . but for the philosophic and aesthetic complexity of the form as a whole. Partly because the manifest tautology of dance is a paradigm of the essential tautology of all art: of its inherent tendency to offer a hundred different treatments of the same subject, to find a thousand different forms of expression for the thoughts and feelings common to all men.[23]

The *Aesthetic Letters* have a structure based on threes. Not only does Schiller reiterate the same concerns almost exactly every three letters, in each of these iterations the Letters demand a "third thing:" a "third character" combining the virtues of both the animal and rational sides of human nature (Letter III); the clarification that the "third character" will differ from the Greek notions of wholeness and harmony (Letter VI); the call for a third term to resolve the dilemma that, to Schiller, characterizes human nature (Letter IX); the argument for the "third drive" conjoining the heterogeneous form and sense drives (Letter XII); beauty is identified with the third drive (Letter XV); a "middle condition" between activity and passivity, combining the advantages of each, is proposed (Letter XVIII); the aesthetic mode of the psyche, the "third state," is defined (Letter XXI); a description of the "third state" to which both individuals and cultures must pass, each moving through a three stage cycle, to achieve full potential (Letter XXIV); and, finally, all the "third things" come together in Schiller's conception of a "Third State," an "Aesthetic State," which fulfills all the previous ideals.[24]

In all of these domains, the "third thing" arises as the interplay of two others. The "third thing" is that which conjoins, with vitality but without synthesis, two heterogeneous, even opposing, structural elements. The "third thing" is always double-faced; at once a warning of the dangers of collapsing or diminishing complexity and a demonstration of the dynamism and vitality of the structural dynamic the "third thing" makes possible.

It is the cross connection of two heterogeneous structures that Schiller presents both in substance and in structure in the *Aesthetic Letters*. His favorite rhetorical figure is chiasm: the rhetorical inversion of the second of two parallel phrases, clauses, and so on.[25] Again he anticipates Merleau-Ponty.

Schiller's paradigmatic play chiasm is: (put positively) the form drive achieves its fulfillment only through the sense drive, the sense drive through the form drive; (put negatively) without the sense drive the form drive runs amiss, the sense drive runs amiss without the form drive. The chiasm is redoubled, but not double-crossed: the chiasm that conjoins yet distinguishes the form and sense drives is the play drive; chiasm is itself a "third thing," play.

Schein, as discussed by Schiller, has two distinct, even opposing, meanings: "to shine" and "to appear or seem." In some usages they are synonymous or at least closely related. In senses related to light, for example, things appear as they shine or are shined upon. But the second sense of the word holds the key to the ambiguity, for there are multiple senses of "to appear or seem." A thing may appear to be what it in fact is, but it may seem to be what it is not. *Schein* may be identified with both *Erscheinung*, "appearance," and *Tauschung*, "deception."[26] Schiller's use of *Schein* in his discussion of aesthetics anticipates, and may serve as a critique of, Gadamer's conception of "mimesis." The peculiarity of the term, which seems to differ from itself (or, to maintain consistent language, to shine upon its appearances) is in the spirit of and anticipates Derrida's "différance." Further, *Schein* cannot be adequately understood apart from "play," or perhaps "play" apart from *Schein*. Chiasm.[27]

Near the end of the *Aesthetic Letters* the discussion has shifted to the achievement of the full potentiality of the human species. Striving for "aesthetic semblance" is, for Schiller, a key to human advancement, since it

> demands higher powers of abstraction, greater freedom of heart, more energy of will, than man ever needs when he confines himself to reality; and he must have already left this reality behind if he would arrive at that kind of semblance. (XXVI.1)

Before the rise of semblance, Schiller argues, humankind is chained to a brute material existence. The emergence of semblance is an advancement because it marks the rise of human invention, the abstraction of the ideal from the brute reality of nature, of form from substance. In the last chapter I argued that it is the felt experience of self-othering that is distinctive of dancing that is a necessary condition for the rise of aesthetic semblance. Semblance is wholly the work of humankind and exists only in the realm of ideas and forms. "Aesthetic semblance" (or variously "autonomous semblance" or "pure semblance") is based on maintaining a clear distinction between "semblance" and "actuality" and "truth." It "neither seeks to represent reality nor needs to be represented by it." (XXVI.13) "Logical semblance" in contrast, is confused with actuality and truth. It is mere deception.

Aesthetic semblance is key to the rise of art, to the aesthetic perspective, to human development. Where it exists "we shall see actual life governed by the ideal, honor triumphant over possessions, thought over enjoyment, dreams of immortality over existence." (XXVI.12)

"Play" is supplementary to "aesthetic semblance." In distinguishing aesthetic from logical semblance Schiller wrote, "Only the first is play, the later is deception." (XXVI.5) He held that the play drive begins to stir at the stage of development when it becomes important to distinguish semblance from reality, form from body. (XXVI.7) What I believe he means is that there can be no play when the sense drive alone is operative, when, in his conception, human beings were at the stage of unreflective brute material sensuality. But then there is no play in logical semblance because this determination of truth and certainty removes the play from the structurality and the results are *dead* certainty. There is no play in a single pole structure for it functions as a center which takes the play out of the structure. "Aesthetic semblance" is one of the ways that Schiller expresses the importance of play. The structural dynamics of the meanings of *Schein* are an illustration, an exemplum, of the structural dynamics of play.

Truth is never endangered by attaching value to semblance, because the clear distinction of semblance and reality prevents any danger of substituting semblance for truth. Though Schiller warns that "it sometimes happens that intelligence will carry its zeal for reality to such a pitch of intolerance, that it pronounces a disparaging judgment upon the whole art of aesthetic semblance just because it is semblance."(XXVI.5)[28]

Schiller's understanding of play is essential to our developing understanding of dancing. Dancing is the play of self-othering. Dancing is the experience of aesthetic semblance, the felt lived experience that the co-presence of identity and difference engenders the playful movement of aliveness, vitality. It is a late eighteenth century articulation of play that connected it with beauty and gives us insight into dancing and why we have such a strong urge to connect dancing with "beauty."

PLAY: HANS-GEORG GADAMER

The movement which is play has no goal which would bring it to an end.
The original meaning of the word spiel *[is] "dance".*
Hans-Georg Gadamer[29]

On many occasions in his writings of the 1960s and 1970s German philosopher Hans-Georg Gadamer turned to the subject of the ontology of the work of art, most particularly in his important 1960 book, *Truth and Method*. Remarkably, in these works he considers play to be the "clue to ontological explanation." Like Schiller, Kant, and others before him he turns to play as the way to articulate some aspect of aesthetics. Play is, it seems, for Gadamer, a metaphor for art. He therefore discusses play in preparation for considering the ontology of art. Like Schiller he writes of play as though there is no ambiguity to the commonsense view. He is not ad-

vancing any new theory or understanding of play; he is merely calling
forth the obvious. Introducing a long discussion of play in *Truth and
Method*, Gadamer writes, "If, in connection with the experience of art, we
speak of play, this refers neither to the attitude nor even to the state of
mind of the creator or of those enjoying the work of art, nor to the freedom of the art itself."[30]

Whereas Schiller was interested in the contribution that beauty makes
to the achievement of human potential and in acknowledging that the
manifestation of such fulfillment is the distinguishing characteristic of
beauty, Gadamer is interested in the mode of being of the work of art
itself, which he understands as necessary to free art from the subjectivist
base it has had since Kant. He wrote, "I wish to free this concept [art]
from the subjective meaning which it has in Kant and Schiller and which
dominates the whole of modern aesthetics and philosophy of man."[31] To
overturn the subjective view of art, which is that art is the "variety of
changing experiences whose object is each time filled subjectively with
meaning like an empty mold,"[32] Gadamer argues that art has a distinctive mode of being and that is representation, an idea he derives from his
understanding of play. "The playing of the play is what speaks to the
spectator, through its representation, and this in such a way that the
spectator, despite the distance between it and himself, still belongs to
it."[33]

By "representation" I think Gadamer means something other than to
present something again, but something more like presenting itself only
for the presentation of it. This is a critical point in our consideration of
dancing, because I believe it is clear that dancing, existing only in the
dancing, cannot be re-presented; indeed, it is the very presence, immedia-
cy, aura, inability to replicate or duplicate, that dancing has its distinctiveness. To re-present dancing, as say in film or photography or art, is to
shift dancing into a subject of some other art, to backfill it in the grids of
another form. I believe that because of our familiarity with the incipient
vital aspect of dancing, we often experience the dancing even when it is
re-presented in other forms, but this is primarily then due to the gestural
conditioning we have in seeing/experiencing the re-presentation of dancing. We tend, for example, in experiencing dance in films to be absorbed
through the medium, to find the film medium to be transparent to us, to
feel that moving itself aspect of re-presented dancing while this aspect of
movement has been shifted to the film. There is then a fascinating play
between dancing and the re-presentation of dancing in film and art; a
self-othering to be sure but of a different sort.

Being the clue to the ontology of art, Gadamer considers play at some
length.[34] The first thing about play, according to Gadamer's understanding, is

the to and fro of constantly repeated movement [and] . . . what characterizes this movement back and forth is that neither pole of the movement represents the goal in which it would come to rest . . . a certain
leeway clearly belongs to such a movement . . . This freedom is such
that it must have the form of self-movement.[35]

Play then appears as self-movement, movement without purpose or
goal.[36] It renews itself through repetition. Play absorbs the player into its
movement. It takes on itself the burden of initiative. Every playing is a
being played. Play does not allow the player or the spectator to act toward it as if it were an object. It cannot be understood as a kind of
activity, nor can it be subjectively determined. Play is not frivolous; it is
not opposed to the serious. Gadamer holds that "play is really limited to
representing itself. Thus its mode of being is self-representation."[37] Play
exists "to play." Gadamer commonly uses the examples of game play to
illustrate his discussion. He notes, for example, that games often indicate
a goal, a solution, an ordering that seemingly directs the play. Yet he
argues that in play the purpose really becomes the movement of the
game itself, that is, the play, the self-presentation.

Play is inseparable from freedom and risk. According to Gadamer,
play must be conjoined with the freedom of choice among serious possibilities. Wherever there are choices there is risk. The attractiveness of
play is in the danger associated with this risk.[38]

Gadamer insists that play is not special or peculiar to human beings or
even to the animal kingdom, for nature "is without purpose or intention . . . is without exertion, a constantly self-renewing play."[39] Thus, he
argues, extending the metaphor of play to art, nature may serve as a
model for art, though art differs from nature in its being a "representation for someone." Art is not "the mere self-representation of an ordered
movement, nor mere representation."[40] Art, in Gadamer's view, has its
being in its performance or presentation—what he calls a "transformation into structure"—and, importantly, this incorporates the spectator as
an aspect of its mode of being. The image of theater is illustrative of
Gadamer's understanding of this aspect of the mode of being of art. In
theater the opening of the fourth wall is part of the closedness of theater.
The audience completes what the dramatic performance as such is. Gadamer centers on the primacy of the medial sense of play, that is, its to-
and-fro movement. The original meaning of the word *Spiel*, Gadamer
reminds us, is "dance."

The spectator and even the chance conditions in which art appears
cannot be isolated from the mode of being of the work of art for these are
inseparable from the presentation or performance itself, that is, the being
of the work. The spectator is part of the being of the work of art. Gadamer
argues further that "the true being of the spectator, who is part of the

play of art, cannot be adequately understood in terms of subjectivity, as an attitude of the aesthetic consciousness."[41]

Art, understood as play, finds its true perfection in a "transformation into structure." Citing Aristotle, Gadamer connects movement, particularly self-movement, with vitality. Play, as unmotivated undirected self-movement, is synonymous with vitality, with life force. Thus Gadamer reasons that "the being of play is always realization, sheer fulfillment, *energia* which has its telos within itself."[42] Realization gains its fullest achievement in art's medial process of "transformation into structure." To the question, "What is mediated by art?" Gadamer responds, "Truth." In its self-presentation occurs the transformation from *energia* (energy) to *ergon* (a work or a creation). Gadamer notably suggests that "creation," *Gebilde*, would be preferable to "work."[43] The work of art is appearing structure, "a structure [that has] found its measure in itself and measures itself by nothing outside it."[44] "The world of the work of art, in which play expresses itself fully in the unity of its course, is in fact a wholly transformed world. By means of it everyone recognizes that that is how things are."[45] Through the play of art reality is transformed into structure. Gadamer understands art "as the raising up of . . . reality into its truth."[46]

Applying Gadamer's notion of "transformation into structure" to dancing, which Gadamer did not do, we must identify the *energia* of dancing, which of course is self-movement, but it is not so easy to be satisfied with this self-movement being transformed into *ergon* (a work). The dance, unlike a painting or even a piece of music or theater, is ephemeral. The dance seems never to show a structure that emerges from this transformation. To be a showing, dancing is the showing of the *energia* of movement itself more so than some resulting object or creation. Dancing considered as art has a primacy among art forms in this respect. Dancing as the presentation of self-movement itself only teases the possibility of *ergon* while hiding any work or creation in the playful flow of promised possibilities. Dancing seduces by suggesting a transformation into structure yet the emerging structure always recedes as it manifests in drawing forth movement that continues so long as it is a dancing. Dancing always reflects or shows *energia* rather than *ergon*, vitality rather than work.

It may appear that Gadamer holds a rather traditional ontological view, that is, that reality is grounded in a hidden, stable, perhaps mystical, realm from which all manifestation is imitation, a pale and imperfect reflection of the hidden. Indeed, Gadamer refers to art as revealing what remains otherwise hidden. But his ontology is more radical than might first appear. This is clarified in his understanding of mimesis,[47] a concept essential to his understanding of art. It is to the communication of his special understanding of mimesis that play serves metaphorically so importantly.

The Greeks, Gadamer recalls, recognized two kinds of productive activity. One was ordinary manual production, but the other was

> mimetic production which does not create anything "real" but simply offers a representation . . . [that is] it represents itself as something that it is not. A role is "played," and this implies a unique ontological claim . . . Imitative representation is . . . a play that communicates as play when it is taken in a way it wants to be taken: as pure representation.[48]

Mimesis is no deception, according to Gadamer's understanding. There is no intent to be believed. Imitation is a showing, or as he puts it a "true showing," an "appearance," a "self-presentation;" this is its mode of being.

Importantly, Gadamer argues that mimesis has nothing whatever to do with the relation between copy and original. It is a showing and

> showing something means that the one to whom something is shown sees it correctly for himself. . . . What is shown is, so to speak, elicited from the flux of manifold reality. Only what is shown is intended and nothing else. As intended, it is held in view, and thus elevated to a kind of ideality. . . . An act of identification and, consequently, of recognition occurs whenever we see what it is that we are being shown.[49]

All true mimesis is a transformation, perhaps more than an imitation; a primordial phenomenon that constitutes the experience of art.[50] Gadamer calls it "aesthetic nondifferentiation," that is, that which is represented in art is not distinguished from the representation. Imitation presents a "transformed reality in which the transformation points back to what has been transformed in and through it."[51] Imitation is an explorative self-presentation of reality. In mimesis is reality intensified, writ large.

Imitation must always be complemented by "recognition." Gadamer holds that the essence of imitation consists in the recognition of the represented. Through the act of identification, the cognition of the true, one knows the represented as something, that is, the represented is something already known. What imitation reveals then, Gadamer argues, is the real essence of the thing.[52] In art the truth is recognized as it only there presents itself.

Despite the tendency to understand mimesis as copy as re-presentation suggesting always a diminishing of the original, a close reading of Gadamer on mimesis reveals a close proximity between what he terms mimesis and what I have called "self-othering." What Gadamer does not do is to discuss how this ideality is experienced. Here again dancing engages this aspect of arting in a very special way in that the reality self-presented is experienced by the dancer, and by observers or audience, in interesting and complex gestural and neurological ways involving mirror neurons proprioceptively, that is, in the most fundamental manner of human experience.

Gadamer's view of art is similar to the "living form" envisioned by Schiller. Gadamer writes

> the play of art is not some substitute dream world in which we can forget ourselves. On the contrary, the play of art is a mirror that through the centuries constantly arises anew, and in which we catch sight of ourselves in a way that is often unexpected or unfamiliar: what we are, what we might be, and what we are about. [53]

With Gadamer's distinctive interpretation of mimesis he points out that the being of art is in the play of its self-presentation. In mimesis art is at play. Mimesis is the self-othering play of art. In art there is an "acting as if," a fabrication that is not to be taken for anything other than itself. "It 'intends' something, and yet it is not what it intends." [54] It is wholly self-referential, yet "shows" a reality beyond itself.

Presentation and performance constitute the base for Gadamer's ontology. Things are as they present or show themselves in the world. Art shares this ontological base with all of nature whose purpose it is only to present itself.

The thrust of Gadamer's discussion of the ontology of a work of art is an attempt to push away from a classical ontological position in which reality stands somehow behind what is apparent and transient. The characteristics of play—the absence of subjective and objective contingency, the lack of outward and inward necessity, the to-and-fro movement that is itself life—are to Gadamer clues to the ontology of art. Play is at once metaphor for art and a description of the structure of art. Art gains its being in its self-presentation.

Still, Gadamer has not achieved the abandonment of a ground of being behind self-presentation. His position seems to necessitate there being a reality beyond art and nature. It is hidden; it needs to be shown. The truth of this reality must be illuminated by art. Yet, he also holds that neither art nor nature is a reflection of a reality to which it must be compared. Reality has its being in its manifestation, even and perhaps most powerfully, in the being of a work of art. Though Gadamer insists that art does not invoke a comparison of original and copy or imitation, it is very difficult to simply dismiss an important ontological difference between reality hidden and reality shown. While it appears that Gadamer intends to diminish the significance of difference by concentrating on self-presentation or self-representation, his conceptions and the language by which he expresses them—imitation, self-presentation, recognition, and hidden reality—are dependent in a fundamental way on difference.

Gadamer's understanding of play is notably similar in some respects to Schiller's. Furthermore, Gadamer utilized play in much the same manner that Schiller did, that is, as a metaphor for or illustration of a kind of relationship, a kind of structuring principle. Both depend on an aspect of the common understanding of play by which to articulate and investigate the being of the aesthetic. Gadamer's advances in the realm of aesthetics were to move from the consideration of the path to human perfection to the mode of being of an art creation. In the realm of philosophy, Gadamer moves away from a traditional ontology, yet remains attached to the foundational structure of such a perspective.

It may appear that Gadamer was right in describing Schiller as using subjectivist criteria in art. Semblance is, after all, described as a human construct, a human perception, not a state of being. Semblance, artistic semblance, is one of those "third things" that are not things at all, that cross connects, without syntheses, heterogeneous drives or structures. Semblance is how Schiller refers to the play of art, it is how one keeps straight the worthiness of aesthetic semblance from the deceptiveness of logical semblance. As a critique to Gadamer's position, it may be suggested that Schiller, by holding to the importance of distinguishing "semblance" and "reality" (however unsatisfactory are these terms) he can save the play that both he and Gadamer agree distinguishes the fine arts. Gadamer, worrying about the conflict of *Schein* and *Sein*, attempts to collapse this distinction, but loses the play that characterizes the mode of being of art (or at best reconstructing it in the conjunction of art and spectator); he muddles the distinction between the fine arts and nature; and without acknowledging their playfulness he uses terms that are inherently double-faced: imitation, representation, recognition, hidden reality.

Gadamer's "aesthetic nondifferentiation" is shown in a critical light by Schiller's discussion of *Schein*. By "aesthetic differentiation" Gadamer refers negatively to the abstraction of art from all of the conditions of its accessibility. This aesthetic consciousness divorces art from everyday life and also from issues of truth. Seen in isolation, Schiller's discussion of semblance might be understood as contributing to aesthetic differentiation, but seen in the context of the *Aesthetic Letters* it cannot. In fact, these concepts are focused at different points in the realm of art and the experience of art. Gadamer, reacting to the tendency he feels has wrongly influenced aesthetic consciousness to separate the meaning of a work of art from its particular experience, proposes "aesthetic nondifferentiation" which "clearly constitutes the real meaning of that cooperative play between imagination and understanding."[55] He wrote that

> it is invariably true that when we see something, we must think something in order to see anything. But here it is a free play and not directed toward a concept. This cooperative interaction forces us to face the question about what is actually built up in this process of free play between the faculties of imagination and conceptual understanding.[56]

Gadamer is concerned, I believe, not with what distinguishes art, its mode of being, but with how we experience art and discern its meaning. Schiller's discussion of semblance is focused more on the importance of the distinction humans make between semblance and brute sensual reality, by which art is distinguished in the first place. There is no play without this distinction. Gadamer tends to shift the arena of play, in the context of this discussion at least, to the subjective realm of imagination and conceptual understanding, while for Schiller play is made possible by the basic distinction of aesthetic semblance, that is, form abstracted from the domain of sense.

In my discussion of dancing I have drawn attention insofar as meaning is concerned to that ontogenetic realm that makes meaning possible, yet itself has no meaning. In the terms of play dancing is the oscillatory structurality, the playful self-movement, the seductive failed promise of transformation into form, the looping *energia*, that is the ontogenesis of possible meaning. It is fascinating to me that both Schiller and Gadamer were familiar with dancing and connected it to the vitality, the *energia*, of playing, yet neither went on to consider dancing in the depth that would have served both of them well in their discussions of art. I suppose this is not really so surprising given the pervasive Western attitude toward dancing.

There are indeed many other discussions of play that would be necessary should my principal concern here be the history of the philosophical discussion of play; however, this is not my purpose. So I'll consider only one other discussion of play and that is by Jacques Derrida who places, if one can call it by such a definite term, play in that ceaseless, and often irritating, endless movement that characterizes a postmodern perspective. Still, it offers much to our efforts to illuminate aspects of dancing as playing.

PLAY: JACQUES DERRIDA

To risk meaning nothing is to start to play.
Jacques Derrida

Jacques Derrida strips away the grounding to which Gadamer seems inextricably bound and sets play free in the joyous Nietzschean affirmation of the play of the world, a world without truth, without origin. Derrida does not see play so differently from Schiller and Gadamer, yet he thinks of play in a radical way, consequently presenting a mature and more sophisticated understanding of play. Perhaps it is more accurate to say that play allows Derrida the language for the radical messages of postmodernity. We could say that Derrida takes play most seriously. Derrida often uses the word "play" (*jeu*), though he rarely directly discusses play as a concept. However, in "Structure, Sign, and Play in the Discourse of the Human Sciences"[57] (1970) he explicitly discusses play.

Derrida's subject is the challenge to the fixedness of structure that he understands to characterize our epoch, a challenge he sees exemplified by Nietzsche's critique of metaphysics, Freud's critique of self-presence, and Heidegger's destruction of the determination of being as presence. The rupture in the way of thinking about structure was a shift from the structure to the principles that govern the structure, that is, a shift to what he terms "structurality." I have adopted this term and used it throughout this book. According to Derrida, structure has always been

> neutralized or reduced, and this by a process of giving it a center or referring it to a point of presence, a fixed origin. The function of this center was . . . to make sure that the organizing principle of the structure would limit what we might call the freeplay (*jeu*) of the structure.[58]

A structurality characterized by the fixation of a center or an origin is given a foundation, a certitude, beyond the play of the structure. The center or origin, which is of the structure, is also outside of the structure. While the center permits the play of the structure it also closes off this play.

Play, for Derrida, is a "disruption of presence," "an interplay of absence and presence," conceived even before the alternative of presence and absence.[59] This disruption is coincident with the realization of the concept of the centered structure. This is a movement from structure to structurality, that is, from thinking about form to thinking about principles, such as understanding a center as the designation of a principle that governs the character of a structure. This shift in thinking leads to the realization that structures are of the process of signification and that the center of a structure, for example, is a surrogate for some central presence. But this presence is always transported outside itself into its structural surrogate. From here, Derrida argues,

> it was probably necessary to begin to think that there was no center, that the center could not be thought in the form of a being-present, that the center has no natural locus, that it was not a fixed locus but a function, a sort of non-locus in which an infinite number of sign-substitutions came into being.[60]

The concept of play casts the light in which Derrida is able to illuminate the vitality of such structures as language or any code system. The field of language is that of play, by which he means "a field of infinite substitutions in the closure of a finite ensemble."[61] It is not that the field of language is inexhaustible that it permits infinite substitutions, but because it is missing

> a center which arrests and founds the freeplay of substitutions. . . . This movement of the freeplay, permitted by the lack, the absence of a center or origin, is the movement of *supplementarity*. One cannot determine

the center, the sign which *supplements* it, which takes its place in its absence—because this sign adds itself, occurs in addition, over and above, comes as a supplement.[62]

Play then is a decentering movement; the movement of an infinite number of sign substitutions; the movement of the difference that must precede even the distinction of presence and absence.

Rather than play being a certain class of movement as Derrida seems to see it, that is, a decentering movement, play understood as an aspect of the movement of dancing is moving as moving itself before and apart from it being backfilled into some thing that might be called by the name "movement," or the name "dance." The affinity between play, better playing, and dancing is much more appropriate to Derrida's description of play as "the movement of the difference that must precede even the distinction of presence and absence." Because dance, as a presence as some thing (*ergon* or work) is ephemeral, more seduction than form, it distinctively always rivets attention to the incipience of its own movement rather than anything manifest. As Gadamer reminded us play and dance, or better, playing and dancing, have common etymological roots.

These characteristics of structurality that are designated by the term play are also evident in Derrida's discussion of "*différance*" (the "a" being an intentional anomalous spelling of "difference" with a silent effect). Of the French, Derrida notes that "the verb 'to differ' [*différer*] seems to differ from itself."[63] On the one hand, it is differ, the "difference as distinction, inequality, discernibility." On the other hand, as defer, it "expresses interposition of delay, the interval of a spacing and temporalizing that puts off until 'later' what is presently denied." "*Différance*," neither a word nor concept, is used by Derrida to identify the commonness, the relatedness, of the two movements of differing to one another. "*Différance*" is "the sameness which is not identical" or "the play of differences." Importantly, characteristic of the rupture with structure that characterizes our epoch, *différance* "*is not*, does not exist, and is not any sort of being-present (*on*). And . . . has neither existence nor essence. It belongs to no category of being, present or absent."[64] "*Différance*" designates the movement by which language or any code becomes constituted as a fabric of differences. It is this movement that Derrida commonly calls play (*jeu*). And it is this sort of understanding of play that corresponds well with dancing.

By its anomalous spelling, "*différance*" as a signifier has a sense suspended between two verbs "to differ" and "to defer." With the signifier "*différance*," Derrida designates the shading of one sense into the other in signification where meaning is always deferred by an endless supplementarity, yet meaning also depends on distinctive oppositions (differences). As Christopher Norris says, "*Différance* not only designates this theme [of the supplementarity of difference and sameness] but offers in its own unstable meaning a graphic example of the process at work."[65] Dancing, I argue, is so important because it offers the proprioceived felt experience of this process. And this is a fascinating attribute of dancing in the context of Derrida's challenge to a being presence. The experiential character of dancing which includes the proprioceptive experience of an other amounts to a felt confirmation but not of some stable being presence out in the world that grounds truth. Rather it confirms through experience the play structurality of dancing as the *energia* of life both for the individual and for existence.

Play designates the vitality, the movement that arises in differences. Play is movement in that sense described by Gadamer as the to-and-fro of constantly repeated movement, as back and forth movement where neither pole of the movement represents the goal, an unstable movement among poles that cannot coexist. In terms of our discussion of dancing this is the to-and-fro that interconnects, yet separates, dancer and dance that we call dancing or self-othering. These two cannot coexist, yet they are also inseparable in this moving.

The loss of center, the embracing of the play of *différance*, of supplementarity, need not be met with nostalgia for presence or origins. Nor is there any intent by Derrida to discover some alternative logic of play. He lucidly articulates the alternatives in the context of interpretation:

> There are thus two interpretations of interpretation, of structure, of sign, of freeplay. The one seeks to decipher, dreams of deciphering, a truth or an origin which is free from freeplay and from the order of the sign, and lives like an exile the necessity of interpretation. The other, which is no longer turned toward the origin, affirms freeplay and tries to pass beyond man and humanism, the name man being who, throughout the history of metaphysics or of ontotheology—in other words, through the history of all his history—has dreamed of full presence, the reassuring foundation, the origin and the end of the game.[66]

Though it might appear that Derrida opts for the second interpretation of interpretation, he says that there is no question of choosing between them.[67] Such a choice would be trivial, for we must "first try to conceive of the common ground, and the *différance* of this irreducible difference."[68] In other words, we must engage the play between these two irreconcilable interpretations of interpretation. In this play between play and not play, Derrida invokes radical imagery to capture some sense of it: "the species of the non-species, in the formless, mute, infant and terrifying form of monstrosity."[69] Perhaps Derrida might have better invoked dancing in that it affirms in the human experience of playful movement the *energia* of vitality.

Derrida brings to fuller maturity the way that Schiller and Gadamer have understood "play." In positing the play impulse Schiller sought to show the impossibility of choosing between the formal impulse and the sensual impulse, to illuminate the vitality of the interplay between these irreconcilable impulses. Schiller would surely have readily appreciated Derrida's discussion of *différance* and supplementarity. Whereas Gadamer attempted to move toward being in self-presentation, Derrida, by taking play radically, moves wholly away from the ontological language that tends to take the play out of play.

Whereas Schiller and Gadamer see play as fundamental to understand what distinguishes art, Derrida pushes the play of play, a structurality, to its limits where the only way to "grasp" the notion is to invoke the shocking affect of the unthinkable, the monstrous. His strategy is to make unimaginable what we are imagining, to force us always back into the to-and-fro, into the playing of play. As I have been attempting to show, the academic inclination to cease the dancing by focusing on the dance, to stop the moving by backfilling it into movement, to miss the ontogenetic structurality that makes meaning possible by demanding specific meanings, is very much the inclination we have to stop the play of playing. We'll not glimpse the richness of dancing in culture and religion until we allow ourselves to allow the play of the dancing.

LILA, NATARAJA, AND DANCING AS PLAYING

According to the Rig Veda, an ancient Sanskrit text, Lord Brahma, the cosmic self, is a unity, that is, it is undifferentiated and undivided and unreflective, yet Brahma is described as breathing or pulsating by itself without breath. Then, at some moment Brahma began the process of differentiating itself with the rise of creation, agency, and cosmic processes including even destruction. Importantly in this act of self-differentiating the cosmic self, which can only be a unity, simultaneously became one thing and another, that is, self and other. It is perhaps best not to think of this in a temporal and sequential way, but rather in structural terms. Not first there was unity and then there was differentiation into multiplicity, but rather that there is self that is also always other and that such a perspective is not possible in any static sense, but only in movement. It is a being that is also always a becoming. The movement itself is the stability, if one should need it, in (or rather embracing) the cosmic order.

The ancient Hindus described this self-othering (my term) in terms of the concept of *lila*, a Sanskrit term that means play or sport in the sense of diversion, amusement, fun. *Lila* also connotes effortless, rapid movement. The third century text, the *Vedanta Sutra*, states that the creative activity of the gods is *lila* in the same sense as is play in ordinary life.[70] Or as relevant to Brahma, Thibault writes, *lila* "the process of inhalation and exhalation is going on without reference to any extraneous purpose, merely following the law of its own nature. Analogously, the activity of the Lord also may be supposed to be mere sport, proceeding from his own nature, without reference to any purpose."[71] Thus for the Hindus, *lila* or play refers to that paradoxical structurality in which the cosmos is whole yet divided, the divine is one and completely whole and necessarily inclusive, yet differentiated and othered in such distinctions as self and other. Play (*lila*) is what points to this paradox that allows the ideas of creation and cosmos and gods without dismissing them as simply impossible or incredulous. Play points to a self-referential paradox on the order, as Don Handelman suggests, of Epimenides' paradox put one way as "all Cretans are liars; I am a Cretan." This reminds us as well of Zeno's Paradox. The non-resolving resolution to such paradoxes is to embrace the movement that is fueled by the paradox. We can embrace the paradox as opening us to the forced acceptance of something like perpetual motion, or movement itself. And, of course, since we may embrace the primacy of movement we can embrace the paradox as offering insight into more than cosmic processes, the conditions that seemingly impossibly provide context for cosmic processes; for ontogenesis.

Hinduism has a good many ways of articulating or, perhaps better, embodying this idea of *lila*. Handelman has developed a couple of these. While the Hindu concept *maya* appears to have no linguistic connection with *lila*, Handelman finds the two terms related in important ways. The word *maya*, by itself, means craft or skill, yet Handelman finds that when connected with deities it connotes their mysterious management or manipulation of the forces of nature. *Maya* is thus connected with the force of continuing change and becomes associated with the power of illusion, which may not have such a negative connotation as it is often given in Western interpretation. *Maya* then is, Handelman writes, "full of the powers that move the phenomenal cosmos and keep it in motion, in accordance with its own nature; that nature is of 'something constantly being made' (O'Flaherty). *Maya*, one may say, is the management of motion."[72]

Handelman, along with co-author David Shulman, studies in some depth play as a fundamental Hindu concept in their 1997 book *God Inside Out: Siva's Game of Dice* that focuses on, as the subtitle indicates, the Hindu deities engaging in games of chance.

As a quick, but relevant, aside, this may remind us that the late choreographer Merce Cunningham often used chance, including the throw of dice, to determine the movement of his dancers. This strategy surely was to force us to fold our attention back to the dancing and away from some backfilled constructed form. Cunningham was then getting at not some message or meaning to convey to an audience, but to sheer movement or creativity in itself.[73] Years ago I had postmodern dancer Michelle Ellsworth teach a studio in my "Religion and Dance" class. There were 90 of us in a huge studio space. She set forth principles of movement based on the digits in our personal telephone numbers; I don't recall specifically, but something like odd number means move to your right and the value of the digit indicating the number of steps to take, or something on that order. Then all ninety of us, spread throughout this space, moved together with evolving suggestive and chaotic patterns.

An example of the Hindu embodied *lila* is in the story where Krishna as a child holds the whole universe in his mouth. Such common imagery grasps in some measure this inside-outside reversibility associated with play and self-othering. In the self-othering of playing, the gods turn themselves inside out and outside in. Maurice Merleau-Ponty adumbrated reversibility as an aspect of his "ontology of flesh" based on touch and on movement. And interestingly, often when I talk excitedly of such modern, indeed postmodern, ideas to my colleagues who study East Asian traditions, they often look at me with the expression that reads, "Duh! Where have you been?" They have a point.

Even in the broadest terms the paths or ways of life articulated in Hinduism reflect the same *lila* structurality. *Dharma*, which is often associated with the word "duty," is the most common lifeway intent upon following the law, doing one's duty, accepting one's place in the rise and fall of repeating cycles of existence, *samsara* and *karma*, so that the great wheel of existence will continue on forever. Yet, there is no salvation in such an approach, only the evolution and devolution of forms through the endless cycle of life. Even the gods are subject to this cycle. Thus, the alternative to *dharma*, yet only possible if earned through repeated existences in *dharma*, is *moksha* or release. *Moksha* is to assimilate into being which is the still center of the wheel of becoming or understood differently to be one with becoming, or we might say movement itself. There is play (*lila*) in the interdependent ways of *dharma* and *moksha*. They are antithetical, they other one another, yet they are inseparable and interdependent. They are reversible and this reversibility is understood in terms of playing. Much of Hindu literature, I think of the *Bhagavad gita* in particular, spins out the tensions and interconnections, these structuralities that constitute the dynamic in which Hinduism gains its many identities.

It is little wonder that there is an ancient tradition in Hinduism of pointing in the direction of *lila* through reference to dancing as in the figure of Shiva as Nataraja, Lord of Dancing. I introduced and described Nataraja at the beginning of this chapter. I turn now to interconnect the perspectives on playing that I have developed with the Hindu concept of play (*lila*) along with related concepts especially as exemplified or embodied in the figure Nataraja, so that I might enrich this connection of dancing and playing.

Handelman did not do more than mention Nataraja in either his book *God Inside Out* or his article "Passages to Play," yet he discusses the Hindu concept play (*lila*) in the context of Western theories of play, particularly based on the work of Gregory Bateson, and paradox, based particularly on the studies of Rosalie Colie. While I presented a number of ideas of play in earlier sections, I did not include Bateson's although it is certainly among the most cited and influential works on play during the last half century.[74] Bateson's essay, "A Theory of Play and Fantasy," was published in 1955. A key principle of play was developed by Bateson exemplified by his reflection on the experience of watching playing monkeys in a zoo. He understood that their playing was premised on their understanding that the actions they were seemingly performing, such as biting, were not what those actions appeared to be, that is biting, but rather they were playful nips or play bites. He then held that there was a meta-message communicated in the context and actions, and that message is "this is play." Bateson argued that all play includes the message "this is play." Handelman focuses heavily on this insight of Bateson in his discussion of *lila*. He believes that the distinction between "this is play" and "this is not play" is key and thus his article title "Passages to Play." In the movement from not play to play, Handelman dwelled on the boundary between them and conceived the boundary itself as a place, thus in this passage there is in his terms a "way station . . . inside the boundary itself."

Once in the boundary, Handelman holds that three things happen: a frame is created, a paradox of the frame is created, and the paradox is overridden opening the way into play. Handelman charts the passage from not play to play with attention to how fascinating is that non-space in the boundary between play and not-play. Yet, at least from my perspective, completing the passage into play, into Bateson's domain distinguished by the meta-message "this is play," seems to me to lose much because it resolves the paradox, which is equivalent to stopping the play. Derrida, in particular, focused on how the two strategies of interpretation, one to play and the other to stop play, seem most directly relevant as a critique of Handelman's interpretation of *lila* as emerging from a passage. Derrida explicitly rejected this notion of passage that attempts to embrace play, or "this is play," only and he did so in order to defend and preserve the endless oscillatory movement character of play itself. Handelman runs afoul when the paradox encountered in the boundary non-space is more playful than is the play to which he understands it providing a passage into. The play/not-play distinction must not be resolved by a choice or a passage from one to the other; this would be a special case of actually stopping play. Play is then always already there as the vitalizing perpetually moving interactivity that gives energy and potential to all things.

The ancient Indian wisdom *lila* or play corresponds closely with the wisdom that Schiller, Gadamer, Derrida, and others sought to articulate in terms of a discourse on the term "play." It is notable that Schiller wrote a poem on "Dancing," yet he did not connect it with play, and Gadamer acknowledged that there is an etymological link between "play" and "dancing," yet he did not include dancing in his discussion of play, and while the Hindus articulate *lila* so eloquently in the figure of Nataraja, Handelman did little more than mention Nataraja; all these suggest an important, if overlooked, connection between dancing and playing. To adopt Handelman's boundary terminology in the context of Hindu *lila* as presented in the dancing of Shiva, the boundary is that distance that has no dimension but the desire to cross that energizes the dancing movement. In the terms I have been developing an understanding of dancing throughout this book we can see how perfectly it serves to catch the creative endless movement of the paradoxical structurality that is at the core of Hinduism.

To continue to balance the rather abstract philosophical discussion of much of this chapter I will consider another extended cultural example focusing on several Native American communities in the American Southwest. I will also continue to develop the correlation of masking and dancing that I introduced in the Javanese example.

GO UP INTO THE GAPS: PLAY AND NATIVE AMERICAN RELIGIONS

It was a dark and misty winter afternoon. As I crested the hill east of Zuni the familiar sights of Corn Mountain to the south and Zuni village nestled in the valley below greeted me. I thought of Frank Hamilton Cushing's description of Zuni as it first appeared to him in 1879:

> Below and beyond me was suddenly revealed a great red and yellow sandplain . . . To the left, a mile or two away, crowning numberless red foot-hills, rose a huge rock-mountain, a thousand feet high and at least two miles in length along its flat top, which showed, even in the distance, fanciful chiselings by wind, sand, and weather . . .
> Out from the middle of the rock-wall . . . flowed a little rivulet. Emerging from a succession of low mounds beneath me, it wound, like a long whip-lash or the track of an earth-worm, westward through the middle of the sandy plain and out almost to the horizon, where . . . it was lost in the southern shadows of a terraced hill.
> Down behind this hill the sun was sinking, transforming it into a jagged pyramid of silhouette, crowned with a brilliant halo, whence a seeming midnight aurora burst forth through broken clouds, bordering each misty blue island with crimson and gold, then blazing upward in widening lines of light, as if to repeat in the high heavens its earthly splendor.
> A banner of smoke, as though fed from a thousand crater-fires, balanced over this seeming volcano, floating off, in many a circle and surge, on the evening breeze. But I did not realize that this hill, so strange and picturesque, was a city of the habitations of men, until I saw, on the topmost terrace, little specks of black and red moving about against the sky. It seemed still a little island of mesas, one upon

the other, smaller and smaller, reared from a sea of sand, in mock rivalry of the surrounding grander mesas of Nature's rearing.[75]

It is now more than a century later and everything appears the same. Perhaps, I thought, this scene is little different from that seen by Fray Marcos de Niza in May of 1539 when he made the first European contact with native peoples in what we now know as North America. Zuni is on an ancient road traveled by many. Coming here is like traveling back nearly half a millennium. Zuni is fitting to be preserved, as did Aldous Huxley in *A Brave New World*. I began to look forward to seeing religious events out of the past.

But wait! I was brought out of this foolish romantic reverie by a traffic jam. Sitting in my car. Waiting. I felt irritated. I was eager to get to the village. What might I be missing? It would be my first time to experience Shalako. I had read so much about Shalako, a grand ceremonial affair, one of Zuni's most important, occurring early each December. What could be holding up traffic in so remote and ancient a place? Seeing the flashing lights of a police car I concluded it must be an accident. Surely traffic would soon move along. The police car moved very slowly parallel to the line of traffic. Why so slow? As it approached me I could finally see. The police car was escorting a small troupe of Zuni figures along the highway. At the head of the group was a Shalako, a twelve-foot tall feather-topped, bird-headed, beautifully costumed figure. Slowly the procession passed and I was able to move along, park, get a quick bowl of chili, and prepare myself for a magical night at Zuni. Well a little has changed since Cushing's day.

Some years before, I sat atop a pueblo in the Hopi village of Hotteville. The occasion was Niman, the home dance. This stately early August event marks the closing of the kachina season that begins in December. Kachinas, messenger spirits, appear as masked dancers for the last time before returning to their homes in the San Francisco Peaks some ninety miles to the west, easily seen on this brilliant hot day. The sounds—clack, jingle, clack, jingle—announced their arrival. As they entered the village plaza I recognized them as my favorite, Angak'china, the Long Hair kachina. To me, their beauty is somehow in their simplicity. Oh they are elaborate enough with feathers and jewelry, kilts and sashes. But their faces are simple, a small turquois rectangle with simple markings for mouth and eyes, set against long hair flowing from the crown of the head nearly to the waist in front and back. They brought gifts of food. They brought dolls for the children. Their dancing brought life and happiness to everyone. I could feel their power then. As I remember them I feel that power now.

Then there was the time, I've forgotten the year, I visited the Franciscan Fathers at St. Michael's near Window Rock on the Navajo Reservation. I enjoyed the hospitality of the Fathers, though awestruck by the sheer fact that I was walking the same grounds, sleeping under the same roof, where Father Berard Haile had lived so many years of his life. He was a sensitive and insightful friend to Navajos, a devoted inquirer about their religion, though he never participated in nor even directly observed their rituals. The second or third day I was there, after an appropriate time for us all to get acquainted, I was asked if I wanted to see the Navajo ritual art collection. It was not a public display. I felt honored. Once in the little room burgeoning with shelves, cabinets, and drawers I was enthralled by the marvelous things about me. We talked easily of these things. I was invited to look at a set of Navajo *ye'ii* masks kept in a drawer. As the drawer glided open, suddenly it came to me. I knew these masks. They had been given as a set to Father Berard by the family of a deceased singer, or medicine man, who feared, because of their power, to keep them. Father Berard had studied and photographed these very masks in the preparation of his book *Head and Face Masks of the Navajo* (1947). I gazed on the familiar empty buckskin bag-shaped masks. Compared with masks made by most other Native Americans these seem so crude. They are not beautiful, yet they are haunting. I don't know whether it was because I know how powerful Navajos consider these masks or that Father Berard had been involved with them, but I couldn't bring myself to touch them, or even to look long upon them. These same strangely ambivalent feelings returned when, some years later, I was shown two Navajo masks by an art dealer in Chicago.

Masks worn, masks danced, are captivating. They take hold of us. They mesmerize. Their power is both that of beauty and that of darkness. We are attracted, fascinated by masking, yet somehow they also frighten. What is this power? How might we appreciate it even if we know we'll never be able to understand it? These examples of masks used in ritual dancing by Native American cultures are three among hundreds. As introduced in my consideration of Javanese masked dancing (*wayang topeng*) there is a homology and compatibility between the masking structurality that interconnects masker and mask and the dancing structurality that interconnects dancer and dance. It is not surprising that masking and dancing are conjoined in self-othering cultural and religious activities. The perspective drawn on to help illuminate Javanese masking and dancing was Merleau-Ponty's flesh ontology. Here I will approach these Native American maskings and dancings from the perspective of play.

If anything distinguishes a mask as an object it is that it is a rigid sculpted face. This characteristic holds for these Native American masks as well. It is like a face in form only; it has facial features but no facial sensuality. Notably most masks are self-consciously false; that is, mask makers appear to take every opportunity to make a mask so it will never be mistaken for a living face. Masking is not disguise.

Yet a mask without a masker, the one who bears the mask, is inanimate, a piece of sculpture, an unused prop. Such objects are often used as wall decorations. Masking, as a ritual and cultural activity, is always the conjunction of the two, the mask and the masker. At the basic definitional level the concept mask requires the conjunction of these two elements. Even the English word mask holds this structurality. The word mask may be a verb meaning "to mask," yet it may also be a noun referring to a physical object. There is a double nature necessary to the very mask idea. It is not a doubling that is eventually resolved, but is ever at play.

This simple observation of the double nature of masking, that is, the interplay of masker and mask, suggests the immediate relevance of play as I have presented and discussed it. I will pursue the conjunction of playing to masking. A mask as an object, rigid and fixed, and artificial in form, is often used to present the eternal and universal idea of a given figure, the figure the mask presents. Apart from the masked presentation this figure has no physical, no sensuous nature, but remains pure form, idea, concept, or virtual. Hence the masking presents rather than represents. The masker, apart from a mask, is a living breathing sentient being. As a human being, he or she, in Schiller's terms, most fully realizes him or herself in the interplay of sensuous and formal impulses. Yet, as masker, the formal drive of the masker is made subsidiary to the sensuous self, since in donning a mask one gives up the form that identifies the human individual. The formal character of the masker becomes coincident with the being presented as the mask, that is, the masker is othered. Masking heightens some aspects of human sensuality. Behind the mask a human masker is, in one sense, reduced in the direction of his pure sensuality. The physical mask at once limits and controls the sensual perceptual faculties that distinguish the nature of the masker as a human being. The masker's vision is impaired, as are his or her senses of hearing and touch, as are his or her abilities to communicate through speech and facial expression. But as the masker's sensual faculties are altered he or she provides a sensuality, a living existence, to an otherwise lifeless form, the mask. This sensual element tempers the pure formality and changelessness apparent in the mask by bringing it into concrete actions, movement that is identified with the mask entity, in a specific time and place. Both mask and masker must exist. Each exerts influence on the other. Masking brings self-moving, sentient, sensual, and physical existence to the pure form of deity, spirit, or concept while at the same time stripping the human masker of his or her own formal self only to engage him or her with another form.

The interconnection of masker and mask and the actions of masking constitute a field of play. The gap between the entity presented through masking and the human being underlying the presentation is a field of play; a space in which the figure presented comes into physical being; a field in which humans come to know through experience, from the inside out (proprioception and touch), the spirits and deities on whom their lives and world depend. In this play between the two something emerges, comes to life, that is much greater than either one separately or even by the simple addition of the two. In the oscillatory movement of play that is masking, the virtual is animated and manifested.

Schiller wrote that play is a reciprocal action between two drives (the sensual and formal, in this case), reciprocal action of such a kind that the one both gives rise to, and sets limits to, the activity of the other, and in which each in itself achieves its highest manifestation precisely by reason of the other being active. If a spirit, a deity, a mythic figure, is formalized in a mask, the represented entity becomes manifest, comes to life, through the interplay with the sentient human masker. While one may contemplate and study the forms of the spirits, gods, and mythic figures, in the activity of masking a human being actually manifests these figures, stands inside of them, giving them sensual existence. The masker fills up and comes to know the form represented by the mask, a feeling experiential kind of knowing.

Masking is a remarkable example of what Schiller recognized as play. He called it "living form," a term that would serve well as a synonym for the *energia/ergon*, as Gadamer put it, of masking. And to continue to follow Schiller, it is "living form" that is beauty. It is the moving in concert of the sensual and formal drives that gives rise to the play drive and hence to beauty. This vital conjunction is also necessary in masking. If the masker does not know the figure whose face he or she is bearing; if the masker refuses to yield his or her personal identity to play the mask (though this is unbelievably difficult to do); the masking is likely to appear false, awkward, anomalous—the sensual aspect of the masking prevails over the formal. If the mask as a form, as an ideal, so overwhelms the masker as to render him or her lifeless, unable to move or act, stricken under the weight of the idea that must be made manifest, the masking fails; it is but a tableau. Here the formal aspect of the masking prevails over the sensual. It is only in the oscillation, the vitalizing reciprocal self-moving engagement of the mask and masker, the formal and the sensuous, that masking achieves "living form," that masking becomes beautiful, manifests beauty.

Entrainment is perhaps another way to describe this working together that yields living form, a way of understanding what Schiller meant by "in concert." When two people walk together, they almost immediately begin to match strides. When a number of people are hammering together, they will fall into a hammered rhythm.[76] This is entrainment and it occurs with masking as well. Once in costume, masked, and in the masking events, the masker's movements, gestures, and postures entrain with the character of the masked entity, as it is understood by the whole masking community. When entrainment occurs in masking, the entity presented by the masking comes to life and the maskers achieve experiential knowledge of this entity. This is "living form"; this is beauty.

Around the world cultural and ritual practices commonly conjoin masking with dancing. This should be no surprise because both masking and dancing exist as structuralities characterizable as playing and self-othering. For both there are the two that are also always one. For both there is a gap, a distance that is filled, but never crossed by living movement. This distance is virtual in dancing where the dancer and dance are one body; the distance is a slight opening, like synapse, in masking where mask and masker, like puppet and shadow, are physically separate yet inseparable. The entrainment of mask/masker is most readily enacted in dancing where the playing self-othering multiplies and compounds.

With this exciting way of understanding masking and masked dancing I want to return to Zuni at the time of Shalako. Late that December afternoon crowds gathered along the Zuni River at a place where a tiny bridge had been constructed of mud and stone. In time a procession of masked figures, called the Council of the Gods, crossed the bridge and entered the village. Leading the group was a young figure carrying a firebrand, Shulaawisi, the fire god. His mask and body were painted black with blotches of light-colored dots all over. Next came Sayatasha and Hututu, the Rain Gods of the North and South. Two yucca-carrying whippers, Salimopiya, came last. The group proceeded to six locations in Zuni Village where holes had been dug, representing the six directions. At each hole the group deposited prayer plumes and sprinkled corn meal. These rites blessed the village, bringing it into correspondence with the order of the whole world in accordance with myth and history. The procession ended at one of the Shalako houses prepared for this event. Here Sayatasha faced Hututu and called "Hu-u-u." Hututu responded "Hu-tu-tu, Hu-tu-tu." Then the group entered the house.

Later that evening I stood for hours in cold ankle-deep mud outside this house enthralled by what I was seeing and hearing. Inside this Shalako house was a long rectangular room. On one end were an altar and a place designated for singers and drummers. Many Zuni people had gathered in the large open portion of the room sitting on chairs and benches. A dance corridor remained open along one long interior side of the room. It was along this dance corridor sitting on benches that the Council of the Gods took its position.

With their masks propped atop their now strangely human heads, members of the Council began to chant in unison. This rhythmic flow of speech continued hour after hour throughout the evening. Not only was this most wonderful, but amazingly the Council shared the house with a pair of Shalako dancers who were performing their own, yet different, chant; two groups, occupying the same space, chanting different words, hour upon hour. The overlapping sounds, in a language I did not understand, were enchanting. I could not seem to stop watching and listening.

Near midnight, the chanting complete, all took a break from the ritual intensity to eat and to rest. Finally the dancing began featuring the wonderful swooping dances of the Shalako. The Koyemshi, a troupe of mud-head clowns, performed their buffoonery in another house a short walk away.

The complexity of Shalako is daunting. Shalako is actually a many day performance culminating nearly a year of extensive preparation. The members of the Council of the Gods spend much of their time for a year enacting the responsibilities of their offices. Shalako requires the building, or at least the refurbishing, of six to eight dwellings in which to house the event. And Shalako is but one of many Zuni masking rituals performed throughout the year.

Confining our attention to but one figure, Sayatasha, we may begin to appreciate more deeply the play of masking. Around the time of the winter solstice, shortly after Shalako is performed, the members of the Council of the Gods who will serve the following year are chosen. After these men are chosen they make offerings to the ancestors at the river, a first performance of the ritual acts they will conduct daily until they perform Shalako almost a year later. Every night they meet to discuss aspects of Shalako and late at night they learn the prayers they will recite during Shalako. Every morning they arise before dawn and prepare to offer prayer meal to the rising sun. Each month at the time of the full moon they offer prayersticks to shrines and at the new moon they travel many miles to plant prayersticks at springs in the mountains south of Zuni.

The Zuni man who will portray Sayatasha, the leader of the Council, is called by the title Sayatasha Mosona and in all that he does during this year he must act in an exemplary manner. He must work hard physically, socially, mentally, and religiously. He is responsible for the Zuni religious calendar, reckoned primarily by the position of the moon. Sayatasha Mosona must notify all parties at the appropriate time to prepare for ceremonial occasions. This man must even walk like Sayatasha, a gait that is ponderous, with exaggerated strides. Sayatasha walks slowly, poising each foot in the air momentarily before bringing it heavily to the ground. Like the Rain Priest he will portray, this Zuni man is sought out for counsel and pointed to as an exemplar of Zuni life ways. Sayatasha Mosana is building through extensive repetition deliberate movements constituting the gestures and postures distinctive to Sayatasha. In this long process he is becoming Sayatasha in his bodily tissues.

The Sayatasha mask and costume are elaborate. To examine the appearance of Sayatasha demonstrates the many attributes of Zuni culture and religion that are brought into play in his masking. Sayatasha is both Rain Priest of the North and Bow Priest. He is the Chief of the Kachina Village which lies beneath a lake two days walk to the west of Zuni, the home of Kachinas and the home of the dead. This remarkable figure, who appears but one time each year at Zuni on this Shalako night, is thus associated with both agriculture and hunting, with both life and death, with both the human Zuni world and the world of kachinas and the dead. The mask and costume reflect the conjunction and interplay of these associations.

The mask is bell jar shaped. Atop the head are downy feathers, blue jay feathers, and feathers of summer birds all fastened to a prayerstick attached to the head, a designation of a Rain Priest. Sayatasha means "Long Horn," a name he is sometimes called when Zunis use English. This designation refers to his distinguishing feature of a single long horn extending outward from the right side of his head. This horn is for long life. A large flat "ear" extends outward from the head on the left. The right eye is a short slit, short, according to Zuni reckoning, for witches that their lives be short; the left eye corresponds with a long line that extends outward into the "ear," long so that the lives of good people will be long. Black goat hair hangs from the horn and over the forehead. A white cotton thread hangs down behind. The elk skin collar is stuffed with wool.

Sayatasha wears a white cotton shirt cut full over which he wears an embroidered white blanket fastened on the right side. He wears a white cotton dance kilt with a blue band, an embroidered sash, a red women's belt, fringed white buckskin leggings, and blue dance moccasins. The cotton dance kilt and shirt and the dance moccasins are those of a Rain Priest and are associated with bringing rain. He carries a fawn-skin quiver over his right shoulder. He wears many necklaces and bracelets. In his right hand he carries a deer scapulae rattle and in his left a bow and arrow and many prayersticks. The quiver, bow and arrows, prayersticks, and rattle identify Sayatasha as a hunter and warrior.

Though this is but a superficial consideration of a single figure in the complex Shalako rituals placed loosely in his cultural and religious contexts, it is clear that Sayatasha is not merely a man wearing a mask and costume. Sayatasha as a Zuni kachina engages a vast field of play that is the vitality of Zuni culture and history. A particular Zuni man has practiced and played almost constantly for a year to present Sayatasha in living movement and form. This field of play is activated and realized in the concentrated form of Sayatasha through the masking. It is the contrasting and even contradictory aspects which, when brought together in this masking, initiate a play that has the potential to produce a living form, to be experienced as beauty.

Sayatasha is at once Sayatasha and Sayatasha Mosona: spirit and human, eternal and mortal, form and sense, of the domain of the dead and of the living. Sayatasha is at once Rain Priest and Bow Priest; at once hunter and warrior; bringer of rain and long life, controller of weather, while at the same time killer of witches, protector, deer hunter, and killer of enemies.

Indwelling Sayatasha's form is, for a Zuni man, an entry into Zuni philosophy and belief, but it is also to bear the responsibility and to be the vehicle for transforming these formal aspects of Zuni religious life into the experience and history of the Zuni people. Masking Sayatasha is, through play, to bring into concert many pairs of mutually exclusive attributes that constitute Zuni reality. The play does not resolve these attributes into unity; the play demonstrates that Zuni religious culture is given vitality in the interaction among these forever opposing and contrasting values and attributes.

Other Native American masking examples will be useful to expand and enrich the nexus of dancing and masking, but first I want to comment on how I see this notion of play as characterizing much of Native American religious experience. To focus on the play of Native American religious action is to articulate the dynamics of what Jonathan Z. Smith meant when he said, "it is precisely the juxtaposition, the incongruity between the expectation and the actuality that serves as a vehicle for religious experience."[77] When we think of religions, especially Native American religions, we tend to think of principles like balance, harmony, centeredness, piety, respect for the earth, kinship with the animals and plants. What we often fail to realize is that a religion characterized in this way would scarcely be either alive or real. Holding this romantic image, we fail to see that religion generally, and most certainly Native American religions, is a process of manipulation and negotiation and application. It is a process of playing in which the many formal dimensions of tradition are strapped on like masks and made to dance and have presence in an ever changing and always demanding world. It is interplay in this gap that gives life to any religious tradition and it is the extraordinary playfulness of Native American religions that distinguishes them among religions.

For a number of years I lived in Tempe, Arizona, just three miles from the Yaqui village, Guadalupe. Every year during the season of Lent I would drop by Guadalupe now and then to observe the various events of their Easter celebration. The Yaqui people lived for centuries in Sonora, Mexico before many were forcibly displaced. Some established communities in Arizona. Their history is remarkable. Yaquis effectively maintained separation from the Spanish for nearly a century after the first contact in 1533. After shunning Spanish influence for nearly a century, suddenly, it would seem, early in the 17th century they requested missionaries be sent to them. The Jesuits arrived in 1617 and in two years the Yaquis had undergone remarkable transformation in their cultural and religious lives. They became Christian at that time, but in their own way. For one hundred fifty years they allowed missionaries to live among them, but finally in 1767 they found Mexican pressure so great that they expelled the missionaries. More than a century followed during which the Yaquis enjoyed an autonomous existence. However, though they fought gallantly, in 1887 they were overcome by Mexican troops and dispersed far and wide.

In time, having formed communities near Tucson and Phoenix, some of the Yaquis began to revive their cultural and religious practices, especially those associated with Yaqui Easter. The whole season of Lent is filled with ritual and ceremony centered on the small Yaqui church in Guadalupe, standing in the shadow of the larger Catholic mission church just to the north of it. I will not describe the complex of events enacted throughout the whole Easter season, only those of the climactic day, Easter Saturday.

During Easter week the attention of Guadalupe is focused on the Yaqui church and the plaza which extends to the east in front of it. Many of the events—the processions around the way of the cross, the capture and crucifixion of Christ, the control of the church by the evil Chapayekas—are somber and heavy in tone. Yet adjoining the plaza in the area in front of the Catholic mission church, a carnival with rides and booths seems to foreshadow and presage the coming victory over evil and its celebration in fiesta.

Easter Saturday is the dramatic climax of this old struggle between good and evil. Early Saturday morning the fearful Chapayekas, who have captured and crucified Christ and taken over the church, leave this domain and in procession escort an effigy of their leader, Judas, into the plaza and affix it to a large cross. They retire to the fringes of the village. Throughout the morning people from the community gather. Many Yaquis approach the anti-Christ to affix a token of penance to him, usually a scarf.

Pascola dancers, with their small masks on the sides or backs of their heads, mingle among the crowds with coffee cans receiving donations as a man, speaking alternately in Yaqui, Spanish, and English, informs the visitors about what is happening and repeatedly asks for donations. Vendors sell food and drinks. There is an air of expectation. Late in the morning the Maestro, or leader of the Yaqui church, along with a small group of worshippers carrying a cross, appears in the plaza and begins a worship service read from a Yaqui book of worship. The group proceeds slowly in the direction of the church. Once they reach the church they enter followed by many women and children. A curtain is drawn across the door.

At the east end of the plaza appear black-garbed Pilates, representing soldiers. In two lines, one formed on each side of the plaza, they march slowly forward to a drumbeat with an occasional eerie flute melody. The Chapayekas follow, prancing and playing, firing toy cap guns and clacking their wooden daggers on their wooden swords. They often stop to wiggle their hips to awaken their belts of horn rattles. The long bands of cocoon rattles wrapped about their ankles emphasize in sound their every step.

The masks of the Chapayekas are wild and colorful. Many look something like cow heads, but others clearly represent stereotype images particularly of ethnic groups: a yellow-faced Chinaman with pigtail; a red-faced, big-nosed, cigar store Indian with long braided black hair. European Americans are not always absent from masked representation. At the end of the Nixon era one Chapayeka was an unquestionable representation of Richard Nixon. Chapayekas are a strange mixture of fearfulness and humor.

This huge procession of perhaps a hundred men marches forward into the plaza. Then retreat. Again and again. On each advance they move closer to the church. Finally, at mid plaza, the lines stop moving. They wait in silent readiness. Suddenly the church bell begins rapidly tolling. Simultaneously the lines of Pilates and Chapayekas rush noisily toward the church. As they approach the church the curtain covering the door flies open and the Pascolas along with many women and children rush out, filling the area immediately in front of the church. They are armed with hands full of flower petals and green leaves. As the evil ones approach they are pelted with flowers and leaves, the transformed blood of Christ. Repelled, the Chapayekas return to their positions mid plaza and reassemble for another attack.

As the women and children return to the church, some of the Chapayekas, those newest to this role, fall to the ground in the area around Judas. They crawl forward. There, met by their family sponsors, they remove their masks under the protection of a blanket or an overcoat. They leave their masks and their daggers and swords at the foot of the Judas effigy. With unmasked heads covered, the sponsors rush these maskers at a full run to the church where they are rededicated to Christ. Other sponsors approach the remaining Chapayekas who remove some aspects of their costumes—rattles, blankets, sandals; an apparent sign of their loss of power.

Quiet returns. Once again the bell rings. The second attack is launched. Again the women and children are successful with their flowers in repelling the onslaught. Other Chapayekas give up their masks. Those remaining remove even more of their costumes.

One final attack is carried out. On its failure even the last of the Chapayekas remove their masks and are rushed to the church.

Chapayeka masks now surround the huge straw-stuffed Judas figure. The swords and daggers are all propped in a line around this figure. As the last of the head-covered figures reaches the church, the Judas effigy surrounded by the masks, swords and daggers, and boxes of debris generated by all these events is set afire. It is quickly an inferno.

Simultaneously, a troupe of Matachini Dancers enters the plaza and begins to dance and the Pascolas joined by a Deer Dancer appear with their musicians immediately in front of the church. It is fiesta time.

There is really so much to be considered in terms of the play of the Yaqui masking on this occasion. There is the play of the past and the present. The ancient Pascola masks representing animals appear in the same event as the Chapayeka representations of contemporary stereotypes. The Yaquis seem masterful at playing the past and the present in the same plaza as a way of vitalizing a hopeful future. Other Yaqui masking features are of special interest to me. The men who mask the Chapayekas comprehend the power of the mask. It is a power that threatens to overwhelm the masker with the character and attributes that the mask presents. In recognition of this power and as protection against it, the masker wears a rosary about his neck. All the time that the mask is on his head, he places the cross of the rosary in his mouth. Constantly he must pray or say the name "Jesus." This is his protection. It is also essential to the *energia* of the masking, the interplay of the masker and mask, the back and forth between all of the opposing valences represented. There is always a fearful or negative element of playing and self-othering. This fear or risk is the qualitative opening manifesting as living movement. Derrida wrote that "to risk meaning nothing is to start to play." The Yaqui masker, by carrying a rosary cross in his mouth, is demonstrating a determination to maintain that masking is and must be maintained as a double identity. Indeed those who portray Chapayekas often talk of the difficulty, but necessity, of having to act in ways that oppose their personal behavior. This reminds me of the same concern expressed by trance dancers in Bali. The masker is not the entity presented by the mask, yet clearly the masker is that entity for the Chapayeka cannot exist without the masker. And the masker experiences being a Chapayeka in his masking activities. The mask form is understood as a powerful presence, especially when enlivened through masking and worn by a human masker. This conjunction of form (the presentation of evil) and sense (the religious Yaqui) must remain at play. Each one both limits and makes possible the existence of the other.

Another very moving aspect of this event is when the Chapayeka maskers remove their masks and are rushed with their heads covered to the church. It is as though the masker, once free of the Chapayeka mask, the form assumed for the masking event, is pure sense, that is, formless, a moment of mere sensation. Certainly with head covered he is faceless, he has no identity. He must be rushed to the church, the opposite pole from the Judas effigy and the Chapayeka mask that has been his form, to acquire another form, this one in the church in the image of Christ and the good.

Finally, in its annual enactment of the Easter pageantry, the Yaqui demonstrate the importance of the play between good and evil. Every Easter, good is victorious. That much is certain. But what makes this victory powerful correlates directly with the eternal presence of evil. If the evil is not powerfully present, how can the victory of good have meaning? And, of course, the struggle continues year after year in the play of masking.

There is one final example of masking that will further illustrate how Native Americans commonly see the double nature of masking, the double nature that I am articulating in terms of play. In northern Arizona Hopi children are carefully protected against seeing the masked kachinas, spirit messengers, without their masks as they are guarded against seeing masks not in use. They understand the kachinas to be exactly what they appear to be, spirit beings who come to Hopi bringing rain, food, and life. At the age of eight to ten, children are initiated into the Kachina Cult and thereupon formally begin their active religious lives.

The climactic event of this initiation rite is when the children are invited into a kiva, or ceremonial chamber, to witness a dance they have never before been permitted to see. The kachinas enter the kiva climbing down a ladder extending into the kiva from a rooftop hatchway. As the kachinas appear they come without masks. The children suddenly recognize their male relatives and neighbors. Many experience this event as a horrible disenchantment. They feel the adults have lied to them and they wonder whether they will ever be able to trust them again. In a short time, of course, all of these children are involved in the practice of Hopi religion. The boys will soon begin to be maskers themselves.

What is remarkable from the perspective I am developing is that this disenchantment is structurally parallel to a demonstration that the mask and masker must always be understood as a field of interacting play. It is difficult to imagine how the distinction between masker and masked identity could be more dramatically established than in this initiation event. Where from the children's perspective there was wholeness and unity of these entities in their midst, initiation divides them, breaking them in two, divided by a space, a gap that seems unbridgeable. All the more remarkable is that by conjoining this revelation with the commencement of the formal religious life, it must be concluded that the Hopi recognize the religious importance of the play between mask and masker, that in this gap is the play that provides energy to ongoing cultural and religious life. Though the children feel the possibility of truth has been lost for them, they will soon experience that it is in this field of play, in the gap between mask and masker, that the vital character of Hopi religious life is experienced. They will come to know the power of this play in their experience of masking the kachinas.[78]

We are accustomed to various metaphors to describe the character of Native American religions; many are romantic projections. Harmony, as it occurs in music, may be a better metaphor than balance, though both are so often used. Musical harmony requires the interplay of wave patterns that modify one another to produce a whole array of overtones. Harmony occurs through the interplay of separate yet interacting vibrations, not through their resolution into a single tone. Sound is always in process, always passing away as it is coming into being, always creatively interacting with other sounds. Sound is oscillation, movement. Sound is impossible to freeze or to stop without losing it all together. Various notes when played together, interact, create harmonics, produce living form, or beauty as Schiller put it, but only because there are gaps, differences, between the tones that interact. It is in these gaps that not only Native American religions, but also all religions, exist. Only here in these gaps is there the potential for play, for movement, for vitality.

Indeed, gap is a provocative metaphor that invokes the dynamics and vitality of Native American religions. So where, beside maskings and dancings, are these gaps to be found? Mythology and ritual, by their natures, create gaps. They are distinguished by their being at once apart from what seems necessary to life and the basis for all of reality, essential to a meaningful life. Many view mythology and ritual as guidebooks, charters, or paradigms for proper living. In this limiting view the religious objective would be to diminish the gap between life and these religious forms. Any disparity between the two is somehow a human failing. Such views remove the play, stop the movement, end the dancing. It is much more fruitful to see mythology and ritual as, even by their natures, gap creators. To understand that the very character that distinguishes myth and ritual is to acknowledge that they open gaps between them and life as lived in which the cultural tradition is played out. The gap created between the mythic and the quotidian worlds, between ritual and non-ritual life, affords human beings the opening in which they must play out their destinies. To close the gap, to live in myth, to make every act a ritual act, is tantamount to destroying human life altogether, certainly it would be the end of religion.

While I believe that to view religion from the perspective of play I have here developed may serve to illuminate the religious vitality of all human beings, there are many signs that Native Americans have very playful religions. Dancing is a near synonymy with religion for Native Americans. Among the religions of the world, few have so elaborate or extensive a use of masking. Native Americans incorporate, in some of their most important religious ceremonials, the performances of clowns. The story traditions about fools and tricksters are widely understood as essential to the proper development of life. The ritual arts are rarely confused with the fine arts, though in form they may be indistinguishable.

The religious value of ritual art forms is assured in widespread practices of destroying ritual art in its use or after it has served its purpose. Navajos never keep sandpaintings nor even allow them to be photographed. Pueblos whitewash and repaint kiva walls, so richly decorated every season with murals. Yaquis burn the Chapayeka masks. Ritual masks are carefully stored by the Pueblos and in some cultures, the Seneca for example, masks are fed and considered to be alive. Pipes are disassembled and kept in bundles. Of course, many Native American cultures have developed craft arts that parallel these ritual arts, but most make very clear distinctions between objects made for sale as crafts and authentic ritual art forms. Such acts assure that form does not appear alone, but that it is always conjoined with the sensuous. It is in the interplay that these objects are religiously powerful, that they become truly beautiful.

Native American religions are distinguished in a playful celebration of the gaps, whose spirit and vitality is nicely caught in a provocative passage written by Annie Dillard:

> Ezekiel excoriates false prophets as those who have "not gone up into the gaps." The gaps are the thing. The gaps are the spirit's one home, the altitudes and latitudes so dazzlingly spare and clean that the spirit can discover itself for the first time like a once-blind man unbound. The gaps are the clefts in the rock where you cower to see the back parts of God; they are the fissures between mountains and cells the wind lances through, the icy narrowing fiords splitting the cliffs of mystery. Go up into the gaps. If you can find them; they shift and vanish too. Stalk the gaps. Squeak into a gap in the soil, turn, and unlock—more than a maple—a universe. This is how you spend this afternoon, and tomorrow morning, and tomorrow afternoon. Spend the afternoon. You can't take it with you.[79]

NOTES

1. Ananda Coomaraswamy, "The Dance of Shiva," (New York: Sunwise Turn, 1924), 69-70.

2. Coomaraswamy, "The Dance of Shiva," 70. The text is Kadavul Mamunivar's *Tiruvatavurar Puranam*.

3. Coomaraswamy, "The Dance of Shiva," 72.

4. Coomaraswamy, "The Dance of Shiva," 74-75.

5. Schiller does not discuss what he means by concert.

6. See Elizabeth M. Wilkinson and L. A. Willoughby, translators and editors, *Friedrich Schiller, On the Aesthetic Education of Man in a Series of Letters* (Oxford: Clarendon Press, 1967), p. clxxxvi; and Susanne Millar, *The Psychology of Play* (Baltimore: Penguin Books, 1968), 15.

7. Johan Huizinga, *Homo Ludens: A Study of the Play Element in Culture* (Boston: The Beacon Press, 1950, trans. of 1944 German edition), 168.

8. Huizinga's book may be cast in a much needed critical light once the discussion of play from Schiller to Derrida has been traced.

9. Immanuel Kant, *Critique of Judgment*, translated by J. C. Meredith (New York: Oxford University Press, 1973) as quoted in Mark Taylor, *Deconstruction in Context: Literature and Philosophy* (Chicago: University of Chicago Press, 1986), 39.

10. Schiller here anticipates Baudrillard's distinction between seduction and production.

11. Kant, *Critique of Judgment*, 47.

12. Kant, *Critique of Judgment*, 56.

13. All references to Schiller's letters will be made in the text referring to Letter and paragraph. The source is *Friedrich Schiller, On the Aesthetic Education of Man in a Series of Letters*, edited and translated by E. M. Wilkinson and L. A. Willoughby (Oxford: Clarendon Press, 1967).

14. Reminiscent of Maurice Merleau-Ponty's "lived body" and his rejection of a simple mind/body duality.

15. Anticipating Merleau-Ponty's distinction of the interdependence of the visible and the invisible.

16. The word "structurality" is an abstract noun denoting the state, condition, or quality of having the character of structure. Having come to believe that play is not best understood as a thing, experience, state of mind, or kind of activity but rather as a particular kind of condition of a thing, an experience, a state of mind, or activity, it requires this peculiar sort of nondesignation.

17. Anthony Savile, *Aesthetic Reconstructions: The Seminal Writings of Lessing, Kant and Schiller* (Oxford: Basil Blackwell, 1987), Chapters 7 & 8.

18. Hans-Georg Gadamer held a similar view as will be discussed below.

19. He anticipates Bateson's discussion of playing containing the metamessage "this is play."

20. "The play of substitution" has been used to describe Schiller's style and structure. Wilkinson and Willoughby indicate their preference for the term "tautology" in the attempt to counteract what they see as the tendency others have had to make too much of some ponderousness of Schiller's style. It seems to me that their reticence to use the term "play" is consistent throughout the work with their basic misunderstanding of it. They tend to equate play with the light, the trivial, even in contrast with Schiller's much more complex understanding.

21. See Wilkinson and Willoughby, *Friedrich Schiller*, 322-6.

22. Wilkinson and Willoughby, *Friedrich Schiller*, cxxii.

23. Wilkinson and Willoughby, *Friedrich Schiller*, lvi. And, of course, this metaphor is especially appropriate since the original meaning of *Spiel*, as Gadamer reminds us, is dance. It is also notable that Schiller wrote a poem titled "The Dance."

24. This structure is the observation described by Wilkinson and Willoughby, *Friedrich Schiller*, li.

25. His use of chiasmus is discussed in Wilkinson and Willoughby, *Friedrich Schiller*, lxviii-lxx and in Elizabeth M. Wilkinson, "Reflections After Translating Schiller's *Letters On the Aesthetic Education of Man*," in *Schiller Bicentenary Lecture*, edited by F. Norman (London: University of London Institute of Germanic Languages and Literatures, 1960), 63-66. It should be read with Merleau-Ponty's and Bateson's separate discussions of chiasm.

26. See the discussion of *Schein* in Wilkinson and Willoughby, *Friedrich Schiller*, 327-9.

27. This consideration of chiasm anticipates Merleau-Ponty's "flesh ontology."

28. This suggests a relation to the distinction of trompe l'oeil (see Baudrillard's discussion in *Seduction*] and to the "reality" model for film.

29. Hans-Georg Gadamer, *Truth and Method* (New York: The Seabury Press, 1975), p. 93.

30. Gadamer, *Truth and Method*, 91.

31. Gadamer, *Truth and Method*, 91.

32. Gadamer, *Truth and Method*, 91.

33. Gadamer, *Truth and Method*, 91. This discussion ought to be related to the concepts of "pure depth" and "flesh."

34. Gadamer's discussions of play may be found principally in *Truth and Method*, 91-119, and in "The Relevance of the Beautiful," 23-30, and "The Play of Art," 123-30, both appearing in *The Relevance of the Beautiful and Other Essays*, translated by Nicholas Walker, edited by Robert Bernasconi (Cambridge: Cambridge University Press, 1986).

35. Gadamer, "The Relevance of the Beautiful," 22-23.

36. Movement, particularly self-actuated movement, has become an important consideration for much of my current work. It should more extensively inform this discussion of play.

37. Gadamer, *Truth and Method*, 97.

38. Of course it was Derrida who wrote "to risk meaning nothing is to start to play." I think this idea of risk is also related to that of "incomplete reversibility" which should also be a consideration related to play.

39. Gadamer, *Truth and Method,* 94.

40. Gadamer, *Truth and Method,* 97.

41. Gadamer, *Truth and Method,* 111.

42. Gadamer, *Truth and Method,* 102.

43. Gadamer, "The Play of Art," 126.

44. Gadamer, "The Play of Art," 101.

45. Gadamer, "The Play of Art," 101-2.

46. Gadamer, "The Play of Art," 101.

47. Gadamer frequently discusses mimesis. See "The Festive Character of Theatre," 64; "Art and Imitation," especially 98-99; "Poetry and Mimesis;" "The Play of Art," 127-9; and *Truth and Method,* 104-5. This discussion anticipated Baudrillard's seduction/production (see below Chapter 5 *Seducing*) distinction and relates to Walter Benjamin's discussion of "aura" in "original" art in his essay "Art in the Age of Mechanical Reproduction," 1929.

48. Gadamer, "The Play of Art," 127.

49. Gadamer, "The Play of Art," 128-9.

50. Gadamer, "Poetry and Mimesis," 121.

51. Gadamer, "The Festive Character of Theatre," 64.

52. Gadamer, "Art and Imitation," 99.

53. Gadamer, "The Play of Art," 130.

54. Gadamer, "The Play of Art," 126. My discussion of "self-othering" in dancing is related.

55. Gadamer, "The Relevance of the Beautiful," 29.

56. Gadamer, "The Relevance of the Beautiful," 29.

57. Jacques Derrida, "Structure, Sign, and Play in the Discourse of the Human Sciences," in *The Languages of Criticism and the Science of Man,* edited by Richard Macksey and Eugene Donato (Baltimore: The Johns Hopkins Press, 1970), 247-265.

58. Derrida, "Structure, Sign, and Play," 247-8.

59. Similar to Jean Baudrillard's discussion of seduction as an oscillation of presence and absence in *Seduction* (New York: St. Martin's Press, 1990)

60. Derrida, "Structure, Sign, and Play," 249.

61. Derrida, "Structure, Sign, and Play," 249.

62. Derrida, "Structure, Sign, and Play," 249.

63. Derrida, *"Différance,"* in *Speech and Phenomena: And Other Essays on Husserl's Theory of Signs* (Evanston: Northwestern University Press, 1973), 129.

64. Derrida, *Speech and Phenomena,* 134.

65. Christopher Norris, *Deconstruction: Theory and Practice* (London and New York: Metheuen, 1982).

66. Derrida, "Structure, Sign, and Play," 265.

67. Derrida's discussion of interpretation parallels Jonathan Z. Smith's discussion of "locative" and "utopian" mapping strategies.

68. Derrida, "Structure, Sign, and Play," 265.

69. Derrida, "Structure, Sign, and Play," 265.

70. Donald Handelman, "Passages to Play: Paradox and Process," *Play & Culture,* 5.1 (1992): 8.

71. Quoted in Handelman, "Passages to Play," 8.

72. Handelman, "Passages to Play," 9.

73. See José Gil and Brian Massumi's discussions of Cunningham's choreography in Brian Massumi, *Semblance and Event: Activist Philosophy and the Occurrent Arts* (Cambridge: MIT Press, 2011),138-44.

74. Handelman also mentions Huizinga's *Homo Ludens,* which I think is not a very useful or insightful book, yet it remains broadly influential it would seem.

75. Frank Hamilton Cushing, "My Adventures in Zuni," *Century Illustrated Magazine* 25 (1882). Reprinted *Zuni: Selected Writings of Frank Hamilton Cushing,* edited by Jesse Green (Lincoln: University of Nebraska Press, 1979), 47-8.

76. I experienced this entrainment personally when I visited a black smithy in Bamako, Mali.

77. Jonathan Z. Smith, "Map is Not Territory," in *Map is Not Territory* (Chicago: University of Chicago Press, 1990).

78. Sam Gill, "Disenchantment." *Parabola* I:3 (1976): 6-13. Reprinted in *I Became Part of It: Sacred Dimensions in Native American Life*, edited by D. M. Dooling and Paul Jordan-Smith (New York: Parabola Books, 1989), 106-119; and Sam Gill, "Hopi Kachina Cult Initiation: The Shocking Beginning to the Hopi's Religious Life," *Journal of the American Academy of Religion* XLV 2, Supplement (June 1977), A: 447-464.

79. Annie Dillard, *Pilgrim at Tinker Creek* (New York: Bantam Books, 1974).

FIVE

Seducing

BOLERO

When I was studying dancing in Costa Rica a few years ago I fell in love with bolero. It must be considered the national social dance of Costa Rica, yet it is not well known in North America. It is sensuous and romantic to the point of being sappy, but I love it. My Costa Rican teachers taught me all sorts of "moves" and fancy stuff, but when I went out dancing in Costa Rica I found that most people simply hold one another as closely as possible and dance it in the most basic sense. I am aware that most non-Latin North American young people find this music almost intolerable, but then for me the popular reggaeton grinding dancing has none of the subtlety of bolero and surely little of the romance. A couple of years ago I went to a large concert venue in Broomfield, near Boulder, to see a Luis Miguel concert. Miguel is a popular handsome Mexican bolero and *balada* singer. My date and I were among about half a dozen non-Latin people there, yet I surely enjoyed it as much as any.

Bolero is a Latin American romantic style of music and social dancing[1] that emerged, so far as it can be traced, in Cuba around 1885 or 1886. Soon thereafter it developed also in Puerto Rico and Mexico and spread throughout Latin America. The music is played slowly and features romantic and dramatic, even melodramatic, lyrics. It is typically danced in closed frame with the partners holding tightly, their legs intertwined to achieve the closest possible full body contact. Many bolero dancers do no break-aways and those who do often keep their heads in contact as much as possible. Erect upper body and long parallel lines accentuate the elegance of the dance. Dancers use pauses and dips to interpret the music. The rhythmic step of the basic bolero[2] is similar to the basic rhythm pattern of contemporary salsa dancing and its predecessors and relatives *son* and *danzon,* yet stylized differently to produce an elegantly romantic affect in contrast with the high energy sexuality of salsa.[3] Africa[4] and Spain (and more broadly Europe) are the principal cultural ingredients in the Cuban and Latin American crucible that created Latin American music and dancing, but as Ned Sublette has shown this mixture is certainly not simple.[5]

There are several styles of bolero dancing from the cultural forms found in social venues all over Latin America to the highly stylized forms that occur in competitive ballroom dancing and Dancesport. There are several distinct styles of bolero danced in Costa Rica.

With her strongly feminist and minority-sensitive perspectives, Frances Aparicio presents an extensive analysis of bolero[6] in her 1998 book *Listening to Salsa: Gender, Latin Popular Music, and Puerto Rican Cultures.* Aparicio focuses on bolero lyrics[7] which she analyzes and interprets in the context of Latin American, specifically Puerto Rican, social and cultural history. Her concern is the representation and impact on gender roles and their construction.[8] Aparicio finds bolero lyrics to be

> a musical space in which Woman (or the feminine) is constructed mostly as absence, an absence that stimulates the expression and articulation of male desire through the text/song and through the act of singing. . . . This romantic musical genre has been a central subtext of heterosexual love and an influential tradition that informs the discourse of desire and sexual politics in salsa music.[9]

For the most part boleros have been sung by men and the subject of the lyrics is almost invariably woman. She is often depicted as an ideal woman, sometimes so superior as to be an unattainable goddess. But some bolero lyrics construct woman as a witch or temptress. As the woman is the object of unquenchable desire, unfulfilled desire, love in bolero lyrics is invariably unrequited. The woman is absent. Rarely does she actually fulfill male sexual desire and erotic pleasure. Aparicio finds that "the separation motif is central to most boleros"[10] with the lyrics and record jackets (album art) depicting the lonely abandoned drinking and smoking male singer.

Yet, Iris Zavala has pointed out that, despite the absence of the woman, she is made a presence as she is evoked in the lyrics of the male bolero singer. This theme of absence and presence offers a fascinating framework for the understanding of bolero in the context of Latin American cultures. In one frame the theme of absence and presence reflects the dynamics of courtly love where the indifference of the beloved, often reflected in physical illness, is cause for increased longing and desire. Aparicio also sets this theme in the modern social context of the Latin American domestic space where it is most commonly the male who is absent, who abandons the family thus diminishing his own power and influence.

Bolero is seduction. Zavala noted of the lyrics that they are the "words about absence [that] seduce us into a presence."[11] Key to Zavala's depiction of bolero lyrics is her understanding of seduction: it is, building on the terms related to self-othering, the reversibility of the woman's absence and presence, that seduces; it is the presence of the promise of fulfillment, always denied, absented, that engenders desire; it is the reversibility that fascinates, that seduces.

Taking inspiration from bolero social dancing and bolero music, I want to study more deeply what distinguishes bolero, but more importantly, I want to continue to build on my discussion of what distinguishes dancing itself. Seduction even in this barest introduction refers to engendering a desire that is never fulfilled. Seduction is only seduction so long as it continues to seduce. Thus, as Renaud Barbaras discussed, as I presented above, movement is the desire to cross distance to fulfill a need, yet desire and movement continue only as the absence of fulfillment persists. Seduction directly addresses this persistence, this absence of fulfillment that is living movement. Barbaras might well have discussed movement in terms of seduction. A remarkably provocative consideration of seduction is found in Jean Baudrillard's 1979 book *Seduction*. I will consider his views more fully, but first I want to consider Aparicio a bit more particularly in her scant consideration of bolero dancing.

In the only reference, slight as it is, Aparicio makes to bolero dancing, she writes, "Woman as sign of absence becomes present through language, through the act of singing, and through bolero as performative act. The sensual evocation of the lyrics allows the heterosexual couple to give meaning to dancing and intimacy 'in the squared eternity of a floor tile' as foreplay and anticipation of sexual pleasure."[12]

With no analysis or even description of bolero dancing, Aparicio believes that in this musical-dance-social context, it is the lyrics that "give meaning to dancing and intimacy." Ironically, especially given the strength and emotion of her feminist perspective, it seems her views betray in this instance a surprisingly male-centered understanding. Her focus primarily on lyrics is logocentric and she seems to hold that the performative act, the dancing, cannot make sense or exist as meaningful apart from its conjunction with the lyrics, with how she interprets the lyrics, and with sexual pleasure. Indeed, given her broad analysis, I am not all that sure I know what she means in the passage I have just quoted. It appears that she thinks bolero dancers must listen to the lyrics so they will understand that what they are doing is foreplay to actual sexual pleasure to be experienced later. Bolero dancing is, it seems she is saying, sexual foreplay. How does the depiction of woman as absent communicate this to the couple with the woman so obviously present? Does it somehow inspire the couple to reject this imagery and use the dancing as a way of being together? It would seem that for Aparicio bolero dancing that does not produce sexual pleasure would be rather meaningless, although surely she does not mean this.

An understanding and appreciation of bolero dancing, as all dancing, must be approached independent of associated lyrics, yet address the significance of the interplay between lyrics and dancing, all, of course, in the context of culture and history. The most obvious observation is that in bolero dancing the woman (and the man)[13] is anything but absent. The man and woman hold one another as closely as possible. There is nothing more certain in bolero dancing than the presence of woman and certainly also the presence of man for woman. So how might we understand that bolero dancing is seductive, which I believe, indeed I know from experience that it is? Where is the absence that creates desire that remains unfulfilled? And, to take a feminist position, how is this not the experience of the woman as much as the man?

The seduction of bolero, I suggested above, is a way of understanding dancing itself. One rather graphic way of clarifying is by considering, in this particular case, what distinguishes the interaction of the man and woman as a couple dancing bolero from a couple unclothed in a private space holding one another in the same embrace. The difference is enormous, but how to articulate it? The unclothed couple holding one another in embrace interacts with the other's body in *actual* foreplay creating full sexual arousal leading to a *real* sexual act. This outcome is not a possibility in bolero dancing, though, of course, it may occur later. Bolero can be foreplay, but that is not what it is. The interaction of the partners in bolero dancing is intimate, it is romantic, it is a kind of body play, it may allow partners to experience a kind of physical unity with one another, but the dance is over when the music ends. As a particular dance form, the bolero enacts the signs of intimacy, yet in sustaining the seduction the dance prevents any connections beyond the world of the seductive signs it has created. Bolero then seduces at two levels: the conventions of the particular dance form in its seductive play of signs and in the seductive structurality that distinguishes dancing as a particular human form of movement.

In contrast with Aparicio's understanding of bolero as principally foreplay, I prefer to take away the "fore" and see it as play,[14] to invoke a perspective I developed in the last chapter. Bolero dancing is rule-bound and the rules do not permit actual foreplay or real sexual contact. In bolero all is appearance, all is sign, and the rules prevent any breach of actual sexual reality. Bolero dancing—like game, like play—is in a way focused on itself, on the world of signs it creates, not anything external to it. The end of a bolero dance does not have the same release that accompanies sexual orgasm; indeed, the end which is cessation of dancing movement and the physical separation of the dancers may heighten the seduction. It does so because, by rule, the experience of intimacy, unity, romance is confined to the dancing; in dancing the desire is never fulfilled. When the dancing ends the desire does not. The end of the dance shows the lie of the experience as union.

What is absent in bolero dancing is the correspondence in reality (sexual, even social, actuality) to all the signs being played during the dancing. The dancing is directed principally toward the mastery of the play of signs. This is not a sex act; it is the play of sexual signs clearly distinguished from sexual actuality. Dancing bolero plays with the signs of a relation of intimacy, but with no bridge or correspondence to any real relationship. The absence that seduces is what distinguishes and also enables the dancing. Bolero dancing, though fully bodied, exists in the world of signs, signs that seem to correspond to the real world outside dancing, but do not, indeed, are prevented by the rules of the dance from realizing the connection. Bolero may lead to or even express male-female relationships of intimacy and sexual union, but these, strictly speaking, are never part of the dancing. The dance seduces by what it intimates, or signifies, but only by always keeping the actuality absent. It is what is intimated but missing that makes the heart sing while dancing bolero, but the missing is all the more powerful, the more bittersweet and heart-wrenching, by the overwhelming presence, presence of body touching body. The dance is over when the music stops; as a result the seduction never ends. In bolero dancing most of the human senses—certainly touch, smell, vision, hearing—scream of presence, but the dance seduces by a designed prevention of the fulfillment of these sensual signs in a non-symbolic world, in the world of sexual actuality. There is no cathartic orgasmic release to dancing; the only choice is the response to all seduction, to continue to be seduced and to seduce by dancing, dancing all night. Seduction/being seduced is autotelic, sufficiently motivated[15] in the doing/being done. The explicit seduction of bolero correlates with the implicit seduction that distinguishes all dancing.

Thus, bolero dancing accomplishes this absence made present in a way much more powerful than the lyrics and, importantly, it has a rather different gender dynamic than do the lyrics. The lyrics make the woman present only by describing her in her absence. The lyrics facilitate an imagined presence. Dancing makes her, and his, presence/absence felt by both partners, known by the bodies aching with the physical experience of the signs that exist only in the world of artifice. While the male still leads in bolero dancing, both male and female are wholly present to one another, yet, by the rules of the dance, both are, outside of being signs, also absent.

The explicitly seductive character of bolero dancing may, I suggest, serve as a metaphor for the structurality of all dancing. Dancing seduces by its creation of postures and gestures that appear to invoke domains of meaning and/or emotion. The body is always engaged in postural and gestural movement that is associated with meaning and value, yet dancing as moving body prevents postural and gestural movement that ever gets beyond self-reference. In its pointing beyond (othering), yet folding back on itself, it seduces. It offers, thus engendering a need to be fulfilled by moving across a distance (the distance of desire) to satisfy a need, yet seductively the goal sought always recedes; the moving that at once offers and recedes is the movement of dancing. The containing movement of dancing is its seduction constantly renewing itself.

Dancing is then a rule-bound form of play that constructs a world of gestural postural movement that points beyond the dancing to the other, yet always denying the achievement of this other. Any realization of these referents would end the seduction, stem the desire, close the gap, collapse the distance, end the play, stop the dancing. As with bolero, it is precisely because the "fore" of foreplay, or at least the "aft" promised by the "fore," is denied by the rules of dancing that it is seductive. It is the full bodied experience of the reversibility of presence and absence that so heightens the seductivity of dancing. And it is in considering dancing as seducing that we begin to comprehend the enormity of the power it provides access to. The seductive aspect of dancing is inseparable from a sense of incipience, the energy of potential, a sense of the almost manifest, yet holding the manifestation, the realization, always in process, a promise, an almost. Dancing.

SEDUCTION: JEAN BAUDRILLARD

Seduction often bears a negative valuation. It is associated with deceptive women and men. Jean Baudrillard's *Seduction* (1979) explores the dynamics of seduction, offering a fuller richer understanding expanding our common usage. While Baudrillard does not include dancing in his discussion of seduction, his exploration of seduction will enhance the connections I have already made between seduction and movement and dancing. At least in my experience, connecting dancing and seduction helps to more fully appreciate and comprehend Baudrillard's understanding of seduction.

Baudrillard understands that seduction has the capacity to "deny things their truth and turn it [sic] into a game, the pure play of appearances, and thereby foil all systems of power and meaning."[16] Appearances have the quality of both showing or revealing what is actually there as well as presenting something that is not connected to truth or reality. These two meanings are reversible, that is, they always contain their own denial, their own opposition.[17] Baudrillard understands this reversibility as "the sole force that is equal and superior to all others, since with a simply play of the *strategy of appearances*, it turns them upside down."[18] Superior to truth and reality because it raises the question of truth and reality, seduction remains at play; seduction remains in motion, cannot be stopped, frozen, by truth by meaning by reality. And superior I would suppose in that the bare truth is often less than we had imagined it to be; yet, even that experience of disenchantment can be a movement and emotion.

This understanding of seduction is apparent in Baudrillard's discussion of how seduction fits in the scheme of time. Seduction's reversibility places it at once in all time and outside of time altogether.

> There is neither a time of seduction, nor a time for seduction, but still it has its own indispensable rhythm. Unlike instrumental strategies, which proceed by intermediary stages, seduction operates instantaneously, in a single movement, and is always its own end . . . It is an endless refrain. There is no active or passive mode in seduction, no subject or object, no interior or exterior: seduction plays on both sides, and there is no frontier separating them. One cannot seduce others, if one has not oneself been seduced.[19]

Baudrillard's description of seduction correlates closely with the structurality I have been developing for dancing. Dancing is movement for its own end, that is, it is about the energetics of self-movement, living movement. It is autotelic in that as living movement it folds back on itself in the seductive persistence that is movement. Its rhythm is its own end.

Baudrillard continues,

> Because seduction never stops at the truth of signs, but operates by deception and secrecy, it inaugurates a mode of circulation that is itself secretive and ritualistic, a sort of immediate initiation that plays by its own rules. . . . Seduction is immediately reversible, and its reversibility is constituted by the challenge it implies and the secret in which it is absorbed.[20]

Quite in contrast to the phrase "movement never lies," made so famous by Martha Graham, dancing differs perhaps from quotidian movement in exactly this respect. It plays by its own rules which are founded in secrecy and deception. It could hardly be an art form without artifice. We may hold with Graham's dictum as it is relevant to dancing only by recognizing that the appearances of the postural gestural movements of dancing are signs that certainly may appear to connect to some value and significance beyond the dancing. These are felt by the audience and perhaps the dancers. Yet it is distinctive to dancing that these signs remain in circulation in a reality of only signs in the dancing.

Seduction turns what appears into its opposite. It is the play of absence and presence, of visible and invisible. In its deconstructive capacities, putting the *not* to every *is*, it is also the root source of power, of creativity, of meaning, and certainly the movement we call dancing, while itself holding no power and no meaning.

Baudrillard describes seduction as a kind of "flickering" or an oscillation of presence and absence.

> The prismatic effect of seduction provides another space of refraction.
> Seduction does not consist of a simple appearance, nor a pure absence,
> but the eclipse of a presence. Its sole strategy is to be-there/not-there,
> and thereby produce a sort of flickering, a hypnotic mechanism that
> crystalizes attention outside all concern with meaning. Absence here
> seduces presence.[21]

A significant motivator for me to want to think and to write about dancing, a reluctant tearing myself away from dancing and teaching dancing,
has been an eagerness to try to comprehend and articulate my fascination
with dancing (both doing it and observing others doing it, and even
thinking about both), a fascination I believe I share with many. I have
wanted to understand what there is about dancing that I find so seductive. I don't believe that this understanding is often considered or has for
me yet to be adequately articulated. Baudrillard's *Seduction*, my reading
of it anyway, when related to dancing suggests some profoundly shocking and deeply revelatory characteristics, shocking in being unexpected
from the perspective of our received views of dancing. Suppose that my
(our?) fascination with dancing is because dancing is seduction. If this is
so, then dancing is comprised of "the pure play of appearances" and
rather than meaning as we expect of it, dancing "fail[s] all systems of
power and meaning" and "operates by deception and secrecy." Do we
dare allow ourselves to travel this challenging road, one that, it would
seem, threatens our most unquestioned and cherished understandings of
dancing?

In, for me, one of his most clarifying discussions of seduction Baudrillard opposes seduction to production. He explains what he means, production's

> original meaning, in fact, was not to fabricate, but to render visible or
> make appear. . . . To produce is to materialize by force what belongs to
> another order, that of the secret and of seduction. Seduction is, at all
> times and in all places, opposed to production. Seduction removes
> something from the order of the visible, while production constructs
> everything in full view, be it an object, a number or concept.[22]

As our society is one that worships production, the deep cost, in Baudrillard's view, is dramatized by him in identifying production with pornography, that need to lay all bare, to see it all, to expose every secret, to
articulate every meaning, to reveal every truth. Ours, he writes, is

> a pornographic culture *par excellence*, one that pursues the workings of
> the real at all times and in all places. [It is] a one-dimensional culture
> that exalts everything in the 'concreteness of production' or of pleas-
> ure—unlimited mechanical labour or copulation. What is obscene
> about this world is that nothing is left to appearances, or to chance [that
> is, to seduction].[23]

Further, he writes:

> No seduction here [that is, in production], nor in pornography, given the abrupt production of sexual acts, and the ferocity of pleasure in its immediacy. There is nothing seductive about bodies traversed by a gaze literally sucked in by a vacuum of transparency; nor can there be even a hint of seduction within the universe of production, where a principle of transparency governs the forces belonging to the world of visible, calculable phenomena—objects, machines, sexual acts, or the gross national product.[24]

Certainly as we begin to appreciate Baudrillard's understanding of seduction over against production, we may begin to see the promise, the unexpected wisdom, of rethinking, reseeing, dancing as seduction. Dancing, quite in contrast with pornography and the characteristics Baudrillard articulates as distinctive of pornography, seems to hide, to obscure— at least to compound possibilities. It is a play of appearances, sometimes accompanied by story and text and clear referent, but even the danced elements tend to ambiguate rather than clarify these links to non-dancing reality. Dancing leaves much, perhaps everything, to be said; its showing is also a hiding. What is revealed, shown, produced, is ephemeral; leaving but a trace on the emotion, on the memory.

But Baudrillard's understanding of seduction inspires more. Seduction is powerless, yet, remarkably the source of power itself. As Baudrillard writes:

> Seduction is stronger than power because it is reversible and mortal, while power, like value, seeks to be irreversible, cumulative and immortal. Power partakes of all the illusions of production, and of the real; it wants to be real, and so tends to become its own imaginary, its own superstition. . . . Seduction, on the other hand, is not of the order of the real—and is never of the order of force, nor relations of force. But precisely for this reason, it enmeshes all power's *real* actions, as well as the entire reality of production, in this unremitting reversibility and disaccumulation—*without which there would be neither power nor accumulation.*[25]

In considering dancing as seduction, what happens to our common understanding that dance is expression, that dancing is a language, that dance is "so meaningful"? Can we begin to realize that these widely-held views, seemingly unthinkable to challenge, might merit a good bit of reconsideration—indeed, possibly even rejection? Might we begin to catch a glimmer of the possibility that our world, our culture, so bent on production, has seduced us into seeing and understanding dancing, no matter how contrary to our experience of it, largely in terms of production? Certainly much of dancing has taken on the trappings of "production": dancers are members of companies that create productions whose worth and success is measured often in terms of money, evidence of a product sold. Of course our production-obsessed culture places great pressure on us to appreciate dancing in terms that tend to deny it as seduction.

Despite our culture marginalizing dancing, why do we always stop and watch dancing, almost any dancing, with rapt attention? What keeps us social dancing all night long even if we don't even know that many steps or moves? Why do so many dancers commit themselves to a life of physical exhaustion with so little hope of making a living as a professional dancer? Seductive is synonymous with alluring, beguiling, bewitching, captivating, enticing, provoking, attracting, fascinating, desirable, tempting, titillating, tantalizing, inviting. To consider dancing as seductive goes a long way in allowing us to understand its allure. We can describe this fascination in terms of the seductive reversibility: dancing is provocative in that it seems to be full of meaning, yet actually absorbs and obscures meaning rather than giving it full expression. Dance may be understood as absorbing meaning in that it gracefully receives most interpretations or analyses offered to it. Dancing bewitches by seeming to be making work,[26] yet it produces nothing real, nothing but the play of signs, the play of appearances. Dancing beguiles in suggesting that the dancer, by dancing, is achieving something like the fullest realization of self (and, of course, it does so but in ways we had not anticipated), yet in dancing the dancer becomes something other. In its möbiatic oscillation dancing seduces us, fascinates us, reveals through what it hides.

Consider the role of the audience, particularly in art and high cultural forms of dancing, from the perspective of dancing as seduction. We are often confounded by this relationship between dancers and audience, between dancing and observing dancing.[27] There is much on this subject to be considered. To see dancing as seduction suggests that the dancer-audience relationship be understood in the terms of the same structurality, that is, by considering the relationship between dancing and audience as möbiatic, as reversible, as chiasmatic, as playful. The play of signs, the play of appearances, in pointing to a reality yet denying a connection with that reality opens to imagining and feeling limitless possible connections with it. Where audiences are present to dancing, members of the audience are seduced by the promise of meaning in the play of signs. Observers of dancing identify and feel signs, signs that interrelate to one another and often even point beyond themselves seemingly toward some reality. As this play of signs "speaks to" each member of the audience it appears to produce meaning for him or her. Members of the audience may be moved, may find revelation, may be changed and charged.

Yet, never in the dancing itself does the play of appearances confirm or deny any of these "readings." While, as Susan Foster[28] and others show, dances can be "read," given the difference I am maintaining between dances and dancing, I suggest that in light of understanding dancing as seduction, as seduction being dancing's distinction and its function as a source of power, we gain much more appreciation for what distinguishes dancing by looking rather at how (and that) dancing prevents and confounds being read, at least in some final sense of being clear, being finished, being captured, in producing some explicit meaning, in laying it bare. Indeed, to read, to capture, to make clear dancing's meaning in this sense is, I believe, to take the dancing from the dance, to end the dancing.[29] Dancing seduces by offering the promise of meaning—how often do we hear the meaningless statement made of a dance "oh it was so meaningful"—yet, it never delivers any explicit statement of meaning. Rather it absorbs meanings offered it and endlessly seduces observers and dancers to continue observing and dancing and seeking meanings that are never adequately fulfilling.

Considering dancing as seduction there is a circulation, an oscillation, a reciprocation, a reversibility between dancers dancing and the audience. It is rather like they are partners in a dance, that is, there is dancing taking place between dancers and audience members. Metaphorically it is like they are dancing bolero. This relationship can be experienced as confounding and confusing—partners out of sync, stumbling over one another's feet—as certainly as it can be an experience of unity and complicity, crystallization of unity, familiar to dancers and members of dance audiences. But this too is seduction for the unity is but a play of signs. Baudrillard says that the best way to seduce is to be seduced. The audience is seduced in the rapt attention and fascination demanded by the play of signs, postural gestural movements, projecting meaning yet being open to the mystery and deception of the illusion. Dancers too experience this circulation. But it should be suggested that this seduction-by-being-seduced occurs in the complicity, the conspiracy that while all appears drenched with meaning (and it is), while all appears to speak to the deepest nature of reality (and it does), while the power generated by the dancing is palpable; in fact, there is nothing real, it is all a lie, a deception, artifice. That this aspect of dancing is known but never spoken of is the heart of dancing being seductive. All—dancers and members of the audience—are so thoroughly seduced that there is no thought of exposing the secret. And I have no reluctance to expose it here in this non-dance context, being confident that in the presence of dance and dancing we will happily be seduced again.

DANCING IS AURA

We can understand this circulation of seduction between the partners dancing bolero. With every invitation and acceptance to dance goes the tacit agreement to play by the rule that all is artifice not real and that the lie of artifice will not be revealed.

Mirrors, mirror images, are like shadows, like masks. They are other, yet they are self. It is common in the West, though relatively unknown throughout the rest of the world, to use mirrors in dancing especially when learning. Apart from mirrors dancers dancing perceive themselves through body awareness, through the subjective proprioceptive bodily experience, through feeling more than seeing themselves as moving bodies. Since sight originates in the body, in the face, there is a highly limited and subjective view of one's own dancing body. One is always looking, if one looks at all, down on the body below the neck and exclusively from the front. Mirrors permit an external view, a horizontally reversed image from the perspective of a separated audience. This reflection empowers the dancer to see and to know the dancing more "objectively" complementing the subjective experience of bodily movement, of one's body image. Mirrors shift the sensory hierarchy—they shift the balance between self and other, feeling and seeing. It certainly makes sense that it is in the West, where objectivity and vision are highly valued, that mirrors are prominent. Brian Massumi distinguished "mirror vision" from "movement vision" on the basis that in mirror vision what is missing is the movement.[30] Certainly it is in the West also that the proscenium stage has evolved distinctly separating audience from performers. While mirrors and separated audiences (and the accompanying implications regarding audience experience and decorum) reflect certain cultural and historical values, these specific features are illuminated further by seeing dancing as seduction. Mirror, like audience, presents other to self, self to other, a projection from the experience of dancing itself. It crystallizes the objective perspective that is necessary to the subjective perspective. Mirrors, like members of an audience, engage the circulation of presence and absence, subjective and objective, internal and external, personal and public—a circulation that seduces.

Often in my teaching I have noticed that many dancers simply cannot take their eyes off the image of themselves in mirrors. It seems they range from a curiosity about themselves—"Is that me?"—to an outright love affair—"Wow am I gorgeous!" Some other dancers have the opposite response to mirrors avoiding them, terrified by the chance meeting of their image in the mirror. Mirrors provide an othering that is clearly seductive.

Many have noted that dancing resists, even confounds, reproduction in film and other media. While this is self-evident in our experience, it may be difficult to grasp and articulate why it is so, especially when we consider dancing only in terms of what it produces. Films of dancing necessarily make something fixed and objective for film can be reproduced. Dancing must be product to be reproduced. To view as product is a common way we approach dancing. If dancing is understood as telling a story, then to recount the story is usually considered an adequate account of its storytelling function. But, clearly this kind of reproduction does not even touch the dancing itself. Baudrillard notes that seduction cannot be reproduced. Indeed, since seduction is contrasted with production, if dancing is seduction rather than production, then *re*production is clearly out of the question. To reproduce is to produce again, to show again, while dancing as seduction opposes production in the first place and at any order. Thus, to consider dancing as seduction allows us to more clearly understand why dancing cannot be reproduced. Dancing has its distinction, as seduction, in the play of appearances, in the *not* to the *is*, in the illusion, in the misdirection, in the oscillating circulation of presence and absence and of the visible and the invisible, in its occlusion that may appear as revelation, in its reversibility, in its möbiatic structurality. Production, reproduction, necessarily eliminates the play, stops the play that is the distinction of dancing. Reproduction takes the dancing out of the dancing.

The ubiquity of video in contemporary cultural life presents a fascinating cultural example. Clearly most knowledge we have of most dances is now limited to watching a video rather than experiencing a live performance. Following Baudrillard's critique of contemporary society, characterized by the worship of production and the loss of reality to a constructed hyperreality, we might be justified in suggesting that the endless video resources available for dance forms from all over the world simply confirm that even dancing has become subsumed in the drive to turn everything into product and it has. Yet, foregrounding the seductive distinction of dancing, it is perhaps possible to understand the obsession with recording dancing as both motivated by its seductivity and as the presentation of images that evoke the elusive seductivity of dancing, even in the produced and reproducible film object.

Once we allow the distinction of dancing as seduction, it is much easier to understand not only why dancing cannot be reproduced, but also why its seduction differs from that of other forms such as music, painting, and particularly photographs, film, and computer generated images. Dancing, while so physically present, is remarkably ephemeral, ceasing at the moment it appears because it is self-movement. This aspect of dancing being seductive is always holding forth the promise of an object that disappears even as it appears. Art forms such as painting, sculpture, even music produce objects in the real world, while dancing only promises to do so, but never does. In a 1939 essay Walter Benjamin addresses the issues of "The Work of Art in the Age of Mechanical Reproduction."[31] For forms like photography, film, and computer generated images, there is no discernible distinction between *original* and *reproduction*. Mechanical reproduction shifts our understanding of art. Whereas in other forms such as painting, Benjamin suggests that the original is distinguished from a reproduction in that it has an *aura*, the presence of originality. And in these terms there arise all of the issues surrounding the terms authenticity and forgery. We might understand aura in terms of its seductivity.

An original painting has aura—that presence of its originality—while mechanically reproduced works of art do not. While works without aura seemingly are not subject to forgery and authenticity, these concerns are present to works with aura. Dancing is interesting in that it logically precedes both of these classes of art. Because in dancing thing made is identical to maker and is inseparable from the making, dancing more than having aura, it seems to me, *is aura*. Aura is the presence of origination, of ontogenesis. Where aura is usually attached to an object, a painting for example, dancing folds aura back on itself. The dancing promises some original thing, yet the thing passes in its appearance leaving behind only a remembered experience of origination, of aura. Dancing can never be faked or forged because it cannot be reproduced. Dancing, seduction *par excellence,* is the human form of action that defies reproduction and thus its originality is always assured. Simply put, reproductions of dancing are no longer dancing, they are better understood as re-presentations that convert dancing to some other form of arting or to a type of production. The ideas of a forgery of dancing and inauthentic dancing are, in important senses, unthinkable. All dancing is original and thus all dancing has/is aura.

Dancing and theater are close kin in respect to aura and, indeed, in many cultures in the world dancing and theater are virtually inseparable.[32] While I believe that there is a continuity between theater and dancing, I think that the distinctive mark is that theater foregrounds the importance of word, of speech, of language which invites, encourages, a reduction of theater to the text/language model so common to Western sensibilities. Theater can be read as text because indeed it is text, script. There is no strict or even close dancing counterpart to script or score. Plays are written and music composed with extensive dependence on script and score. Even formally choreographed dances are not first or concurrently created on paper. They are created on/in/as the body with memory and direct transmission required. And each performance of a dance is in an important sense a seductive original. Dancing is self-referential, autotelic, contained, not about anything outside itself, not by choice or subject matter but by its nature. The performance is something added to the principle creation of the play—performance (even musical arrangement) is secondary in some senses to music—yet for dancing performance and creation come at once and are not distinguishable.[33] Yet, of course, parallel to dancing, theater restricted to the scripts is like dancing being restricted to dance music lyrics. I am astonished by the dozens of studies and other considerations of dance-music complexes that unapologetically, even unwittingly, consider neither music nor dance, but only lyrics. Latin American dance music is an excellent example. Dancing, one would think, and especially dancing that has no accompanying text, tends to foil such reductions.

Dance and text are increasingly interconnected in modern and post-modern dance, and dance and text are interconnected in the dance-dramas common throughout the world. Text is recited by the dancer or a narrator or as an element in the musical score (spoken or sung as lyrics) accompanying dancing. There are many combinations, countless ways in which text and dance are interrelated. From the perspective of dancing as seduction I suggest some criteria for understanding these combinations. In the West, where production is valued and seduction is devalued, I propose that spoken text is often added to disambiguate dancing, to make it speak and relate and function and serve. Dancing is thus justified by using a text to clarify for an audience the meaning of dancing, or better the particular dance. This gain, however, may be won at the price of losing some of the seductive qualities of dancing. The words, in their fixing the meaning (if this is their intent), in their connection to reality beyond the dancing, may suppress the seduction of dancing, of that incipient sense that meaning is always on the verge of coming forth. It is not difficult to understand the motivation to bring clear meaning and value to dancing, the eagerness to have dances correctly read. But this is a masculinization of dancing, an attempt to make dance productive, a conveyer of value, an action of use. Here dancing aspires to use power rather than being the source of power, though it will always in some sense fail in this regard. Words are perceived and processed differently than is dancing's postural/gestural movement. Because, as we are conditioned to believe, words inherently mean, that is, convey meaning, it is difficult not to understand text primarily in terms of the meanings they produce or seem to convey. Literary theory has suggested alternatives to this view and the alternatives are, I believe, precisely in line with allowing literary texts to be seen in terms of their seductive potential. This perspective on word is well known in the sung texts of dance-dramas and the lyrics of dance music. Still, even where texts are read to disambiguate dance, I believe that the seductive aspect of dancing eventually dominates because even when great emphasis is placed on this masculine productive functional effort, the redundancy, the movement, the play of signs that are dancing will wear out, exhaust, and finally deny these other intentions.

Words may seduce as well. After all words are signs, appearances, themselves reversible and as such may be presented in the play of seduction. This is certainly the case with poetic language and sung lyrics. Words may reverse their claim on meaning and value and seduce the auditor. So there are ample possibilities for text to complement dancing as seduction.

SEDUCTION IS FEMININE

Jean Baudrillard published *Seduction* during a period marked by major development of feminism when many important French feminists were writing furiously. Thus it was more than a little bold that Baudrillard would address feminism and seduction in ways that seemed to reprimand the feminists of the day as being shortsighted if not simply wrong, but he did so and on feminist grounds.

Baudrillard identifies seduction as feminine and production as masculine, and argues this alignment based on feminist reasoning.

> All masculine power is a power to produce. All that is produced, be it the production of woman as female, falls within the register of masculine power. The only, and irresistible, power of femininity is the inverse power of seduction. In itself it is nul [*sic*], seduction has no power of its own, only that of annulling [*sic*] the power of production. But it always annuls the latter.[34]

And further, "The feminine knows neither equivalence nor value; it is, therefore, not soluble in power. It is not even subversive, it is reversible. Power, on the other hand, is soluble in the reversibility of the feminine."[35]

Without engaging the feminist discourse of the 1970s or its history, if we acknowledge, for whatever reasons, the correlation of seduction (as Baudrillard understands it) with the feminine and production with the masculine, we may identify dancing, understood as seduction, as decidedly feminine. This identity of dancing as feminine need not be, indeed it is not, principally about the gender of dancers or stereotyped gender images of dancing. Feminine activities, done by either gender, are those that are seductive: not only dancing, but also poetry, theater, the novel, art, music, transvestitism, and so on. That is, the feminine activities are those that enter into and love the play of signs and understand the value of continuing the play without resolution. Masculine activities are those that, through production, seek the end of the game, the resolution, the real, the truth. And, for Baudrillard, it is the feminine that makes the latter even possible. Dancing, among all feminine forms, produces no enduring thing—no script, no image, no score, nothing to frame—and, I argue, consequently stands as the exemplar of femininity as it does of seduction. Too bad Baudrillard was not a dancer.

In the West, dancing has strong correlates with females, the feminine, and femininity in the biological gendered sense. The pervasive tendency to make this strong gender stereotype identification with dancing is more the result of a culture bent on production, a culture that devalues seduction as Baudrillard understands it. As I explored earlier, boys don't dance. Boys that do dance are considered feminine. Among men who dance professionally there is a much higher incidence of gays than in the non-dancing culture. It certainly makes sense that a culture that stresses, seemingly at all costs (the economic metaphor is telling here), production to the exclusion of seduction—Baudrillard, remember, sees this as ob-scene—is a culture that makes simple correlates between the gender of the actor and the value of the action. Women are non-productive (i.e., seductive); men are producers. Production is valued; seduction is deval-ued. Women are devalued; identified with seduction presented only in a negative threat-to-production light. Since dancing is feminine, then it is women who must dance or it is femininity that must characterize those who dance—an unfortunate misunderstanding of so much. Western en-tertainment and cultural forms of dancing attempt to refute the feminine-seductive character of dancing by entering the world of production: dance groups are *companies*, they do expensive *productions*, they charge admission, they distribute printed programs, and they seek published reviews. But the feminine gender identity is more difficult to shake.

Take for example the popular 2000 film *Billy Elliot*. I have discussed the musical version above; here my comments are confined to the film. This film appears to criticize the pejorative aspect of the association of dancing with the feminine. When young Billy finds that he prefers ballet to wrestling, he must hide his interest from his father and family. His friend fears he is a "puff." His father, a coal-miner (a "real" man), is furious when he finds out and forbids Billy to continue dancing. Billy's love of dancing persists.

A female ballet teacher takes him on as a secret private student and eventually his father and family get behind him, supporting his success-ful efforts to gain acceptance in the Royal Academy of Ballet in London. Billy's non-dancing male friend dresses up in his mother's clothing, we suppose to teach us that it is really the non-dancer, not Billy, who is the "puff." At the end of the film, the coal miner father and the coal miner older brother go to London to see Billy perform as a principal dancer in Swan Lake. The boyhood friend is present, now adult too, of course, at first unrecognized by Billy's father because he is a transvestite and Billy is the accomplished, very powerfully masculine, muscular, dancer. The father cries.

The gender constructions with dancing need to be more than reexam-ined. I think *Billy Elliot* does not offer us much on this, seemingly its principal point. Reconsider, to begin, Billy's boyhood friend, the trans-vestite, in terms of Baudrillard's wonderful analysis of transvestitism. He wrote,

> What transvestites love is this game of signs, what excites them is *to seduce the signs themselves*. With them everything is makeup, theater, and seduction. They appear obsessed with games of sex, but they are obsessed, first of all, with play itself; and if their lives appear more sexually endowed then our own, it is because they make sex into a

total, gestural, sensual, and ritual game, an exalted but ironic invoca-
tion.[36]

If we accept this understanding of transvestitism and seduction, *Billy
Elliot* incorrectly identifies the non-dancing transvestite as the feminine
puff, robbing her/him of his/her highly seductive and therefore feminine—in a non-stereotypical, but rather elemental—character. Corresponding with this treatment is its presentation at film's end the adult
Billy, now a ballet principal, who, though in makeup, is athletic, physically ripped, and physically powerful—the very image of productive masculinity. As we study the image that ends the film–Billy's powerful muscular body frozen mid-leap high in the air—we can't help but say to
ourselves, "Wow! What a *man* that little skinny kid made of himself."
And we appreciate all those years of training and work it took Billy to
produce these results. Here again, dancing is forced into being productive. Not only does this dance occur as a lavish production by a distinguished ballet company in an elegant theater, with everyone dressed to
the nines, the principal male dancer is an amazingly powerful man. What
we do not see is that Billy, much like his transvestite friend, is playing
with swans, seducing his audience by entering the world of the play of
signs. Dancing is finally always feminine.

I suggest that, rather than challenging our inappropriate gender align-
ments with dance, as seems to be its intent, the film actually re-affirms,
even deepens, them. And, because it seems expressly to be about challenging our gender associations with dancers, it seduces us into believing
that we are indeed meeting that challenge and makes us feel pretty good
about ourselves as we do it. Yet, transvestitism is confused with sexual
orientation and, by setting it up as the counterpoint to Billy, the film
supports the association of transvestitism with the culturally negative
image of the "puff" and thereby misses how it too is seductive. And it
masculinizes Billy by focusing on his productive aspect which requires
freezing him in a closing image making him cease to be dancing. Seduction is an insightful way to comprehend and appreciate the structurality
that is and distinguishes dancing itself.

DANCING AS MAKING

Against the backdrop of arguing against dancing being associated with
production as contrasted by Jean Baudrillard to seduction, our understanding of dancing can be developed by considering it as a making.
Early in the twentieth century noted dancer Ted Shawn identified the
distinctiveness of dance making I want to focus on when he said "Dance
is the only art of which we ourselves are the stuff of which it is made."
From a physiological perspective Deane Juhan noted, "the medium

through which dancers express their art, the actual artifact that is created, and their own musculature are all one."[37] Dancing is making on and of the body of the dancer; thing made is never an external object. Thing made is continually folded back in the dancing in the endless process of dancing making. *Dancing is making itself on display* and this is the distinctiveness of dancing; if there is anything made by dancing it is the seductive glimpse of making in process, a virtual object.

Writing in 1927 Paul Valéry anticipated a distinction that allows us to understand dancing as making without it being relegated to Baudrillard's production.

> A practical man is a man who has an instinct for such economy of time and effort, and has little difficulty in putting it into effect, because his aim is definite and clearly localized: *an external object.*
>
> As we have said, the dance is the exact opposite. It moves in a self-contained realm of its own and implies no reason, no tendency toward completion. A formula for pure dance should include nothing to suggest that it has an end. It is terminated by outside events; its limits in time are not intrinsic to it; the duration of the dance is limited by the conventional length of the program, by fatigue or loss of interest. But the dance itself has nothing to make it end.[38]

Valéry makes the distinction between the practical or productive which aims at making an external object the terminus of the making process. Yet, he considers dancing the exact opposite, seduction in Baudrillard's terms, which is making without end. He uses the term "pure dance" which aligns with what I have been referring to as dancing in contrast with dance which is the aspect of dancing subject to a particular program.

The insight here is that dancing is a making, but it holds a very special place among all human makings. Dancing, unlike most other makings, can never be separated from the human body in the action of making/dancing. The dancing body is most certainly directed toward making otherness, something other than the quotidian dancer's body. It seduces in the apparent promise for an external object that is never realized. Dancing is often engaged as and identified as art, yet among all art forms, it gets at arting itself, at the creative action that may produce artifact in other forms of art.

Valéry discussed this as well in understanding dancing as "an action that derives from ordinary, useful action, but *breaks away* from it, and finally *opposes* it."[39] Valéry goes on to find the place of dancing in the context of all the arts.

> All action which does not tend toward utility and which on the other hand can be trained, perfected, developed, may be subsumed under this simplified notion of the dance, and consequently, *all the arts can be considered as particular examples of this general idea,* since by definition all

the arts imply an element of action, the *action which produces,* or else manifests, the *work.*[40]

Dancing is not distinct among the arts as being distinguished simply by identifying some difference in form and medium but rather in that it breaks away from ordinary useful action, the action that produces object, opposing it in the sense of being about the action, the making, rather than the terminus in some work, artifact, object made. Dancing's concern is with the action, the process, the creating, the making, the arting itself, that is, with the heart of all the arts.

Insofar as we might consider dancing as making art, artifice, artifact, the object made is virtual and seductive. Dancing is making otherness, but it is the otherness that is experienced as moving rather than object. In dancing the body is bent upon achieving what in some sense it seems it should be incapable of doing; that is, making itself up by making itself into something it is not. Without ceasing to be one body, the body we know as self, in dancing it makes itself into an other; the relationship between them is living movement, vitality.

NOTES

1. The entry on bolero in the *International Encyclopedia of Dance,* ed. Selma Jeanne Cohen (New York: Oxford University Press, 1999) is limited to a presentation of a nineteenth century Spanish dance. The many index entries for bolero extend the coverage only to the use of Ravel's composition "Bolero" as the music for numerous modern and ballet dances. Though bolero is among the older and certainly among the most widespread and important of Latin American dances there is no mention of it in the *IED.*

2. The description here is for bolero classico. There are other forms of bolero that adapt to the slow chachachá and other musical and cultural variables. To my knowledge there is no study of the many variations of the dance, or even the music for that matter, from country to country throughout Latin America.

3. Dance and music identified by the term "salsa" are used here rather broadly according to contemporary use. Actually the term "salsa" arose in New York in the early 1970s and the dance/music forms had predecessors such as Cuban *son.* There is significant variance in opinion about the use of the term and what exactly it refers to. Some say it simply means Cuban music and dance, others see it as a broadly generic term encompassing all recent forms of Latin American music and dancing.

4. While I use the general term Africa here I more specifically indicate the areas of West and Central Africa that were the source of slaves sent to Cuba and Latin America. While I believe it highly inappropriate to generalize about Africa—there are, after all, dozens of countries and many hundreds of cultures—it is in some general sense appropriate to refer to and oppose African to European (which itself is hugely varied). The assumption is that despite the major variations, all Africans, in terms of rhythms and dances, are more closely associated with each other than they could be with any element of Europe, and vice versa.

5. Ned Sublette, *Cuba and Its Music: From the First Drums to the Mambo* (Chicago: Chicago Review Press, 2007). And also in terms of posture and body comportment bolero is closer to *danzon.*

6. Her research is highly influenced by and dependent on Luis Rafael Sánchez's *La importancia de llamarse Daniel Santos* and on Iris Zavala's "De héroes y heroínas en lo imaginario social: El discurso amoroso del bolero," *Casa de las Américas* 30 (March-April 1990): 123-29, and René A. Campos, "The Poetics of the Bolero in the Novels of Manuel Puig," in *World Literature Today* 65 (Autumn 1991): 637-42.

7. Notably a large portion of studies of Latin American dance music, while acknowledging that it is music for dancing, ignores even the simplest descriptions of dancing, and focuses analysis of music heavily on lyrics. As I will show, the ignoring of the musical and dancing dimensions of Latin American dance music is—shouldn't this be obvious—to miss the point. It is to be overwhelmed by the male production centered orientation of Western cultures.

8. Interestingly there are many parallels between bolero and tango lyrics. For an analysis of these see Marta E. Savigliano, *Tango and the Politics of Passion* (Boulder: Westview Press, 1995).

9. Frances Aparicio, *Listening to Salsa: Gender, Latin Popular Music, and Puerto Rican Cultures* (Middletown, CT: Wesleyan, 1998), 125-26.

10. Aparicio, *Listening to Salsa,* 132.

11. As quoted in Aparicio, *Listening to Salsa,* 130.

12. Aparicio, *Listening to Salsa,* 127. Her quote in this passage is from Sánchez and she notes that the timelessness and universality of bolero is also discussed by Héctor Madera Ferrón in "El bolero es eterno," *Un siglo de bolero,* 3-5. The square eternity of the floor tile refers to teaching dancing on black and white checkerboard floors with dancers instructed to stay within a square while dancing.

13. There is another way in which Aparicio's analysis fails to be adequately feminist. In focusing entirely on how the male created and sung lyrics impact female gender constructions, she ignores the female perspective, she too experience of the woman as much as the man? absents the woman. In excluding dancing and focusing only on the lyrics, Aparicio fails to see that the woman is indeed present and present in a much more bodied way than in the lyrics. She is physically present as one of the dancers. A man cannot dance bolero without a female partner. From the perspective of the dance, we can ask "what is the woman's point of view?"

14. Taking away the "fore" shifts the consideration of bolero dancing from an unsatisfying functionalist explanation to address a consideration of what distinguishes bolero as a dance, and, I will argue, what distinguishes dancing among other forms of human action.

15. I don't say sufficiently "satisfied" because it is in the absence of the fulfillment of desire—thus in some sense keeping one unsatisfied, wanting more—that is the attraction of all dancing.

16. Jean Baudrillard, *Seduction,* translated by Brian Singer (New York: St Martin's Press, 1990 [1979]), 8.

17. Perhaps most notable, given its parallel to our earlier discussion of Merleau-Ponty's "flesh ontology," is that Baudrillard identifies seduction with "reversibility."

18. Baudrillard, *Seduction,* 8. The sense of the "elemental" as Merleau-Ponty expressed for flesh is felt in this statement of Baudrillard's.

19. Baudrillard, *Seduction,* 81. For other discussions of the reversibility of seduction see 17, 20, 21.

20. Baudrillard, *Seduction,* 81.

21. Baudrillard, *Seduction,* 85.

22. Baudrillard, *Seduction,* 34-35.

23. Baudrillard, *Seduction,* 34.

24. Baudrillard, *Seduction,* 34-35.

25. Baudrillard, *Seduction,* 46 (italics in original). Merleau-Ponty identified reversibility as the essential feature of his "flesh ontology." The structurality of flesh and seduction are in many ways the same. Reversibility, that möbiatic relationship he illustrated by one hand touching/being touched by the other, is, in his analysis, elemental; it is what makes symbolism, language, art, perception, thought, human life

itself, possible. It is reversibility, flesh, that is elemental. Flesh is the source of the meaning and power of these real things. Baudrillard articulates his understanding of seduction as "reversibility" in much the same terms as did Merleau-Ponty of flesh. Thus, for our consideration, Merleau-Ponty's flesh ontology aligns with Baudrillard's seduction. Considering the two together expands our understanding of both and, of course, of dancing. I think particularly important are Baudrillard's discussions of seduction in opposition to production and the gender associations of this pairing. I will develop this below. Further, since we found dancing to offer insights into "flesh ontology," we might expect that our consideration of dancing as seduction will enhance our comprehension of this seduction-flesh complex.

26. Many choreographers refer to their creative processes as "making work."

27. There is something of this relationship akin to the partnering relationship in social dancing.

28. Susan Foster, *Reading Dancing: Bodies and Subjects in Contemporary American Dance* (Berkeley: University of California Press, 1988).

29. This is quite similar to Massumi's analysis of how we typically take the movement out of movement when we attempt to analyze it.

30. Brian Massumi, *Parables for the Virtual: Movement, Affect, Sensation,* (Durham: Duke University Press, 2002), 48-50.

31. Walter Benjamin, "The Work of Art in the Age of Mechanical Reproduction" in Walter Benjamin, *Illuminations: Essays and Reflections,* edited by Hannah Arendt, translated by Harry Zohn. New York: Schocken Books, 1968.

32. Beth Osnes, *Acting: An International Encyclopedia* (Santa Barbara: ABC-CLIO, 2002).

33. One may argue that a choreographer makes a dance and then this may be performed by various dancers or dance companies, yet the original choreographed work does not take a separate form, a text or score, but is rather only when danced.

34. Baudrillard, *Seduction,* 15.

35. Baudrillard, *Seduction,* 17. Baudrillard took to task the feminist movement at the time, the 1970s, for having what he believed to be a limited understanding and appreciation of seduction. "What does the women's movement oppose to the phallocratic structure? Autonomy, difference, a specificity of desire and pleasure, a different relation to the female body, a speech, a writing—*but never seduction*. They are ashamed of seduction, as implying an artificial presentation of the body, or a life of vassalage and prostitution. They do not understand *that seduction represents mastery over the symbolic universe, while power represents only mastery of the real universe.* The sovereignty of seduction is incommensurable with the possession of political and sexual power." (Baudrillard, *Seduction,* 8).

36. Baudrillard, *Seduction,* 12-13.

37. Deane Juhan, *Job's Body: A Handbook for Bodywork* (Barrytown, NY: Station Hill Press, 2003), 255.

38. Paul Valéry, "What is Dance?" in *What is Dance?* ed. by Roger Copeland and Marshall Cohen (Oxford: Oxford University Press, 1983), 62.

39. Valéry, "What is Dance?" 62. (italics in original)

40. Valéry, "What is Dance?" 63. (italics in original)

SIX

Dancing

Dance fascinates and entertains, yet it is rarely taught in public schools. In cultures throughout the world dance occurs on many religious and ritual occasions, yet dance is largely ignored by the academic study of religion. The distinctive postures and gestures of dance mark the cultural identities of the dancers; it is a hallmark of tradition. Dancing commonly occurs as a force of change, challenging established values, offering alternatives constituting fundamental change. Yet dancing as a cultural, social, historical force is poorly understood and rarely acknowledged beyond its connection with fun and entertainment.

Dancing and studying dancing have revealed to me hints about how to comprehend the amazing profundity and complexity of dancing. My feelings about dancing are those of a new religious convert. I see dancing as at the core of what constitutes us as human beings. I believe dancing to be the realization of human potential. I believe that dancing has the potential to offer new paradigms for the study of culture and religion. I am excited about this adumbrated understanding of dancing and my claims for dancing arise endlessly. I don't apologize. In fact, I think it is the responsibility of scholars to push their claims as far as they can; to have the grand visions and to do their best to establish them. Experience assures me that the academic critical process will soon drag these visions back towards modesty. I am not interested in reserve; I prefer to enjoy the energy of my inspiration and to imagine large. My only concern is the limit of my capacity to adequately express the insights I have glimpsed. I am particularly excited to engage in the interplay between my personal experience, my studies of specific dance traditions in cultures around the world, and my interpretation of the perspectives of scholars in various fields whose work is profound and inspiring even though done mostly without any reference whatsoever to dancing. These scholars are the giants on whose shoulders I have dared to balance, my strange partners in an academic dance. I know that had I greater knowledge and sophistication in a number of fields of study, my understanding of dancing would be richer and my descriptions and explanations more artful. Nonetheless it is what it is at this moment.

In this final chapter I want to focus on some principles that have emerged in this study of dancing that I see as central to not only the study of dancing, but also to the academic study of culture and religion. I want also to engage more explicitly the core topic of this "Body and Religion" series of volumes in such a way that the study of dancing may contribute significantly to the academic study of religion.

It is not difficult to see the affinity between dancing and religion given that dancing is inseparable from human vitality, from the human capacity of transcendence connected with self-realization, from the cultural techniques of body (gestures and postures) that most closely define cultural identity, and from the powerful mechanisms of continuity and tradition as well as change and innovation. Indeed, for most religious cultures in the world, religion and dancing are entwined. It is a concern, especially given the bloody fleshy sensory rich character of the Christ event, that European and American Christianities have held themselves for the most part at a distance from dancing. The explanation of how this antagonism came to pass is the task of others, yet for me here now it is important to recognize that since northern hemisphere Christianities have contributed much to the operative prototype of religion for the academic study of religion, the result is that dancing has been practically invisible to the study of religion. This invisibility contrasts quite remarkably with the high visibility of dancing among religions in cultures throughout much of the world and how this religion/dance connection is acknowledged by most everyone as more or less obvious. And as dancing has been ignored so too have similar and related religious actions such as ritual, drama, and music.

Throughout this book I have been interested primarily in danc*ing*, that structurality that is present in every action that we identify with the word "dance." At least part of my motivation for this emphasis is that it appears that typically dancing is valued to the degree that it is understood as something other than dancing. A basic aim I have maintained throughout has been to *keep the dancing in the dance*. To consider dancing first in the context of self-movement helps us understand how to accomplish this goal, because in the realm of movement there are profound and insightful studies of self-movement, living movement, movement itself. Further, to acknowledge that all dancing is movement allows us to appreciate dancing as enjoying the considerable qualities and characteristics of movement common to animate organisms. Yet, because it is clear that not all movement is dancing, we must be able to specify what distinguishes dancing as a subset of movement. The discussion of movement is framed in the common attributes of all human movement, that is, universal and common to human beings and more broadly that of animate organisms. Dancing as a ubiquitous learned human self-movement activity offers insight about human distinctiveness. Dancing, as a form of human movement where the dancer and the dance are both identical and separate, offers insight into the fundamental structuralities that, in my view, underlie human distinctiveness. It is in the exploration of this distinctive structurality that I believe we have the most to gain and in doing so to comprehend how to keep the dancing in the dance; indeed, to appreciate that dancing structurality generates a distinctive self-movement that is, at core, about living movement itself. This book has centered on exploring this structurality by engaging an expanding vocabulary of terms and ideas—moving, gesturing, self-othering, playing, and seducing—as well as its broad implications for comprehending human nature.

A second general principle that has developed throughout this study of dancing has to do with the role allowed Cartesian divisions. To focus on the structuralities of movement and dancing does not depend on, indeed it alleviates at the outset, any hierarchical divisions such as mind and body, material and thought or belief. The principle is that such divisions are of value only to the degree these doublings help articulate an interactive dynamic structurality and that these divisions are always understood as inseparable one from the other rather than as paired alternatives or options that can function alone. Rather than beginning with a recognition of the limitations of the classic Cartesian divide and to make an effort to either champion the ignored term or to join together the separated and opposing parts and contentious divisions, the movement/dancing approach developed here begins from a position, established even at the level of neurobiology (proprioception, for example), of profound dynamic interrelatedness.

It is of the structure of the academy, reflected in its very furniture and architecture, to proceed from the assumption of the mind/body split. The academy is an institution that traditionally cultivates minds by removing the scholar from the topic of study and disdaining feelings and experiences in order to maintain objectivity. The subject of study is understood as it is territorialized into object grids that allow analysis and determined observation. What is rarely acknowledged is that the perspective of the academy is one that removes the vitality, the self-movement, the living dynamics from the subjects studied. One kills as one dissects.

It can certainly be suggested that something of value might be won by alternatives to the traditional academic approach. Movement and dancing offer, I believe, such alternatives. Approaching religion and the study of religion as I have attempted to do with movement and dancing, that is, as movement, as process, avoids the tiresome and distracting dual structures such as body and mind, material and spiritual or thought, text and action, intellectual and popular. Movement does not put these parts back

together using hyphen glue or slash paste upon having acknowledged
that they have been unfortunately wedged apart; rather, movement and
dancing never allow for any dividing wedge to exist in the first place.
Once Humpty has fallen and broken into pieces the evidence of the pain-
ful fall will always persist as egg on his face no matter how good the
patch job.

I have noticed a welcome shift toward approaches now commonly
collected under the term "body," as in the series this book is part of, but
also "materialist" as in the 2011 book *More Than Belief: A Materialist Theory of Religion* by Manuel Vásquez. These are important developments and
certainly take on the difficult task of contributing important new approaches to the study of religion as well as including much that has been
overlooked and excluded by the study of religion, a daunting task because of the deep establishment of the positions these new perspectives
tend explicitly to counter. For me the concern is that they often play into a
hierarchical dualist dynamic with unfortunate implications of opposition:
body over against mind or spirit or soul and material over against text or
thought or doctrine or belief. My concern is that this new discourse simply plays out the ongoing academic discourse of the last couple of centuries with the terms all remaining pretty much the same, even with the
relative values reversed.

It is possible to consider the character of the modern academic study
of religion as a discourse on where one stands related to the issue of the
accepted mind/body, material/thought, distinction. One persistent discussion has centered on the term "place." Jonathan Z. Smith appealed to
Archimedes' dictum "Give me a place to stand on and I will move the
world."[1] Smith credits Mircea Eliade for teaching us that to ask of the
character of the place on which one stands is *the* basis question we need
ask to understand that person's religion. Place has been an important
term on which the academic study of religion has developed over the last
half century. Eliade's mid-twentieth century understanding of religion
was stated in temporal and spatial place terms: the beginning (*in illo
tempore*) and the center (*axis mundi*). These terms designate the precise
time and space where the gods established the world and its order; these
are the places that are dependable and can hold trusted meaning and
value despite the messiness of history which, for Eliade, is a profanation
and a burden that needs periodically to be absolved by returning to the
center and the beginning.

Smith, developing an alternative view of religion, countered Eliade by
insisting that religion is principally application inseparable from the
messiness of not only history but also of the quotidian; religion has an
everydayness to it and comes to mean anything only as its doctrines,
beliefs, practices are interpreted, selected, and applied. Smith's concern
is, I believe, to shift our attention towards the enactment of religion,
rather than to find ourselves satisfied by the description of objectified

systems or a descriptive account of history. His emphasis is on the dynamics of application which he articulates most powerfully, I think, in terms of "comparison." Relevant to both the religious practitioner and the academic student of religion, principles and ideals are juxtaposed with the exigencies of the moment, engaging the oscillatory comparative negotiative process of religious or academic enactment. Rooted in his study of James George Frazer's *The Golden Bough,* I believe that Smith's comparative method of accounting for the dynamics of enactment might also be effectively articulated in the terms of *play.*[2] The enormous shift, suggested by Smith, is to keep the religious enaction in religion in contrast to the objectified, territorialized understanding of religion that has persisted almost unchallenged to the present.

Yet, Smith's most direct articulation of this understanding of religion as application and enaction was cast in the language of place, specifically "maps." He set forth approaches to the study of religion in the broad terms of *locative* (having a place and experiencing meaning by being in place) and *utopian* (abhorring any restriction to place; considering being in place a threat to freedom and meaning) maps. Thus presented, these terms appear to designate types of religions even though Smith explicitly warns against this implication. As explicit categories they have already taken the enactment out of religion, the religioning out of religion. Furthermore, it is the locative that is the more common of the two maps, that is the map type overwhelmingly represented by religions documented and studied, the map type characterizing the academic perspective. Smith is challenged to find any significant examples of the utopian map. I think that we would be better off considering Smith's discussion of locative and utopian as mapping strategies (keeping the dynamics which I believe is central to him) rather than objective categories or maps. However, even more importantly, Smith's discussion of these two terms seems to me, when considered carefully, of value only in establishing the framework in which to articulate a third, unnamed, dynamic mapping strategy of the cosmos. Here is how he put it.

> The dimensions of incongruity which I have been describing in this paper appear to belong to yet another map of the cosmos. These conditions are more closely akin to the joke in that they neither deny nor flee from disjunction, but allow the incongruous elements to stand. They suggest that symbolism, myth, ritual, repetition, transcendence are all incapable of overcoming disjunction. They seek, rather, to play between the incongruities and to provide an occasion for thought.[3]

Unfortunately, and I think quite remarkably, few have yet to acknowledge or appreciate[4] Smith's discussion of this third unnamed map or dynamic, described as being something like a joke.[5] I can only believe that the inability to even see this dynamic in Smith's discussion is akin to the almost total absence of any studies of dancing in the study of religion.

Both invisibilities are fundamentally the outcome of the same perspective. And Smith's choice of terms tends to support locative preferences; for example his use of the term "stand" and his addressing religious actions in terms of their "incapability of overcoming incongruity" rather than seeing this embracing of incongruity as their vitalizing capacity and access to power. Still, I believe that the anomalous *play* is for Smith, and most decidedly for me, crucial to understanding religion; that is, religion is always somehow a negotiation between being in place and abhorring the consequences of place; religion is always application of the givens of tradition with the experiences of the exigent present. Finally, as inspired by this study of dancing, religion is best understood in its capacity to play in the virtual distance between place and no place, moved by the desire that can never be achieved to resolve the distance, thus fueling the enaction that is religion. My analysis of Smith has led me to believe that practiced lived religion can be adequately accounted for only in the terms of this third, commonly overlooked, perspective that I have called "play";[6] this is a way that we might understand religion where the enaction of religion remains in the religion. It is not a matter of focusing on the body or to construct a materialist approach that will accomplish what Smith imagined, but rather one exemplified by this study of movement and dancing.

The attention students of religion have given Archimedes' statement (or the place concept to which it is thought to relate) seems largely confined to the "give me a place" part, while ignoring the "I will move the world" part. This is consistent with the "locative" preference of the study of religion and to removing the dynamic and living dimension from religions by territorializing or backfilling them into grids. Surely Archimedes' ultimate interest is in moving the world and his interest in finding place cannot be isolated from self-movement. Thus, one must believe that even his concern for place must be seen as including a groping style of self-movement leading toward, while perhaps never achieving, some desired point of leverage.

Perhaps Archimedes' statement should be interpreted differently. Archimedes acknowledges that he is missing something necessary to enact his desire to move the world, that being a place to stand on. The issue for Archimedes is bound in what Barbaras terms as distance and desire. Yet Archimedes seems helpless regarding movement, a pathetic powerless soul seemingly awaiting in some impossible placeless spot something to happen; awaiting someone to direct him to his place or something he might recognize as a place so he might be usefully engaged in moving the world. Surely we have taken Archimedes too simply; his statement is not a call to find one's place, but a comment on the paradox of the very issue of being in place. Archimedes' statement is more on the order of Zeno's paradox in that moving the world is dependent on being in a place, but being in place requires self-movement in and of the world.

Ultimately, as Bergson showed us, moving is never "in" any place, because movement is the very denial of place. To understand movement of the world in terms of place is impossible other than from a backfilled gridified perspective constructed after movement has ceased.

Perhaps the advice we have yet to hear, yet has all along been cleverly suggested by Archimedes, is simply, "exercise the gift of the primacy of human self-movement and go grope about! This groping *is* the moving of the world." Isn't this what, if we care to admit it, religious folks and scholars of religion do most of the time anyway? Place has no point other than in describing what has already taken place; although there is perhaps a place for such accountings. Still, living movement is never *in* any place at all! Self-movement is how we discover the dimensions of self and world. Residing in place is only a scholar's poor construct after the action is but memory or a trace held as artifact or text. Bestowing primacy to place, as we academics have done, has been to adopt a strategy that fails due to the limitation inherent to being in place or mistakenly feeling that place is a fulfillable desire. It is a strategy of removing movement and vitality; a strategy of backfilling or territorializing and thus removing or ignoring what is surely an aspect of human life that is inseparable from vitality. Place, however used, means stability, objectivity, and the uncomfortable and endlessly tiresome discussion and debate about which place to take, where to stand. Indeed, Smith's own discussion of the consequences of this strategy shows this frustration. On quoting Archimedes, Smith wrote,

> There is, for such a thinker, the possibility of a real beginning, even of achieving The Beginning, a standpoint from which all things flow, a standpoint from which he may gain clear vision. The historian has no such possibility. There are no places on which he might stand apart from the messiness of the given world. There is, for him, no real beginning, but only the plunge which he takes at some arbitrary point to avoid the unhappy alternatives of infinite regress or silence. His standpoint is not discovered, rather it is fabricated with no claim beyond that of sheer survival. The historian's point of view cannot sustain clear vision.[7]

Smith seems to be saying that there is no alternative to groping about, yet, and this is the unfortunate part I think, it seems that for him this is an unavoidable unfortunate situation. There remains for Smith, it seems, a nostalgia for permanence and stability; a map that is a territory. We need to get over it. And more importantly, as this study of dancing has shown, the dynamics of religion and the study of religion are that of grasping, groping, enacting, applying, dancing, moving, all of which require a glorious vitalizing messiness. Infinite regress or silence is not the unhappy alternative to a "real" point of view. A "real beginning" is rather simply a romantic impossible constructed to create a distance, a pure depth, a playful gap, for the enaction of religion and the study of religion.

As dancing is so commonly found in religious ritual, drama, and celebration, it is clear that there are mutual and compatible qualities and characteristics between dancing and religion. The fuller dancing is understood the better we are able to appreciate the dancing-religion connection and the more we will find dancing to contribute to our studies of religion.

Dancing is self-movement, but an acquired learned marked form distinctive to humans. As movement, dancing is a structurality about distance and desire—the opening of a virtual distance inseparable from a negative, a need, a gap, a desire which is a way of articulating the movement that is dancing. Religion might well be understood as self-movement in some important sense—or perhaps *enaction* to follow the lead of cognitive science—or *application* or *play* to follow Jonathan Smith. One might well comprehend the distinctive constituents of religion—myth, ritual, transcendence, repetition, belief—in the structurality of living movement and especially dancing. Religion creates gaps, virtual distances, that fuel action, movement. This is the source of the distinctive power and character of religion.

Since dancing is distinguished by a folding back on itself, since dancing is about the energetics of living movement itself, it is particularly adaptable to religious application as well as development into the most abstract inclusive greater-than-cosmic concepts as in the example of the Hindu Nataraja.

Dancing is characterized and distinguished by its remarkable ability of self-othering. Dancing is becoming something wholly other (a deity, a principle, an ideal, a mythic character), yet experiencing this other fully as one experiences one's own self by means of the full affective proprioceptive movement touch human mechanisms. Dancing is a form of knowing, a feeling kind of knowing, a transcendence through other into full self-realization. The self-othering structurality that distinguishes dancing movement is remarkably compatible with religion both to express religious ideas, but more importantly to enact and experience them.

As with dancing, religion is comprised of gesturing and posture, the techniques and attitudes of body[8] that constitute identity. As exemplified in dancing, repetition, even unconscious or mindless repetition of patterned behavior, is understood as foundational to meaning and identity and even the shape of reason. I don't think that the academic study of religion has ever quite known what to do with the highly repetitive character of so much that is undeniably religious. Likely we continue to be influenced by a cultural evolutionist view that identifies such repetitive things as magical and thus belonging to a pre-religious stage of development. Repetition is fundamental to dancing, both its acquisition (one cannot learn to dance other than by highly repetitious practicing) and its cultural/religious affect (its distinctiveness is in the familiar repeated patternings). Gesturing and posture, understood in a rich sense, involves the looping processes fundamental to creating and discovering the world and oneself. Gesture and posture are ways of understanding repetitive self-movement that is at the core of human sensibility and creativity and agency. Gestural and postural repetitive living movement establishes and continually modifies image schemas (body concepts) and basic level categories. Such engramatic dynamics are inseparable from the establishment of the changeable stabilities we refer to as tradition, the enculturation of such patterns in individuals recognizable as cultural and religious identities, and they offer the means by which such patterns are, through living enaction, modifiable either gradually or radically. Dancing, as movement focused on the dynamics of self-movement itself, both shows how this expressive/agentive looping works and also offers itself as a modifiable dynamic that is endlessly adaptable to religious applications and enactions.

As I have shown in my discussion of Jonathan Smith's understanding of religion and the study of religion, play is a term that identifies the negotiative, application, living dynamic of religion. Religion is action, enaction, self-movement that is invariably manifested in the juxtaposed incompatibilities that demand movement. Smith understood the outcome of this incongruity principally in terms of thought, that is, "incongruity gives rise to thought," yet dancing demonstrates that this incongruity is another name for the virtual distance and desire, negativity, gap, pure depth that fuels living movement, that *is* movement. In this view religioning occurs, religious history emerges, in the structuralities of paradox and incongruity that open a gap or distance, virtual and never closable, that gives rise to movement; indeed movement, self-movement, living movement shaped by communities that, by moving together and playing out these incongruities together, have forged a common gestural core of identity. As we have seen in the study of dancing, play is a way of articulating the energetics of this ongoing religious structurality of incongruity and impossibility. To understand religion in terms of play is similar to appreciating dancing as play. Religions take the shapes and play themselves out in gestural and postural forms that distinguish them as dances developed and practiced through the history of religious communities.

A fascinating aspect commonly inseparable from religions is their propensity to promise impossibles: heaven, eternal happiness, peace on earth, oneness with god. One wonders why people buy into such impossibles and shape their lives according to them. They seem as artificial as wooden masks. As suggested by the study of dancing, such impossibles engender a seductive force and quality. Seduction is a structurality that promises the impossible in order to engage interest and motivate self-movement. Seduction then is all about movement, about articulating the conditions that are living movement. Dancing promises the presence of emerging form. Yet, in the dancing, this presence always passes away coincident with its appearance. Dancing seduces by its promise of presence that passes as it appears. The seduction is what distinguishes dancing movement, a collapse of the promise of stability and meaning and presence arising from dancing into the ongoing dance movement itself. The felt vitality of dancing arises in the seduction of promised impossibilities. Should, in the study of religion, the effort focus on explaining or resolving such impossibles, as I think has been our principal interest, religion will always be understood as an inactive objective thing. It is in its seduction that religion constitutes its aliveness, the source of its power, and its incredible capacity to fascinate. Dancing, as the human movement that is about the character of human self-movement, reveals the importance of the seductive strategy so common to religion. Religion is seductive I think in much the same terms as are masks and maskings; they tend to present themselves in terms of the most unbelievables possible, yet while incredulously claiming them to be cosmically foundational. The seductivity of this dynamic is at the heart of the moving enaction that is religion.

I have suggested that dancing, if it is about anything, is about the nature of human self-movement itself. Dancing offers insight into our capacities as self-moving human beings; it offers us a way to comprehend our distinctiveness among animate beings with which we share self-movement. Dancing refers to the dynamic structurality that is common to all forms of movement we call "dance" and by understanding dancing we can appreciate how it functions when manifest in specific application as cultural and religious dances. As dancing and religion are commonly copresent and intimately interrelated, our understanding of dancing may suggest aspects of religion that are consistent with similar aspects of dancing.

NOTES

1. Jonathan Z. Smith, "Map is Not Territory," in *Map is Not Territory* (Leiden: E. J. Brill, 1978), 289. Reprinted in *Map is Not Territory* (Chicago: University of Chicago Press, 1990). At least one version of Archimedes' statement includes the use of a lever to move the world: "Give me a place to stand and with a lever I will move the whole world." I am going to argue that the emphasis should be on the action, the movement, even in determining the place. The "lever" version is equally appropriate in that it is focused on moving the world.

2. See Sam Gill, "No Place to Stand: Jonathan Z. Smith as *homo ludens*, the Academic Study of Religion *sub specie ludi*," *Journal of the American Academy of Religion* 66/2 (1998): 59-88, and "Play" in *Critical Guide to the Study of Religion*, edited by Russell T. McCutcheon and Willi Braun (London: Cassell, 2000), 451-62.

3. Smith, "Map is Not Territory," 309.

4. For example, in his recent book *More Than Belief* Vasquez doesn't see it. In a section titled "J. Z. Smith: The Locative and the Utopian" (289-93), Vasquez provides a summary and critique of Smith's two terms without a mention of the third category.

5. Smith's "joke" and "play" terms were, I believe, deeply influenced by his study of Frazer's *The Golden Bough*. See Gill, "No Place to Stand."

6. Gill, "No Place to Stand," and Gill, "Play."

7. Smith, "Map is not Territory," 289-90.

8. "Body" is Mauss's term and used here simply to remind us of the lineage of gestural studies. I prefer something more inclusive like "movement techniques" which would incorporate the inseparability of nervous and muscular, the visible and the invisible, thought and action. Certainly one could consider "body" as incorporating these dynamic relationships, but, unfortunately, it has not been our practice to do so.

Bibliography

Aparicio, Frances. *Listening to Salsa: Gender, Latin Popular Music, and Puerto Rican Cultures*. Middletown, CT: Wesleyan, 1998.

Barbaras, Renaud. *Desire and Distance: Introduction to a Phenomenology of Perception*. Stanford, CA: Stanford University Press, 2006.

_____. "Life and Exteriority." In *Enaction: Toward a New Paradigm for Cognitive Science*. Eds. John Stewart, Olivier Gapenne, and Ezequiel A. DiPaolo. Cambridge: MIT Press, 2010.

_____. "Life, Movement, and Desire" *Research in Phenomenology* 38 (2008).

Bateson, Gregory. "A Theory of Play and Fantasy." *Psychiatric Research Reports*. 2 (1955): 39-51.

Baudrillard, Jean. *Seduction*. Trans. Brian Singer. New York: St Martin's Press, 1990 [1979].

Bergson, Henri. *Matter and Memory*. London: George Allen and Unwin: 1911.

Benjamin, Walter, "The Work of Art in the Age of Mechanical Reproduction." In Walter Benjamin, *Illuminations: Essays and Reflections*. Ed. Hannah Arendt. Trans. Harry Zohn. New York: Schocken Books, 1968.

Bourdieu, Pierre, *Outline of a Theory of Practice*. Cambridge: Cambridge University Press, 1977.

Campos, René A., "The Poetics of the Bolero in the Novels of Manuel Puig." In *World Literature Today* 65 (Autumn 1991): 637-42.

Cataldi, Sue L., *Emotion, Depth, and Flesh: A Study of Sensitive Space*. Albany: State University of New York Press, 1993.

Cohen, Selma Jeanne, ed. *International Encyclopedia of Dance*. New York: Oxford University Press, 1999.

Cole, Jonathan and Barbara Montero, "Affective Proprioception." *Janus Head*. 9.2 (2007): 299-317.

Coomaraswamy, Ananda K. "The Dance of Shiva." New York: Sunwise Turn, 1924.

Cushing, Frank Hamilton. "My Adventures in Zuni." *Century Illustrated Magazine* 25 (1882). *Zuni: Selected Writings of Frank Hamilton Cushing*. Ed. Jesse Green. Lincoln: University of Nebraska Press, 1979.

Derrida, Jacques. "Structure, Sign, and Play in the Discourse of the Human Sciences." 247-265 in *The Languages of Criticism and the Science of Man*, eds. Richard Macksey and Eugene Donato. Baltimore: The Johns Hopkins Press, 1970.

_____. "Différance." In *Speech and Phenomena: And Other Essays on Husserl's Theory of Signs*. Evanston: Northwestern University Press, 1973.

Dillard, Annie. *Pilgrim at Tinker Creek*. New York: Bantam Books, 1974.

Doidge, Norman. *The Brain that Changes Itself: Stories of Personal Triumph from the Frontiers of Brain Science*. New York: Viking, 2007.

Downey, Greg. "Throwing like a girl('s brain)," Internet, February 1, 2009, http://neuroanthropology.net/2009/02/01/throwing-like-a-girls-brain/ (accessed December 2010).

Ferrón, Héctor Madera. "El bolero es eterno," *Un siglo de bolero*. Mexico City: EDUSA, n.d., 3-5.

Foley, Kathy. "The Dancer and the Danced: Trance Dance and Theatrical Performance in West Java." *Asian Theatre Journal* 2.1 (1985): 28-49.

Foster, Susan. *Reading Dancing: Bodies and Subjects in Contemporary American Dance*. Berkeley: University of California Press, 1988.

Fraleigh, Sandra. *Dance and the Lived Body*. Pittsburgh: University of Pittsburgh Press, 1987.

Gadamer, Hans-Georg. *Truth and Method*. New York: The Seabury Press, 1975.

_____. "The Relevance of the Beautiful," 23-30 in *The Relevance of the Beautiful and Other Essays*. Trans. Nicholas Walker. Ed. Robert Bernasconi. Cambridge: Cambridge University Press, 1986.

_____. "The Play of Art," 123-30 in *The Relevance of the Beautiful and Other Essays*. Trans. Nicholas Walker. Ed. Robert Bernasconi. Cambridge: Cambridge University Press, 1986.

_____. "The Festive Character of Theatre," 64 in *The Relevance of the Beautiful and Other Essays*. Trans. Nicholas Walker. Ed. Robert Bernasconi. Cambridge: Cambridge University Press, 1986.

_____. "Art and Imitation," especially 98-99, in *The Relevance of the Beautiful and Other Essays*. Trans. Nicholas Walker. Ed. Robert Bernasconi. Cambridge: Cambridge University Press, 1986.

_____. "Poetry and Mimesis," in *The Relevance of the Beautiful and Other Essays*. Trans. Nicholas Walker. Ed. Robert Bernasconi. Cambridge: Cambridge University Press, 1986.

Garcia, Guy. *The Decline of Men: How the American Male Is Getting Axed, Giving Up, and Flipping Off His Future*. Harper, 2009.

Geertz, Clifford. *The Religion of Java*. Glencoe, IL: Free Press, 1960.

Gibson, James. *The Ecological Approach to Visual Perception*. Hillsdale, NJ: Lawrence Erlbaum Associates, 1986.

Gil, José. "Paradoxical Body." *TDR: The Drama Review* 50:4 (T192) Winter 2006.

Gill, Sam. *Storytracking: Texts, Stories, & Histories in Central Australia*. Oxford University Press, 1998.

_____. "Disenchantment." *Parabola* I:3 (1976): 6-13. Reprinted in *I Become Part of It: Sacred Dimensions in Native American Life*. Eds. D. M. Dooling and Paul Jordan-Smith. New York: Parabola Books, 1989.

_____. "Hopi Kachina Cult Initiation: The Shocking Beginning to the Hopi's Religious Life." *Journal of the American Academy of Religion* XLV 2, Supplement A (June 1977): 447-464.

_____. "No Place to Stand: Jonathan Z. Smith as *homo ludens*, the Academic Study of Religion *sub specie ludi*." *Journal of the American Academy of Religion*, 66.2 (1998): 59-88.

_____. "Play." In *Guide to the Study of Religion*. Eds. Russell T. McCutcheon and Willi Braun. London: Cassell, 2000.

Grosz, Elizabeth. *Volatile Bodies: Toward a Corporeal Feminism*. Bloomington: Indiana University Press, 1994.

Haile, Fr. Berard. *Head and Face Masks of the Navajo*. Salt Lake City: University of Utah Press, 1996 [1947].

Hall, Edward T. *The Hidden Dimension*. New York: Anchor Books Doubleday, 1966.

Handelman, Donald. "Passages to Play: Paradox and Process." In *Play & Culture*. 1992.

Handelman, Donald and David Shulman. *God Inside Out: Siva's Game of Dice*. Oxford: Oxford University Press, 1997.

Hood, Mantle. "The Enduring Tradition: Music and Theatre in Java and Bali." In *Indonesia*. Ed. Ruth T. McVey. New Haven, CT: Human Relations Area Files, 1963.

Howard, Pierce. *Owner's Manual for the Brain* 3rd ed. Austin: Bard Press, 2006.

Hughes-Freeland, Felicia. "Consciousness in Performance: A Javanese Theory." *Social Anthropology* 5:1 (1997): 55-68.

Huizinga, Johan. *Homo Ludens: A Study of the Play Element in Culture*. Boston: The Beacon Press, 1950, trans. of 1944 German edition.

Johnson, Mark. *The Meaning of the Body: Aesthetics of Human Understanding*. Chicago: University of Chicago Press, 2008.

Juhan, Deane. *Job's Body: A Handbook for Bodywork*. Barrytown, NY: Station Hill Press, 2003.

Kam, Garrett. "Wayang Wong in the Court of Yogyakarta: The Enduring Significance of Javanese Dance Drama." *Asian Theatre Journal* 4:1 (1987): 29-51.

Kant, Immanuel. *Critique of Judgment.* Trans. J. C. Meredith. New York: Oxford University Press, 1973.

Keeler, Ward. *Javanese Shadow Plays, Javanese Selves.* Princeton: Princeton University Press, 1987.

Kendon, Adam. *Gesture: Visible Action as Utterance.* Cambridge: Cambridge University Press, 2004.

Krichauff, F. E. H. W. "The Customs, Religious Ceremonies, etc. of the 'Aldolinga' or 'Mbenderinga' Tribe of Aboriginies in Krichauff Ranges, South Australia," *Royal Geographical Society of South Australia* 2 (1886-88).

Lakoff, George. *Women, Fire, and Dangerous Things: What Categories Reveal about the Mind.* Chicago, University of Chicago Press, 1987.

LaMothe, Kimerer L. *Nietzsche's Dancers: Isadora Duncan, Martha Graham, and the Revaluation of Christian Values.* New York: Palgrave Macmillan, 2006.

_____. *Between Dancing and Writing: The Practice of Religious Studies.* Bronx, NY: Fordham University Press, 2004.

Leder, Drew. *The Absent Body.* Chicago: University of Chicago Press, 1990.

Leroi-Gourhan, André. *Gesture and Speech II.* Paris: Albin Michel, 1964–65.

Lockhart, Robert D., Gilbert F. Hamilton, and Forest W. Fyfe. *The Anatomy of the Human Body.* Philidelphia, PA: J. B. Lippincott Co., 1977.

Malabou, Catherine. *What Should We Do with Our Brain?* 3rd ed. Bronx: Fordham University Press, 2008.

_____. *Plasticity at the Dusk of Writing: Dialectic, Destruction, Deconstruction.* New York: Columbia University Press, 2009.

Manning, Erin. *Politics of Touch: Sense, Movement, Sovereignty.* Minneapolis: University of Minnesota, 2007.

_____. *Relationscapes: Movement, Art, and Philosophy.* Cambridge: MIT Press, 2009.

Massumi, Brian. *Parables for the Virtual: Movement, Affect, Sensation.* Durham: Duke University Press, 2002.

_____. *Semblance and Event: Activist Philosophy and the Occurrent Arts.* Cambridge: MIT Press, 2011.

Mauss, Marcel. "Techniques of Body." Orig."Les techniques du corps," *Journal de Psychologie* 32, 1936.

Merleau-Ponty, Maurice. "The Philosopher and his Shadow." In *Signs.* Trans. Richard C. McCleary. Evanston: Northwestern University Press, 1964.

_____. *The Visible and the Invisible.* Evanston, IL: Northwestern University Press, 1968.

Miksic, John. *Borobudur: Golden Tales of the Buddhas.* Singapore: Periplus Editions (HK) Ltd., 1990.

Millar, Susanne. *The Psychology of Play.* Baltimore: Penguin Books, 1968.

Minkowski, Eugene. *Lived Time: Phenomenological and Psychopathological Studies.* Evanston: Northwestern University Press, 1970 [1933].

Montero, Barbara. "Proprioception as an Aesthetic Sense." *The Journal of Aesthetics and Art Criticism* 64:2 (Spring 2006): 231-242.

Noë, Alva. *Out of Our Heads: Why You Are Not Your Brain, and Other Lessons from the Biology of Consciousness.* New York: Hill and Wang, 2009.

Noland, Carrie. *Agency & Embodiment: Performing Gestures/Producing Culture.* Cambridge, MA: Harvard University Press, 2009.

Norris, Christopher. *Deconstruction: Theory and Practice.* London and New York: Metheuen, 1982.

Osnes, Beth. *Acting: An International Encyclopedia.* Santa Barbara: ABC-CLIO, 2002.

Polanyi, Micahel. *The Tacit Dimension.* Gloucester, MA: Peter Smith, 1983.

Róheim, Géza. *The Eternal Ones of the Dream: Psychoanalytic Interpretation of Australian Myth and Ritual.* New York: International Universities Press, 1945.

Rosin, Hanna. "The End of Men." *The Atlantic.* August 2010.

Sartre, Jean-Paul. *Being and Nothingness.* New York: Washington Square Press, 1966.

Savigliano, Marta E. *Tango and the Politics of Passion*. Boulder: Westview Press, 1995.

Savile, Anthony. *Aesthetic Reconstructions: The Seminal Writings of Lessing, Kant and Schiller*. Oxford: Basil Blackwell, 1987.

Sax, Leonard. *Boys Adrift: The Five Factors Driving the Growing Epidemic of Unmotivated Boys and Underachieving Young Men*. New York: Basic Books, 2007.

Sheets-Johnstone, Maxine. *The Primacy of Movement*. Amsterdam: John Benjamins Pub. Co., 1999.

_____. "Thinking in Movement: Further Analyses and Validations." In *Enaction: Toward a New Paradigm for Cognitive Science*. Eds. John Stewart, Olivier Gapenne, and Ezequiel A. DiPaolo. Cambridge: MIT Press, 2010.

Schiller, Friedrich. *On the Aesthetic Education of Man*. Oxford: Clarendon Press, 1967 [1793].

Smith, Jonathan Z. "Map is Not Territory." In *Map is Not Territory*. Leiden: E. J. Brill, 1978. Reprinted in *Map is Not Territory*. Chicago: University of Chicago Press, 1990.

Sommers, Christina Hoff. *The War Against Boys: How Misguided Feminism is Harming Our Young Men*. New York: Simon & Schuster, 2000.

Spencer, W. Baldwin. *Spencer's Scientific Correspondence with Sir J. G. Frazer and Others*. Ed. R. R. Marrett and T. K. Penniman. London: Oxford University Press, 1932.

Spencer, W. Baldwin and Francis Gillen. *The Arunta: A Study of a Stone Age People*. London: Macmillan, 1927.

_____. *Native Tribes of Central Australia*. London, Macmillan, 1899.

Stern, Daniel N. *Forms of Vitality: Exploring Dynamic Experience in Psychology, the Arts, Psychotherapy, and Development*. Oxford: Oxford University Press, 2010.

Stewart, John. "Foundational Issues in Enaction as a Paradigm for Cognitive Science: From the Origin of Life to Consciousness and Writing" In *Enaction: Toward a New Paradigm for Cognitive Science*. Eds. John Stewart, Olivier Gapenne, and Ezequiel A. DiPaolo. Cambridge: MIT Press, 2010.

Strehlow, Carl. *Die Aranda Und Loritja-Stämme in Zentral Australia*. Ed. Moritz Freiherr von Leonharde. Trans. Hans D. Oberscheidt. Frankfurt am Main: Joseph Baer, 1907-15.

Sublette, Ned. *Cuba and Its Music: From the First Drums to the Mambo*. Chicago: Chicago Review Press, 2007.

Suharto, Ben. "Transformation and Mystical Aspects of Javanese Dance." *UCLA Journal of Dance Ethnology* 14 (1990): 22-25.

Swain, Tony. *A Place for Strangers: Towards a History of Australian Aboriginal Being*. Cambridge: Cambridge University Press, 1993.

Taylor, Mark. *Deconstruction in Context: Literature and Philosophy*. Chicago: University of Chicago Press, 1986.

Valéry, Paul. "What is Dance?" In *What is Dance?* Eds. Roger Copeland and Marshall Cohen. Oxford: Oxford University Press, 1983.

Vásquez, Manuel A. *More than Belief: A Materialist Theory of Religion*. Oxford: Oxford University Press, 2011.

Varela, Francisco, Evan Thompson, and Eleanor Rosch. *The Embodied Mind*. Cambridge: MIT Press, 1991.

Wilkinson, Elizabeth M. "Reflections After Translating Schiller's Letters On the Aesthetic Education of Man." In *Schiller Bicentenary Lecture*. Ed. F. Norman. London: University of London Institute of Germanic Languages and Literatures, 1960.

Wilkinson, Elizabeth M., and L. A. Willoughby, translators and editors. *Friedrich Schiller, On the Aesthetic Education of Man, in a Series of Letters*. Oxford: Clarendon Press, 1967.

Young, Iris Marion. "Throwing Like a Girl: A Phenomenology of Feminine Body Comportment, Motility, and Spatiality." In *Throwing Like a Girl and Other Essays in Feminist Philosophy and Social Theory*. Bloomington: Indiana University Press, 1990.

Index

About the Author

Sam Gill is professor of religious studies at the University of Colorado at Boulder. Native American religions were the focus of his work for twenty-five years. He has enjoyed frequent visits to cultures in the American Southwest—Navajo, Hopi, Yaqui, and Zuni—to observe ritual and dancing. Sam published a number of books on Native American topics: *Mother Earth: An American Story* (1987), *Native American Religions: An Introduction* (1982, rev. ed. 2004), *Sacred Words: A Study of Navajo Religion and Prayer* (1981), *Songs of Life: An Introduction to Navajo Religious Culture* (1979), *Native American Religious Action: A Performance Approach to Religion* (1987), and *Dictionary of Native American Mythology* with Irene Sullivan (1992).

Sam has long been interested in the issues of studying other cultures, and this topic was first presented in *Beyond "The Primitive": The Religions of Nonliterate Peoples* (1982) and significantly developed in the context of his study of Australian Aboriginal religious cultures and the history of the early development of Central Australia in *Storytracking: Texts, Stories, and Histories in Central Australia* (1998).

Since the early 1990s Sam has been an enthusiastic student of dancing. He has studied many dance cultures including travel to observe and study dancing to Bali and Java; Thailand and Nepal; Ghana and Mali; Costa Rica, Dominican Republic, and Puerto Rico. Sam has taught courses on many topics related to dancing, notably a yearlong course "Religion and Dance" that covered over thirty dance traditions and included weekly dance studios taught by artists from the relevant cultures. In the late 1990s Sam founded, with his daughter Jenny, a dance and music school, *Bantaba World Dance & Music*, which attracted artists from all over the world to teach and hold workshops; many of these artists remain residents of Boulder or elsewhere in the United States. He also began teaching salsa dance in various forms as well as other Latin American dances. He regularly teaches salsa in high schools, in his classes at CU, and in the community. He has developed an extensive catalog of salsa dance instructional videos. For years, he has choreographed for and taught a salsa performance group.

Sam's insatiable interest in various fields of study—play, masking, perception, cognitive science, neuroscience, philosophy, movement, gender issues, fitness, gesture, aging—are interwoven throughout this book on dancing.